# SOLOMON SCHONFELD

For my dear sister Valerie

# Solomon Schonfeld
## A Purpose in Life

DEREK TAYLOR

VALLENTINE MITCHELL
LONDON • CHICAGO, IL

*First published in 2009 by Vallentine Mitchell*

Catalyst House,
720 Centennial Court, Centennial Park
Elstree, WD6 3SY, UK

814 N. Franklin Street
Chicago
IL 60610, USA

www.vmbooks.com

Copyright © 2009 Derek Taylor

British Library Cataloguing in Publication Data

Taylor, Derek.
Solomon Schonfeld : a purpose in life.
1. Schonfeld, Solomon, 1912- 2. Rabbis—Great Britain—
Biography. 3. World War, 1939-1945—Jews—Rescue.
I. Title
296.8'32'092-dc22

ISBN 978 0 85303 891 7 (cloth)
ISBN 978 0 85303 881 8 (paper)

Library of Congress Cataloging in Publication Data

*All rights reserved. No part of this publication may be reproduced in any form or by any means, electronic, mechanical, photocopying, reading or otherwise, without the prior permission of Vallentine Mitchell & Co. Ltd.*

# Contents

| | |
|---|---|
| *List of Plates* | vi |
| *Foreword by Lady Jakobovits* | ix |
| *Preface* | xi |
| *Acknowledgements* | xiii |
| 1. The Story So Far | 1 |
| 2. After Victor | 19 |
| 3. 1933–1938: Life Gets More Difficult | 37 |
| 4. The Storm before the Storm | 55 |
| 5. Wartime | 73 |
| 6. The Problems of Peacetime | 91 |
| 7. Two Steps Forward, One Step Back | 109 |
| 8. Surviving a Tumour | 127 |
| 9. Good Growth and Bad Growth | 144 |
| 10. The Final Years | 163 |
| 11. Epilogue | 179 |
| *Bibliography* | 195 |
| *Index* | 197 |

# Plates

1. Rabbi Victor Schonfeld, c. 1905, before his wedding.
2. The Schonfelds in April or May 1914. Left to right: Betti and Jacob (Victor's parents) with Daniel, Ella, Samu (Victor's brother), Solomon and Victor. This was photographed probably in Grosswardein, Transylvania, where the older Schonfelds had moved.
3. The Schonfelds, 1922. Left to right: Moses, Solomon (standing), Akiba, Daniel, Ella, Asenath, David, Victor.
4. Solomon Schonfeld, September 1927, probably before leaving for Trnava Yeshivah.
5. Rabbi Dr Victor Schonfeld, late 1920s.
6. The Adath Yisroel Synagogue, Green Lanes, London.
7. The funeral of Rabbi Dr Victor Schonfeld, outside his synagogue, January 1930.
8. Rabbi Dr Joseph Herman Hertz, c. 1935.
9. The Schonfelds, 1938. Left to right: Moses, David, Ella (seated), Asenath, Daniel, Jacob, Akiba, Solomon.
10. Judith Hertz, September 1939, shortly before her wedding.
11. The wedding in the Hertz's drawing room, 104 Hamilton Terrace, January 1940. Left to right, seated: Kato Weisz (Ella's sister), Ella, Judith, Dr Hertz. Standing: Asenath, Akiba, Dr Solomon Schonfeld, Daniel, Ruth Hertz, David, Josephine Hertz, Ernest Petrie (Asenath's husband), Edith (Daniel's wife), Joir Weisz (Kato's husband), George Weisz.
12. Solomon Schonfeld's self-designed cap-badge. (Photo by kind permission of Ruthie Morris.)
13. Solomon Schonfeld at the inaugural meeting of the Va'ad Hakehilot (Central Committee of Polish Congregations) in Krakow, February 1946.
14. Dedicating the first Synagogue Ambulance. One of few photographs showing Dr Solomon Schonfeld together with Dr Hertz.
15. Dr Schonfeld in uniform at London Docks, discussing the distribution of newly arrived children to waiting adults.

16. Dr Schonfeld with Rabbi Eli Munk and Mr Stanton at a Hasmonean School sports day, Parliament Hill Fields, c. 1950.
17. With Jeremy at the cottage, c. 1953.
18. At a wedding, early 1950s.
19. Dr Schonfeld at the opening of the Northwold Road Synagogue, 1955. (Photo by kind permission of *The Jewish Chronicle*.)
20. A school speech day, showing Schonfeld to the left, H.A. Goodman speaking, Dr Judith Grunfeld in the white hat, and Ella Schonfeld and Joe Loebenstein on the extreme right.
21. Dr Schonfeld in 1964, with Julius Loebenstein (father of Joe) and Dayan Hanoch Padwa.
22. Dr Schonfeld with young visitors on Purim 1978.

*The Lady Jakobovits*
*London*

10 May 2009

How can one possibly do full justice when assessing the character and personality of Rabbi Dr Solomon Schonfeld? Here was a unique human being – literally 'larger than life'. Dr Schonfeld single-handedly saved thousands of Jewish children whose descendents can easily be counted in the tens of thousands and possibly more.

Dr Schonfeld was responsible for saving the life of my own dear husband, Rabbi Lord Jakobovits, a fact that my husband often mentioned when he spoke about his early years. Very few of those Dr Schonfeld saved were as open as he was about their debt to him.

Dr Schonfeld was impulsive, yet motivated every day of his life to save human beings – and he succeeded brilliantly.

My dear husband accepted the call from the Anglo-Jewish community, welcoming the opportunity, inspired as he was by his great teacher, Dr Schonfeld. He saw here a unique opportunity to walk in the footsteps of one of the greatest human beings in our times. It was he that motivated Rav Jakobovits to work single-mindedly in improving both the quantity and the quality of Anglo-Jewry's Jewish education.

In conclusion I wish to thank Derek Taylor, the author of Solomon Schonfeld: A Purpose in Life for the honour he bestowed upon me by allowing me to write these few words and in doing so to recommend every survivor, their children and grandchildren and many, many others to read this book. It makes very easy reading, yet is full of many lessons.

# Preface

It is easier to write a nineteenth-century biography than a twentieth-century one. All the facts are in the public domain, everybody concerned with the events is dead, and there is nobody to upset if some facts emerge which are not quite as favourable to the subject of the biography as had been previously thought.

In writing a biography of the twentieth-century Rabbi, Dr Solomon Schonfeld, there is the additional problem: most of his community do not desire publicity, and would prefer to get on with their lives in peace. This very limited ambition has seldom been easy to achieve, however, and the story of Judaism's Right Wing has been regularly punctuated with horrendous instances of persecutions and massacres, culminating – as for other Jewish denominations – in the Holocaust. As a result they still keep their heads well below the parapet.

However – and it's a big 'however' – Solomon Schonfeld was a great man and fully deserves a balanced biography. I say 'balanced' because he was a great human being, which means that, like the rest of us, he had faults as well as great virtues. Much of the material written about him thus far has been over-critical or hagiographic. He neither deserved the level of condemnation, nor needed uncritical plaudits to underpin his level of achievement. His contribution to the whole Jewish community in Britain is such that his story needs to be told for the benefit of those who did not know him and for future generations.

His life is also a fine example for all ethnic communities of what can be achieved if there is sufficient application, intellectual ability, belief in the cause and determination to succeed.

A lot of people talked to me in confidence. Some were concerned that it would be taken amiss that they had spoken at all. There is, indeed, a Jewish ruling that you shouldn't speak ill of the dead, but there would be no history books if you couldn't tell the story accurately. The Bible itself speaks of the faults of the Patriarchs as well as their merits. The wish for confidentiality I have, of course, honoured and many references are, therefore, not given.

DEREK TAYLOR<br>London 2009

# Acknowledgements

I wish to gratefully acknowledge the continuing patience of my wife – husbands writing books become obsessed with their subjects – and the help I received from Barbara Barnett, Judy Bermant, Dr Gerry Black, Dick Bird, David Black and the Army Chaplains Archives, Ben Davis and the BMA archives, Aba Dunner, the late William Frankel, the late Bernard Garbacz, Dr Michael Grayson, Freddy Greenwood, Victor Hochhauser, the late Rev. Leslie Hardman, Leah Harris, Jonathan Hertz, Ramsay and Nicole Homa, Lady Amélie Jakobovits, David Jacobson, Doreen Joels, Esra Kahn, Hanneli Kohn, Rabbi Ephraim and Sula Kestenbaum, Norman Lebrecht, Rabbi Dr Abraham Levy, Elkan Levy, Rabbi Reuben Livingstone, Joe Lobenstein, Henry Lunzer, Jack Lunzer, Conrad and Ruth Morris, Professor John O'Connor, Dr Ernest Petrie, Rabbi Herbert Richer, Rabbi Meir Roberg, Karen Robson and the University of Southampton's Special Collections Division, Jacob Schonberg, Jonathan Schonfeld, Hadassa Schonfeld, Dr Jacob Schonfeld, Victor Schonfeld, Sir Sigmund and Lady Hazel Sternberg, Aron and Ruth Vecht, Rev. Malcolm Weisman, Deborah Winegar, the late Aaron Winegarten and Erla Zimmels and the London School of Jewish Studies library.

If, at the end of the day, there are mistakes, they are mine.

# 1   The Story So Far

At the beginning of the twenty-first century people with strong religious beliefs often come under attack. The most popular epithet is to dismiss them as fundamentalists. To exacerbate the situation, this word has become almost exclusively associated in the public's mind with suicide bombers, terrorist attacks, a total intolerance of everybody else's views and even ambitions for world domination. The word has been hijacked – it actually means 'a strict maintenance of traditional beliefs' (OED).

Just to survive, Orthodox Jews, over the centuries, have always had to have strong traditional religious beliefs. Not in order to kill others – they seldom had any weapons. Not to dominate the world – at their peak they have never exceeded twenty million people in all. Not to impose their views – they were a small minority in every country in which they lived for nearly 2,000 years, and were often not even allowed to practice their faith. They had to be fundamentalists, and by that I mean fundamentally committed, just to survive as a separate religion. Not as a separate people. If the Jews were a nation, they would have vanished long ago. Why suffer discrimination, heavy additional taxation, pogroms, expulsion, torture and massacre just to be able to fly a flag. Remember too that, to be treated as well as anybody else, all the Jews typically had to do was give up their religion and then they would be welcomed into the Christian or Muslim fold; in every generation for all those centuries, sufficient Jews turned down the opportunity and Judaism survived.

They stayed Jewish over the millennia, that small core who were determined to live their lives by the laws they believed the Almighty had given to Moses all those thousands of years ago. They were a religion. They would suffer anything which was thrown at them rather than stop observing the tenets of Judaism. It might only be tiny in comparison with the world's larger faiths, but they'd see it stayed in existence. The Jews today are, in fact, 0.2 per cent of the world's population.

To survive in a hostile environment involves going to war, sometimes militarily and always intellectually. To win such a war it is necessary to have weapons, vast amounts of money and brave, disciplined and able soldiers. The Jews had the right people but they were opposed over the centuries by overwhelming force: whole empires who wanted to wipe them out. The Greeks and Romans had the weapons and the money. So, later on, did the Spanish Inquisition, murdering Jewis who had been forced to convert, not to mention the Nazis and the Communists. So did any number of vicious, equally determined and now long forgotten dynasties over those 2,000 years. What team could the Jews field to beat such odds? They did have good, intelligent rabbinic generals leading them but, above all, they were inspired by the belief that they had the Almighty on their side. If they confidently believed that to be true, they had to believe they could survive anything.

So this is the story of a British Jew who fought in the war on the Ultra-Orthodox Jewish side for half of the twentieth century. By all the rules, he should have lost. Compared to his opponents, he had no money, and he had only a tiny group of supporters. He was up against the Nazis in Germany when he tried to save Jews from the threat of the concentration camps. He was opposed by the vast majority of his own Jewish community in Britain, who were initially against his aims and objectives in the field of Jewish education. The odds were always heavily stacked against him but, nevertheless, this is the story of how he won.

Not all the time. Not with everybody. There were battlefield objectives he failed to take, retreats under bureaucratic fire, wickedly long casualty lists of those he failed to save. Many of the battles continue to rage today and will do so for further centuries. His victory has to be measured in points scored and in not having been knocked out.

He fought with everything he had and if ever there was a supporter of the belief that the ends justify the means, Solomon Schonfeld was that man. His public behaviour was, on occasions, devious, untruthful, unpleasant and even criminal, but he wouldn't have won as often as he did if he had always obeyed the Marquis of Queensberry's rules. Certainly, his opponents didn't always abide by them. Schonfeld was massively outgunned in every engagement of his war and often by opponents, like the Nazis, who would stop at absolutely nothing. Or who held all the aces of official power, like the leadership of the large majority of British Jews – the non-observant, the half-hearted, the officious and the indifferent.

Yet, as a result of Schonfeld's efforts, people did come through the ordeal; he saved their lives. He also saved the middle-of-the-road Orthodox Jewish community in Britain from the real possibility of self-destruction. He recruited and educated an army of young Orthodox

Jews who would carry on the war and enable the community to avoid ending up as a footnote in history. Jews who would follow in the footsteps of their ancestors since they first came out of Egypt, since the times of the biblical Abraham, Isaac and Jacob. Not for them the fate of breakaway Jewish groups in history, like the Karaites or Sabbateans, who had vanished into oblivion.

Now, the determination to achieve this objective may not seem that important to some, and some could certainly condemn Schonfeld as an extremist. Nevertheless, in carrying on the fight, he hurt nobody, though some of his opponents' egos were certainly deflated. Nobody died as a result of Schonfeld. A lot of people did live on and the small British outpost in the Jewish religious defensive line was markedly strengthened because of his efforts.

In order to understand Schonfeld's brand of extremism, it is necessary to understand the background which formed seriously Orthodox Jewish communities, or as I shall refer to them here, the Charedim. It isn't an exact term. It's a modern term and it covers a large number of minute religious variations. It's certainly about a way of life, every part contained in a body of law called the Talmud, which is an enlargement of the Pentateuch. The Talmud was collated about 1,500 years ago and it includes instructions on every aspect of a Jew's existence. From what they can eat and when they should wash, to the laws which apply to international trading and the rights of women.

In a biblical world which believed in seven-day weeks for servants, the Talmud said they had to have a day off. Jewish people also had to offer any Jewish slave their freedom after seven years. The nineteenth-century founders of the Trade Union movement, more than 2,000 years later, would have approved. At a time when Frederick the Great, like everybody else in the eighteenth century, didn't wash – after thirty years he developed erysipelas and died – the Talmud laid down that the Jews must bathe regularly and wash their hands before eating bread. Modern hygienists would applaud.

Of course, a very considerable number of the laws were inexplicable to the people who carried them out; for example, circumcision, a prohibition on wife beating and the humane slaughter of animals. The Jews obeyed them – and plenty more – because it was in the Talmud. Everything is in the Talmud. However, over the centuries, millions of Jews did give up the faith altogether. In addition, large numbers of them decided that the Talmud was out of date and much of it shouldn't apply to them. They became far less observant than the Charedim. Most American Jews favour this stance.

Obeying all the rules does, indeed, demand a considerable amount of effort, sacrifice and inconvenience. While many laws only affect the individual, the laws of marriage affect the community and, ultimately, the Jewish people as a whole. Primarily, a Jewish man who wants his children to be accepted by any Orthodox community as Jews, has to marry a woman who is legitimately Jewish by the standards of the Orthodox. For a woman to be considered Jewish, she has to have a Jewish mother, who had a Jewish mother, who had a Jewish mother, all the way back, though this lineage could include officially recognized converts.

The Talmud lays down that the status of the father is not relevant. When Jewish men had to choose between the non-Jewish girl they loved and the Jewish legitimacy of any children they might produce in the future, a lot chose the girl. It followed naturally that a high proportion of their progeny would give up the remnants of the family's level of observance and what they saw as the unpleasant results of belonging to the faith. Massacre, intermarriage and assimilation would reduce the number of Jews in the world to only a million in the Middle Ages. The battle to survive took its toll.

Responsibility for obeying the rules lies exclusively with the individual in Judaism. A rabbi cannot intervene with the Almighty on anyone else's behalf. Rabbi means teacher, not intermediary. As Solomon Schonfeld wrote of the majority of British Jews in the early days of his own ministry:

> The tendency to regard the rabbi or minister as a bus driver of the vehicle called Judaism, who takes the fares and delivers the passengers to their destination, must be replaced by a realization that we are all marchers and that our officers merely keep us in step and directions.

Schonfeld's family originally came from Hungary. There were only 35,000 Jews in Britain in 1870 and that was the total after 200 years of being allowed to live peacefully in the country. On the Continent there were far more – the Nazis killed six million of them from 1933–45. The question for so many of the nineteenth-century Continental Jews was what was the best way to survive? There were two possible approaches for the Charedi leaders. One was to try to marry the observance of the rules of the Talmud with the best of the cultures of the countries in which they lived. This party was inspired by a German rabbi, Samson Raphael Hirsch, who argued for what he called *Torah im derech eretz* – Torah with the way of the land. His followers became known as Hirschians. Admittedly, Hirsch approached the host culture with caution. He didn't want it to take a major role in the life of his congregants. As his contemporaries sought academic recognition, it was said that 'since the rabbis became Doctors, the Jewish religion became ill'. Many Charedim communities in Germany came to accept a two culture-stream approach to life, but it was a compromise. To get the best results from such an approach it was sensible to start when the children were growing up. 'To carry his programme into practice, Hirsch established *the* orthodox primary and secondary school in Frankfurt, a prototype that has gained wide acceptance among Western Jewry'.[1]

The alternative for the Charedim was to withdraw into an enclave where their life was structured to concentrate on the Talmud and to, effectively, ignore the native culture around them. Many of those who followed this route were called Chassidim. The East European Chassidim and the German Hirschian communities were both Charedim. Both groupings were tiny parts of the Jewish whole and only parts of what became known as the Right Wing.

It is common outside Charedi circles to talk about the Right Wing as if it was one united body, but this is not the case at all. The main segments of the Charedim are the Chassidim, the Lubavitch – a subgroup of the Chassidim – and the Mitnagdim, the followers of the Vilna Gaon (Rabbi Elijah ben Solomon) and the nineteenth-century Chatam Sofer (Rabbi Moshe Schreiber). Then there are the Satmar, the followers of the twentieth-century rabbi Yoel Teitlebaum, and the Torah im derech eretz Hirschians. They are all very Orthodox and Right Wing in their practices and originally they had their own main geographical centres as well.

The Chassidim were founded in the eighteenth century and emphasize the joys and spirituality of the religion in addition to its learning. The name comes from Chasidut, meaning piety. They were to be found in large numbers in Hungary, Austria and further East. Among them are the Lubavitch who, today, add the importance of evangelizing, but only among non-observant Jews. They will never recruit from the ranks of the Charedim or from other religions. Lubavitch was a small town in Belarus in Russia where the founder lived. Mitnagdim simply means 'opponents'. The very name Mitnagdim defines its followers as those who were against the Chassidic approach. They were strong in Lithuania. In Czechoslovakia there was a mixture of Chassidim and Mitnagdim. The Orthodox Poles were mostly Chassidim while the Hungarians in the Austro-Hungarian Empire included a large number of the Mitnagdim.

The vast majority of the 35,000 British Jews in Victorian times were not Right Wing. They observed fewer and fewer of the Talmudic laws and were on their way to assimilation. It might take one generation, it might take several, but they were on the way out. This also applied to most of the members of the great ruling families in British Jewry in the nineteenth century, who no longer follow the faith today. The descendants of the Montefiores, the Rothschilds, the Sassoons and the Salomans are down to the last few drops in the well which succoured Jewish observance in this country for so long.

The Charedi segment in Britain was revived, however, from the 1880s, by massive immigration from Russia, Poland, Hungary and Romania. In all those countries the treatment of Jews had reached a nadir. They were being massacred by the hundreds of thousands in pogroms in Russia and Poland, they were not considered Romanian citizens even if they were born in Romania, and in Hungary they were second-class citizens. The Jewish people left in droves, vast numbers going to America, with a couple of hundred thousand coming to Britain over the next forty years.

They came to a Britain where lay Jews had traditionally controlled their communities in everything except religious matters. Laymen dealt with government, local authorities, the finances of the congregation and the problems of the community's sick, aged and poor. The rabbis were synagogue officials, apportioned a degree of respect, but mainly there to serve the lay officials.

The only exception at the end of the nineteenth century was the Chief Rabbi. He held an unusual office. There were no other Chief Rabbis outside the British Empire, except in a few German states where relations between Jews and governments were often far less favourable to the Jewish community. Normally, as a rabbi is a teacher, every rabbi has the same authority as any other. Some are acknowledged to be more learned than others and are treated as the equivalents of Courts of Appeal and even Supreme Courts, but each community of Jews is, usually, independent. By contrast, the communities who joined the United Synagogue, which was formed in 1870, were happy to band together under the religious leadership of a Chief Rabbi.

The tiny Charedi community in Britain remained totally independent of anybody. What was more, if they had a rabbi, it would be he, and not the lay officers, who ran the community. The traditional Charedi approach was to have two rabbis if possible; one would be expected to lead the congregation, and to deal with any domestic problems which came up within it, the second would rule on all questions of Jewish law. Occasionally a rabbi would be skilled enough to carry out both functions but, where possible, there would be two of them, simply to deal with the workload and because the optimum personalities and intellects would be different. One was needed to be a leader, the other a sage.

The Charedi lay officers were there to support *the rabbis*. It's a very important distinction in approach. The reaction of the United Synagogue to the future interventions of Solomon Schonfeld was antagonistic, partly because his job specification did not entail being a subservient cleric – which undoubtedly they would have expected of one of their ministers – and Schonfeld was certainly not going to behave like one.

A good illustration of this subservience within the United Synagogue was the fact that the ministers were not even encouraged to be qualified as rabbis. They were to be called Reverend, like a vicar, and wear a clerical collar. To get a rabbinic qualification (semicha) it is necessary to study the codification of the laws of the Talmud, especially in what is known as the Shulchan Arukh, written by Rabbi Joseph Caro in the mid-sixteenth century. Semicha is granted by the rabbinic teachers and supervisors. Some United Synagogue ministers preferred not to undergo the rigorous study and, even if they achieved the qualification, they were not allowed to use the title. Only the Chief Rabbi was called Rabbi.

Schonfeld's community, the Adath, came mostly from the followers of the thinking of Hirsch in Germany. He had been an early contender for the position of British Chief Rabbi when a new one was needed after Solomon Hirschell died in 1842. Another segment of the Jews who had fled to Britain from the pogroms in Eastern Europe in the 1880s had been drawn together at the end of the century into a new body called the Federation of Synagogues. This grouping, while independent and Charedi, maintained closer relations with the United Synagogue, under the Federation Founder, Samuel Montagu MP, later Lord Swaythling.

Initially, the membership of the multi-community Federation was very much larger than that of the single synagogue Adath. Over the years, however, it declined. It was not blessed with particularly able lay leadership after the death of Montagu. He had wanted the Federation members to become anglicized without dropping their level of observance. To achieve this, among other things, he banned Yiddish, the Hebrew-German based language which had been used by Ashkenazi Jews as a lingua franca for centuries. It was considered out of keeping with the desirability of benefiting from both Jewish and British culture. Yiddish was, however, used throughout Jewish circles in Poland, Russia and Lithuania. It had a fine cultural history and retained a great deal of popular affection, similar to languages like Gaelic and Welsh. The hidden agenda was often based on snobbishness. It was decided that Yiddish was not to be used as a means of communication within the Federation. Montagu also refused to allow any discussion of Zionism at official meetings.

A large number of Federation members eventually went off to join the more middle-class United Synagogue congregations in the suburbs of London. The East End, where they had all originally arrived, was, naturally, the dock area and very badly bombed during the Second World War. It would slowly cease to be a Jewish centre and would become the home of many of the next wave of immigrants, this time from India, Pakistan and Bangladesh.

The determination to remain independent was only one cause of public friction between the Charedim and the United Synagogue (US). From the US point of view, the overriding goal was to portray the Jewish community to the wider world as equally Jewish and British. The US considered they were the best qualified to do this, rather than the mostly foreign-born Charedim, who, initially, understood British ways to a lesser extent.

Ultimately, though, as the Jews in both strata had the necessary qualification for membership – they had an Orthodox Jewish mother – they were acceptable as Jews in both communities. That was not disputed. What the Charedim did object to, from their side, was the level of religious observance of the United Synagogue leaders. The Charedim felt that a good leader had to set a good example and had to obey the rules. The original trust document of the Adath stated quite clearly:

> No person is eligible for election as a member of the governing body who openly infringes the Sabbath or partakes of forbidden food or who is not, as far as human knowledge and judgement go, a strictly Orthodox Jew.[2]

Most of the United Synagogue leaders would have fallen well below that standard. Some of the US ministers did not observe the letter of the law either, even if it was only by carrying an umbrella on a wet Sabbath day.

One of the longest serving and most senior Jewish lay leaders in the first half of the twentieth century was Sir Robert Waley Cohen, the No. 3 in Shell Petroleum for many years. As the name implies, he was a Cohen – a member of the priestly tribe who, among other things, are qualified by birth to bless a congregation on a Festival. So he would take his place in the synagogue to do just that. The problem, for the Charedim, was that it was well known that he drove up from his farm in Somerset in the morning to reach the synagogue. And the *din* (the law) forbids driving on a Festival.

As the ultra-Orthodox Adath Rabbi, Victor Schonfeld said in a sermon once:

> There always existed second-class Jews in the community, but in bygone days, the right of the religious and learned to lead was never doubted. It is only this blind civilization of ours which has made it possible for those who stand low in the ranks of Judaism to command. Those who were previously only tolerated are now followed, those who were only suffered to remain within the community now guide and direct. How shall those who stand far from Judaism guide Israel.³

This type of criticism did not make the Rabbi terribly popular with the United Synagogue leaders. In time they would also frown upon his son.

So, by Charedi standards, Waley Cohen was non-observant but it is difficult to define the word 'observant' in this context. The core number of pentateuchal rules total 613, but many of these have been subdivided and updated over the centuries. There are rules for medical transplants, for example, which had to be developed from general biblical commandments. Nobody in Biblical times considered the possibility of transplants, so the modern rules have been developed from a general decision on what would have emerged if the necessary skills had been invented in those days. Or again, some Orthodox communities allow the use of sabbath-compliant electricity time-switches on the sabbath; some do not.

It's more than nitpicking. Not surprisingly, Orthodox Jews of all kinds often make good lawyers because they are brought up in families which have argued on points of Talmudic law for as long as records go back; it's in the blood. It is, however, extremely difficult for anybody to keep every rule, and all of them are equally important. So who is truly Orthodox? The only safe answer is 'that's up to the Almighty'.

It does seem reasonable, though, that leaders should be expected to be role models and while the example given by the United Synagogue Honorary Officers at the time did not fit the bill, it did, on the other hand, reflect the attitude of most of their community. As Solomon Schonfeld pointed out in his 1958 book *Message to Jewry*: 'Judaism has not been tried and found wanting. It was found difficult and not tried.'⁴

All these Charedi movements, bar the Hirschians, had in common that they flourished best in the world of enclosed communities. They believed that the way to ignore the effects of the eighteenth-century Enlightenment movement was to pretend that nothing had changed. The fact was, though, that the Enlightenment brought a vast alteration in the lives of the Continental Jews. It helped to abolish the ghetto and to allow the Jews to enter professions which had previously been barred to them.

Countless thousands of Jews promptly moved into the mainstream societies and gave up Orthodoxy. They either assimilated or decided to join the Reform movement, whose practices were far less onerous to observe and more in accord with the culture of the countries in which they lived. At the time Hirsch set out to create an Orthodox marriage between the Talmud, its codification, the *Shulchan Aruch*, and German culture. The official Reform leaders had abandoned many laws. They had banned *schechita* and the performance of circumcision for their members, closed the ritual baths and clamped down on Talmud study groups. The most precious elements of Jewish traditional practice were under attack from within.

Meanwhile Chassidic spiritual leaders in Eastern Europe, who were totally devoted to study, came to be the better scholars, and when German communities needed a new rabbi, it was often Eastern Europe to which they looked. Among the followers of the Hirschian philosophy were the Schonfelds. Avigdor (Victor) Schonfeld was an anglophile, whose doctorate had been on the seventeenth-century religious philosopher, the 3rd Earl of Shaftesbury, and in 1909 he was recruited from Vienna to be the rabbi of a tiny community in North London.

Known then as the North London Beth Hamidrash, the community held services in the homes of its members, and then, as it grew, Schonfeld transformed it into the Adath Yisroel. Julius Lunzer was its most important lay honorary officer as well as its first President, and, in 1911, the congregation moved into a custom-built synagogue in Stoke Newington. The Adath would be a synagogue in the Hirschian tradition. Like the Federation, meetings were conducted in English, rather than Yiddish, which was frowned upon. The language was considered common. The German Jews considered themselves superior to their co-religionists in Eastern Europe and vice versa.

The Chassidim were less inclined to value German culture and, later on, the more extreme the Nazi measures against the Jews became in that country, the more they felt their view was justified. At the Adath the leaders made sure the Chassidim were welcomed as members of the community and were given facilities for their own services. These were, however, held in the Lachosky Room across the entrance courtyard from the synagogue on the second floor. It wasn't much but it was the best the Adath could do for their Charedi brethren. The Chassidim in the Adath at the time were a tiny minority of a tiny minority, and fully aware that most of the community looked down on many of their practices. If a Chassid came to synagogue in the traditional eighteenth-century Polish dress, he stuck out like a sore thumb. The fur hat, the white stockings and the long coat were very foreign. The Chassidim, themselves, were mostly poor and many were dedicated to lifelong study rather than to earning a living, which could be seen as irresponsible.

It would be foolish to imagine that the attitude of the majority of the community went unnoticed in the Chassidic ranks. They knew that they were, at best, merely tolerated. As they believed they were practising the faith correctly, they stuck to their guns with stubborn resolve. They looked forward to the day when their viewpoint would be that of the majority. When that day arrived – as they were sure it would – it would be their turn to be, at best, tolerant of the Hirschians who remained.

Victor Schonfeld had married Rachel Leah (Ella) Sternberg in the same year he came to London. She came from another very Orthodox family. The Sternbergs were descendants of Rabbi Akiba Eger, arguably the greatest Talmudist of his age. To be able to lay claim to distinguished rabbinic ancestors was a greater honour for a Charedi family than wealthy antecedents. Victor Schonfeld's parents had been very poor. Family folklore had it that the children couldn't all go to synagogue on the Sabbath because there weren't enough shoes to go round. By contrast, the Sternbergs were antique dealers and Ella inherited the strong and persuasive personality needed to prosper in that very personal field. She had a lively sense of humour, but when she had children, there would be no question of who was in charge at home.

Rabbi Schonfeld was six feet tall, erect as a guardsman, handsome, with piercing blue eyes, elegant, cultured and saintly. With those qualities, he had little difficulty in dominating his new London community. As a disciple of Hirsch he also fully accepted that educating the young was the only way to guarantee the continuation of the Charedim in the future; his guru, Hirsch, had given up both the office of Chief Rabbi of Moravia and a seat in the Austrian parliament to run his school in Frankfurt from 1853 to 1871.

The Rabbi knew his prime target market from the beginning. If he could not make Judaism meaningful to the younger generation, all would be lost. His first move was to create a first class youth club for them: the Chevra Ben Zakkai. It would hold debates, organize outings into the country, run a cricket team and study the Talmud. Schonfeld was brilliant at inspiring young people, always remembering their names, though he could be a stern disciplinarian: an incident when he smacked his son, Daniel, in public was long remembered. Those were the days, however, when a popular saying was: 'spare the rod and spoil the child'. The painful results of a father's wrath would have been acceptable in moderation.

Victor Schonfeld was a long-time Zionist but, eventually, the Zionist founders alienated themselves from the more highly Orthodox by their open desecration of the Sabbath and their total disregard of many Orthodox observances, even that of the most holy day in the Jewish calendar, Yom Kippur. Jewish opinion on a National Home in Palestine was deeply divided anyway. There was common agreement that persecuted Jews all over the world needed somewhere safe to live. There was also common ground that Palestine was the Holy Land to which the Jews would eventually return. That was it. The rest was a question of three different opinions.

The first was that of Theodor Herzl, founder of the Zionists, who wanted a National Home but really didn't care if it was in Palestine or, say, Uganda (which the British Foreign Office offered him at one point early in the twentieth century). Herzl was not an observant Jew and most of the early Zionists were secular in their outlook.

The second group were those who were happy in the country in which they lived. They disliked supporting the concept of a National Home because it might throw doubt on their loyalty to the lands of their birth. This group included a very large proportion of British Jews until well after the Balfour Declaration of 1917.

The third section was the Charedim who wanted to return to the Holy Land, but only when the Almighty decreed that this should take place. If they were to live in the Holy Land – and some had continued to subsist in the country since Roman times – then they preferred the idea of it remaining the British mandate it had become after the First World War. They could then live there, but still wait for the Almighty's final confirmation that all the Jews should now go back.

These differing viewpoints made for different agendas and were particularly difficult for the British authorities to reconcile. If the Jews couldn't make up their own minds what they wanted, then the British couldn't give it to them. Which was convenient because the Arabs also wanted the country, where they were far more numerous and far more economically important – their countries had most of the world's oil. They also considered that they had built up a much better claim to the country than the Jews over the previous 1,500 years.

When the State of Israel was eventually founded in 1948 and became a firm ally of the West, the concern about the accusation of dual loyalties would subside in Britain and the distinction between the Zionists and the non-Zionists would become blurred. Some Charedim, however, would remain ambivalent about the State – supporting their co-religionists, but unhappy about the way the State developed religiously and even its existence in the first place.

Victor Schonfeld was unlike the vast majority of the British Jews at the time. He was delighted with the sentiments in the Balfour Declaration, even if 1917 was a bad year for him. He contracted endocarditis and suffered several bad attacks of influenza in the years that followed. Schonfeld was one of those who founded the Mizrachi movement in Britain, and was elected at the Mizrachi World Conference after the First World War to head up their religious school system in Palestine, under the first Ashkenazi Chief Rabbi in Palestine, the renowned Abraham Kook. The Mizrachi were religious Zionists. The members of Agudas Yisroel were religious non-Zionists. The Neturei Karta party would, in the future, be a breakaway from Agudas Yisroel, and would oppose a secular state in Israel.

Schonfeld accepted the school post and left his London congregation. There was a lot of planning to be done and the family spent time in Vienna on their way to Palestine. Their sixth child, David, was born at the end of August 1920. At this time Victor was still Austrian and it wasn't until 1926 that be became naturalized as a British citizen. This, officially, gave the children dual nationality which would come in useful for their second son, Solly, twenty years later.

Father, mother and six children eventually finished up in a three room house in Jerusalem and 'their primitive home near the open hillsides of Sanhedriya in north Jerusalem perhaps inspired the children's lifelong indifference to material comforts'.[5] This might have applied to the children, but it did not apply to Ella. Surrounded by 'primitive' sanitation and the possibility of contracting dysentery – with malaria also a threat – Ella found it difficult to settle down. She considered, reasonably enough, that the children had been less exposed to such diseases in London or Vienna.

Money was, as always, short and so, in 1922, Victor went to America to try and solicit some donations for the cause. While he was away, the Mizrachi executives decided to join together with Keren Hayesod, which was the financial arm of the secular Zionist movement, the Jewish Agency. As a result the rabbi could see that it was now inevitable that the Orthodox approach would be watered down in future compromises. Independence had been sacrificed in order to get financial help: 'The Mizrachi has been making concessions to the Zionist organisation for the last 25 years. It must now do the same towards the Aguda for the sake of a unified Orthodoxy.'[6] That wasn't to happen; the religious and the non-religious still have difficulty in working together.

So Schonfeld resigned after what was a brief tenure. He would never have shifted his views for pragmatic financial reasons and that lesson would not be lost on Solly. Ella was delighted. A free agent again,

Victor could then have accepted one of several offers of senior posts on the Continent and in America, including the office of Chief Rabbi of Salonika in Greece. He preferred, however, to go back to London and the Adath community. He particularly wanted to bring up his children in a Britain to which he was immensely attached and where he was now able to speak good colloquial English. That enthusiasm would be passed on in full measure to Solly as well.

The Adath grew during the 1920s. They bought their own cemetery at Enfield in 1924, which was financially very helpful. A lot of people join synagogues in order to ensure they are buried decently. By paying a small contribution each week, the Charedim could now be guaranteed a sacred resting place. Land bought in acres and sold in small plots is a large source of income. The availability of a suitable cemetery was a key reason for the many small Charedi communities to agree to work together, and in 1926 Schonfeld was instrumental in founding the Union of Orthodox Hebrew Congregations (UOHC).

He still had his dream, though. He wanted to start a school like Samson Raphael Hirsch. He knew what its philosophy should be: to teach pupils the best of British culture and, at the same time, allow a substantial part of the curriculum to be devoted to Jewish studies. In those days, if a Jewish child went to a Christian school, his religious education had to be absorbed outside school hours. It would take place in the evenings when the child was tired, or on Sunday when the child wanted to play. It wasn't conducive to enthusiastic study. What was more, many fine schools were Christian foundations and took the religious views of their founders very seriously. Jewish pupils were expected to conform and were often not allowed to take days off to celebrate Jewish Festivals. Often there was also compulsory Saturday morning school, preventing them going to synagogue. Schonfeld wanted the children brought up in a Jewish environment rather than a Christian one.

Being different at school is never easy. The whole ethos is one of teamwork and maintaining the school's traditions. The fellow pupils of an Orthodox Jew could well find some of his practices eccentric. For example, an Orthodox Jewish boy wears an undergarment called a *tsitsit* which has fringes and was created to apply a biblical rule. As it is often worn under a shirt, it is not always visible. When a boy gets ready for Physical Training, however, it is very visible when he changes. The Jewish child would often be teased for wearing it. The simple way to stop the teasing was not to wear it. Parents often told their children that it didn't matter if they left it off.

What the parents were effectively telling the children as well, however, and at a very impressionable time of their lives, was that the rules could be abandoned if they made their life difficult. By allowing them the choice, the parents were also suggesting that a fine education was more important than following the laws in the Talmud.

If, in later life, the boys fell in love with non-Jewish girls, a large number followed the tenet their parents had taught them all those years ago: if the Jewish law is inconvenient, ignore it. So they married the girl which, illogically, their Orthodox parents usually found totally unacceptable. Family relationships were destroyed, parents were distraught. It was the ultimate disgrace within most Jewish communities. The fact that it was the fault of the parents, who had led the way in breaking the rules in the first place, was ignored.

In 1926 Rabbi Schonfeld proposed starting a Jewish secondary school movement and his community agreed to support him. One of them gave him a typewriter, which the rabbi accepted, an exception to his normal rule not to be beholden to anyone. At the age of 14, his second son, Solly, learned how to use it and became his secretary for the purpose. Victor Schonfeld believed his school would be the route by which the road to assimilation might be avoided, where the rule could be set down from the child's earliest years that the commandments were there to be obeyed. This emphasis on a substantial curriculum of Jewish studies marked out Schonfeld's concept from the one great Jewish school which had existed in Britain since 1817: the Jews' Free School. This had been set up to counterbalance the attempts by Christian conversionists in Regency days to get poor Jewish parents to swap their children's Jewish birthright for a decent lunchtime meal and a suit of clothes. Converting the Jews was an unwavering part of the Church of England's objectives at the time.

The Jews' Free School's colours are blue and yellow; these are the house colours of the Rothschilds and that great family saw to it that JFS not only survived, but grew mightily until, at the beginning of the twentieth century, it was the largest school in the country, with over 4,000 pupils. The objective of JFS had been, however, from the beginning, to educate poor Orthodox Jewish children so that they could earn a living when they left school. It wasn't that JFS was anti-religious; far from it. The governors just felt that helping the children survive in a hostile world was of even greater importance that their Talmudic education. They gave all the time they considered feasible to Jewish studies but Schonfeld regarded both the quality of the Jewish curriculum and the time devoted to it, to be inadequate.

Now, again, a lot of people felt – and still feel – that there is nothing wrong with assimilation. However, it was not acceptable as far as the Charedim were concerned. They wanted Judaism to survive, and were prepared to go to any lengths to ensure this. They did not intend that all their persecutors over the centuries should eventually be victorious. They carried on the war, and there would soon be an appalling and horrendous number of slaughtered casualties.

The main objections to the creation of a new Jewish school were threefold: that it would not be possible to finance the running costs; that it would make it more difficult for the pupils to relate to the non-Jewish majority in the country in later life; and that insufficient numbers of children would be attracted. The first and third objections were to be problems for many years to come.

The school opened its doors in 1929. Schonfeld's congregants, David Gestetner and the Fink family, gave £500 each towards its foundation (the equivalent of £20,000 each today). There was also a goodly list of other generous supporters. In addition, the constitution of the UOHC specifically allocated one third of its annual income from the Burial Society to the support of the school.

The first necessity was to find a good headmaster. Victor was highly competent to look after the religious part of the curriculum he envisaged, but the secular side was not his field. He advertised the position in *The Jewish Chronicle* in May 1929, saying that the school would open in September, which it did, and that the successful candidate should, of course, be a strictly Orthodox Jew. The only problem was that nobody applied who could measure up to that description.

It was for that reason that a non-Jew, C.A. Smith, got the job. As Dr Smith, MA, PhD, recalled in a letter to *The Jewish Chronicle* in 1981,[7] he had not applied for the post and Victor's letter offering it to him came out of the blue. The rabbi knew of him because he had taught the elder Schonfeld boys at the local Highbury County School. From the beginning Schonfeld and Smith got on very well; indeed Dr Smith said they never had a cross word. There were occasions, of course, when Dr Smith was asked a question about Jewish practices by his pupils and was at a loss to give the right answer. He recalled being questioned about what made milk kosher. He did his best and suggested that the cows were milked facing Jerusalem!

Victor Schonfeld knew, of course, that Smith was not Jewish. What he might not have discovered, however, was that Smith was not only non-Jewish, he was actually an agnostic. He didn't believe in organized religion. To make matters worse, he was also a committed left winger and quite prepared to lecture his pupils on the attractions of the Russian system every morning if he could. One of his pupils was Kibo (Akiba), Victor's 11-year-old son. In time, as Smith was an able teacher, he would have a marked effect on Kibo's religious outlook. In 1929 it was not difficult to make Communism sound good as an alternative philosophy to many more traditional beliefs; it had replaced the Czar who had presided over the pogroms. It had many Jewish leaders, like Trotsky and Kaganovich (Stalin's brother-in-law). It also, ostensibly, planned to make the poor rich – and there were plenty of poor Jews in Kibo's part of London. Moreover, its ambition to spread its message internationally seemed a more world-shaking programme than could be found within the confines of North London.

Victor Schonfeld meant what he said when he promised that his school would provide an amalgam of the best in British and Jewish culture. He advertised for a part-time maths teacher and others to tackle science, modern languages, drawing, music and gymnastics. They were all required to have good university qualifications. And to be strictly Orthodox. The rabbi made one distinction, however, between the Jewish and secular studies. For the former, the boys would cover their heads with a kippah, as all Jews do while praying. For the secular lessons they would not wear the kippah. This distinction was obligatory at the school, even for the very religious boys who would normally keep their heads covered at home throughout the day.

Where the children would come from, bringing in school fees which would keep the school solvent, was left somewhat in the air. Certainly, the Rabbi contacted all his many friends, within and outside of the Adath, and asked them to send their boys to the school. He was, as always, offered a hearing, respect, admiration for his initiative and even donations to his new enterprise. What he wasn't offered was many children. The school roll in the first year was around thirty in total and it would be a long time before that figure improved.

Not that Victor would take *any* child. One of the prospective pupils still remembers his interview with his future headmaster.[8] The Rabbi was dressed in a Victorian frock coat and spoke English well. To an 11-year-old he was, naturally, an imposing figure and he tested the boy on the portion of the bible which had been read on the previous Sabbath in the synagogue. This the lad could deal with, as his father went over it every week for two or three hours on the Friday night. He was accepted as a pupil in a class of ten boys.

Then, unexpectedly, in the autumn of 1929, Victor fell ill and a few months later, he died. It was a terrible shock to the Ultra-Orthodox community as a whole. Schonfeld was only 49 and although he always worked himself to a frazzle, he had seemed healthy enough. In October 1929, though, he found he had haematuria, blood in the urine. Within twenty years the condition could have been dealt with easily enough with antibiotics, but it was too early for penicillin. His doctor, Bernard

Homa, a great friend of the family, did everything he could and wouldn't take a penny in payment.⁹ Leading specialists were called in, including Lord Dawson of Penn and experts from the Continent. The cost of £500 (some £20,000 today) was covered by his friend, David Gestetner, who had made a fortune with a copying process which involved duplication from a stencil.

Nothing did any good. Towards the end of the year Victor suffered angina attacks and he died early on 1 January 1930. The Charedi educational ship was hardly out of harbour and, in one man, both the captain had departed and the Hirschian pilot.

### NOTES

1. Josef Burg, *Historical Essays to Honour Rabbi Dr. Israel Porush* (Australian Jewish Historical Association, 1988).
2. The Silver Jubilee Book of the Adath Yisroel Synagogue (Adath Yisroel Synagogue, 1936).
3. Victor Schonfeld, *Life's Purpose* (London: Jewish Post Publications, 1958).
4. Solomon Schonfeld, *Message to Jewry* (London: JSS Books, 1958).
5. *The Jewish Chronicle*, 16 February 2001.
6. Naphtali Lipschutz (ed.), *In Memoriam – Rabbi Dr. V. Schonfeld* (London: 1930).
7. *The Jewish Chronicle*, 27 March 1981.
8. The late Aaron Winegarten in conversation with the author.
9. Bernard Homa, *Footsteps in the Sands of Time* (London: 1990).

# 2  After Victor

When Victor died, his third son, Daniel, was 17 years old. He wrote of his father's death years later: 'I do not recall the departure of any man from his earth's existence accompanied by such love and respect.' Daniel remembered that during the illness a medical bulletin was posted outside the house and updated every day. In addition, the local authority had straw laid down in the street on both sides of the house to deaden the traffic noise and bus drivers were told to drive slowly.

Victor left a widow and seven children: Moses, Solomon (Solly), Daniel, Asenath (Senath), Akiba (Kibo), Aaron Eliezer David, (known as David) and the youngest, born little more than two years earlier, Jacob.

The synagogue in Green Lanes was packed for the funeral service. No fewer than 1,000 mourners came to the cemetery in Enfield for the interment. Mounted police carefully marshalled the crowds in Lordship Park where the family lived, at No.35. Even church bells tolled. There were, of course, a number of speeches and eulogies, including two from Victor's sons, Moses and Solomon, but it was noticeable that the Chief Rabbi, Joseph Hertz, was not invited to contribute. His former opposite number in the Sephardi community, Haham Moses Gaster, did give an oration, but the relations between the Adath and the Chief Rabbi's United Synagogue were only correct at best. There had been lengthy disputes about shechitah (ritual slaughter), the quality of the legal skills of the United Synagogue Beth Din and marriage authorization.

Haham Gaster found the right words, as he usually did: 'You are not dead, my friend', he said. 'You are living; your work lives after you, and you will be remembered not only by this generation but by generations to come.'[1]

Who would succeed him? The wish of most of the Adath Yisroel congregation was that the religious leadership should remain within the family. As Rabbi Hirsch Ferber said at the funeral, 'on his seat no stranger shall sit'. The only question, therefore, was which son? The oldest was Moses, who was 20 years old, committed, but not really the right calibre to make a top quality rabbinic leader of the community, or sufficiently inclined in that direction. He would always take an interest in synagogue affairs and, in his youth, he enthusiastically supported the Chevra Ben Zakkai club at the synagogue, serving it as both Secretary and President. There was one particularly interesting debate in 1931 which illustrated the dedication of the young people of the time to the teachings of Samson Raphael Hirsch. The motion was 'that the salvation of the Jews does not lie in a return to the ghetto'. Moses spoke and the motion was carried. In the future there might be a change of heart in the community, even if any retreat to ghetto-type isolation would be voluntary rather than imposed by non-Jewish authorities.

The problem with Moses might well have been that he was considered haughty in his youth and this could have been due to the fact that he had a good brain and did not suffer fools gladly. It was something of a family trait. Overall, Ella decided, the successor would have to be her second son, Solly. He had wanted to be a lawyer – he was articled to a very good Jewish practice – but he would have to abandon his proposed career. Solomon accepted the challenge, though he would never lose his fascination for the courts. It was a real sacrifice and he probably remained a frustrated lawyer for the rest of his life. He loved his father, though, and was steeped in his teaching, and if Victor was going to be the hardest of acts to follow, Solly was prepared to give it his best shot. He always remembered one of his father's favourite sayings: 'We do not just want life. We want a purpose in life.' Solomon Schonfeld would always have a purpose in life. For most of his years, it would be the development of the school project.

Solomon Schonfeld was born on 21 February 1912, and on his birth certificate the family name is spelt Schoenfeld. He grew to be nearly six feet tall, was immensely charismatic, blue eyed, extremely handsome and totally confident in his own ability. All just like his father. He had been educated at Highbury County School, which most of the brighter Adath children attended. It was a foundation of the Grocers Company in the City of London and past pupils were known as Old Grocers. There was no problem about taking the festival days off and no Saturday school. The Jewish boys took packed lunches or went home at midday, so the problems of what they could and could not eat did not arise either. The school took an enlightened attitude towards its Jewish pupils, which was more than could be said for many even more illustrious establishments.

After school, the Charedi boys would go on to Hebrew classes between 5.00 and 7.00 on four evenings a week, and there would be other classes on the Sabbath and Sunday. It was a packed curriculum. It ensured that if they ever thought of giving up Judaism, they would at least know what they were giving up. For most, the education they received as a child was the foundation of their beliefs throughout their lives. For some, it was all too much and they drifted away when they grew up and could make their own decisions. Solly was not one of these; he had a comfortable relationship with the Almighty and he believed in the cause.

Even so, everybody who would like to be a great man – and Solly was always ambitious – is, first and foremost, in need of a variety of mentors; people who will help and train, encourage and advise. For Solly, among the first was a successful clothing manufacturer called Harry Goodman. Solly met him at the age of 12 when Goodman joined the Adath congregation. The older man told him of the difficulties facing those who wanted to be Charedi in a non-Charedi world. On Goodman's 50th birthday, Solly wrote to him:

> When I was 12 (you) took the trouble to argue with me seriously about the battle of Orthodoxy ... we enjoyed our rows. When I was fifteen, you encouraged me in my first efforts at communal work and teaching, at public speaking and writing. When I was seventeen you sponsored me as the potential rabbi. When I was twenty, you welcomed me to a position for which I was hardly equipped and you used your astute powers of influencing opinion to build up the name and authority of the rabbi of the Adas and Union.[2]

Goodman was a leader of the anti-Zionist Agudists. He once said that if Chaim Weizmann went to plead the cause of the Zionists with the government, he, himself, would be in the waiting room, ready to go in next and put the alternative non-Zionist point of view. Goodman would later publish a Jewish newspaper and was chosen by the government to broadcast to Jews in occupied Europe during the war. It was not a popular choice with his many opponents within the community. Nevertheless, he would have had many useful contacts and Schonfeld wrote, 'for the last fifteen years we have become partners in practically every field of Jewish life'.[3]

Solly took his matric exam – the equivalent of today's GCSEs – gaining two distinctions and five credits. One of the distinctions was for Elementary Maths, a skill he would need continuously in the years to come, but was often accused of lacking. From school he went on to enrol at the London School of Economics in 1928 to read law and he did some courses at Vienna University. In June 1929 he passed his Intermediate Exam and was articled to Herbert Oppenheimer Nathan

& Vandyk. He also spent many months at a good yeshiva in Nitra in Czechoslovakia, but he was back in London when his father died.

During the period of mourning there were floods of well-wishers calling at the family home, and among them was the Chief Rabbi, Dr Hertz. Two weeks later, on 18 January, Solly visited Dr Hertz's home to offer his condolences on the death of Rose Hertz, the Chief Rabbi's wife. This was the first occasion that Solly had seen Hertz's daughter, Judith, a shy but attractive 16 year old. Judith remembered the effect of first seeing what she described as the laughing blue eyes of the handsome young son of the late Adath rabbi. Whatever attraction there might have been between the pair, however, a Chief Rabbi's daughter was far above a yeshiva student and articled clerk in those class-conscious days.

So Solly resigned from Oppenheimers, packed his bags and set out for Europe to obtain a rabbinical diploma. In his absence the pulpit at the Adath was occupied by a German refugee, Rabbi Eli Munk, but it was made clear to him that this post would be his only until Solly came back to England.

Rabbi Munk was eleven years older than Solly and had far better qualified for the Adath post than the former rabbi's son. Munk was married to the daughter of the Chief Rabbi of Hamburg, his father was a rabbi in Berlin and he had, himself, already held down rabbinic posts in Germany. He had worked closely with his father as a teacher and on matters of kashrut. In 1932 he would publish a work in Germany which refuted suggestions that Jewish laws were biased against gentiles. He had strong support for taking on the Adath post permanently and he was incensed when it was suggested that, when Solly took over, Munk would agree not to establish a synagogue in or near the borough. That clause in his contract was rescinded.

However, from Munk's point of view, he was convinced it was high time to get out of Germany while it was still possible to do so. The writing on the wall was invariably anti-Semitic graffiti and Jews were already suffering from new laws being passed against them in many German states, even before the rise of the Nazis. Hitler may not have been in power yet, but his invective in opposition against the Jews found much support among German politicians. So Munk gladly accepted the job that was offered. He did his job conscientiously and when the time came to leave, became the rabbi of a small synagogue in Golders Green which became a major bastion of the Charedim in London. He served it from 1934 to 1968 and it is still referred to as 'Munks'; no other British synagogue has ever been consistently referred to by the name of its rabbi even long after his death. Munk never expressed any bitterness or regret that he was replaced by Solly, and they would work together harmoniously many times in the future, though, naturally, they would not always agree on everything.

After seven days, the initial statutory period of mourning for Victor was over. For the family, it would, of course, last much longer and the children were always to be strongly influenced by Victor's credo; like him, wandering through life would never be their style; they would always have to be pursuing that singular objective. This was the philosophy which he had drummed into them. It was partly because of this that all the Schonfeld children achieved so much.

Kibo was 12 years old at the time of his father's death. When a boy studies for his bar mitzvah, his religious faith usually reaches its first – and sometimes last – peak. For many months after his father's death Kibo prayed fervently to the Almighty. He can still be remembered[4] swaying deeply over his prayers, in the traditional manner. There are, however, two reactions to grief for a child in a religious setting. The first is to accept the will of the Almighty, on the principle that, 'For My thoughts are not your thoughts, and your ways are not My ways, saith the Lord' (Isaiah 55:8). The other is to reject your God on the principle that what has befallen you is entirely unfair and all His fault. Religious beliefs can be strengthened, weakened or destroyed in such cases. When the grief subsided with the passing of time, Kibo considered the left-wing teaching of Dr Smith and when he later went up to Oxford, his strictly religious upbringing was challenged by all these influences. He had no equivalent of Harry Goodman as a religious support; in fact, just the opposite.

At school, the teaching must have been rudimentary in many subjects, as Ella Schonfeld struggled to keep it going after Victor's death. Even so, Kibo managed to win a Senior Foundation Scholarship at St Pauls when he was 16 in 1933. All the other successful candidates except Kibo had the benefit of a St Pauls education that year. Kibo had extra tuition from a first rate academic, Herbert Loewe, later Reader of Rabbinics at Cambridge, but he must also have had a remarkable brain. He left St Pauls in 1935 and spent some months at the same yeshiva as Solly before he went on to Magdalen College, Oxford when he was 19 years old.

The yeshiva had little positive effect on his views. He decided that the world was bigger than what he saw as the narrow boundaries of the Adath. He gave up his father's Charedi practices, married Zuzanna Przeworska, a non-observant Jewish girl, and became an internationally famous economist. His wife had come from Poland shortly before the war and found herself at Somerville College, Oxford when war broke out. Zuzanna was always proud of her Jewish background and became a distinguished social historian in her own right. The *Dictionary of National Biography* says of Kibo: 'He was a rebel against tradition who had escaped after great struggle.'[5] That struggle was mostly within him, although his mother also fought hard to save him for the ultra-Orthodox. Certainly, the 1930s were not a good time for introspection; the clash of the massive forces of Communism and Fascism and the probable approach of war, meant that, for many, action seemed more imperative than the imponderables of religion.

In the army Kibo changed the spelling of his name to Shonfield and eventually changed his name by deed poll to Andrew, though some of his friends continued to call him Aki. The BBC had chosen the name Andrew because they felt Akiba was too foreign. Shonfield's subsequent indifference to all religious observances could lead to difficulties. He once agreed to take part in a radio programme which would be pre-recorded but broadcast on Yom Kippur. Ella was initially horrified at what might well have been seen in her circle as desecration of the holy day and took a lot of persuading that he would not actually be in the studio himself at the time.

Andrew was knighted late in his life in 1978 and eventually was buried by his family in the Liberal Jewish cemetery; theologically a very long way indeed from his father's resting place. He always maintained good relations with Solly though. Solly would eventually go to his funeral, even though the Charedim do not usually go to Liberal services. Kibo admired Solly. In one letter he wrote in 1960, he told his brother that he had a 'special quality of impetuous generosity ... and I have always admired – even envied – your incaution'.[6] On other occasions he said that, although he had met many world leaders in the course of his work, Solly had more charisma and leadership than anybody else he had come across.

In 1933 Daniel was 20 years old, a tall, strapping man who had decided to become a surveyor. He was proud of the Schonfeld name but not deeply involved in the community. Asenath (Senath) had left her Quaker School and was now 16, helping her mother at the JSS where David was 10 and a pupil. She would go on to do some teaching at the school for a while, until she went to University College London to study psychology. The cost of her studies was initially paid by two of her former Quaker teachers. She subsequently got her PhD at the Maudesley Hospital in the department of the famed Dr Hans Eysenck.

Jacob was still a baby and, as Ella set out to keep the school alive and carry on Victor's work, he grew up to feel neglected. He only remembered being brought up by a nanny but, in fairness, that was standard practice at the time in middle-class homes and relationships between parents and children were seldom undermined by it.

It was a past president of the Adath, Israel Kestenbaum, who officially interviewed Solly to see whether he would be a good candidate to succeed his father, in spite of it being a foregone conclusion. Kestenbaum had been Victor's choice to look after the school's finances and he was still an Honorary Officer of the synagogue. He was aware that the 18 year old in front of him had no rabbinic qualification, but he did have the magic Schonfeld name. What was more, he was obviously going to be a magnetic personality and a charismatic leader. Anybody could see that in his demeanour, in his self-assurance, in his personality and in his fine physique. It was also not unusual for Jewish communities to be served by successive generations of one family. The rabbis of the Conquy family in Gibraltar served the community for more than 100 years. All the Ashkenazi Chief Rabbis in Britain from 1705 to 1911 could trace their ancestry back to the famous seventeenth-century scholar, Rabbi Zevi Ashkenazi.[7] So choosing Solly, without advertising the post, would raise few eyebrows and would help Ella to cope financially. Kestenbaum also lent Ella £100 later, so that Solly could complete his studies.

Kestenbaum thought that, if the lad was prepared to study hard, it might work. Solly was positive in his approach and convinced Kestenbaum that he was indeed the man for the job. It was agreed that he would set off straightaway for the yeshiva in Nitra. Ella was delighted. One of Solly's secret weapons within the community was that the powerful figure of his mother always stood behind him in the early years. If Kestenbaum had demurred, it was Ella with whom he would have had to deal.

Victor was dead and, officially, Ella was simply the widow of a much beloved rabbi. A short, attractive woman in a sheitl, the wig did not diminish her charm. She was extremely pushy and ruled any roost on which she decided to perch. She had a strong Hungarian accent and, with verve, flair and presence, she dominated any room she entered. Deprived of a power base by the death of Victor, she took the only available option. She persuaded all around to accept her at her own valuation. She behaved as if she was important and, *ipso facto*, she was accepted as important. It became generally agreed that no one ever said 'no' to Mrs Schonfeld, and behind her back she became known in her community as 'the Queen Mother'.

In Solly's early days as the Rabbi of the Adath community, the most frequent question he was asked was 'Does your mother agree?' Ella did not adopt a low profile. She was very hospitable; the house at Lordship Park was always buzzing and one of the social centres of the community. She had always been a dominant influence on her children and she continued to be devoted to their interests. Even as a relatively penniless widow, she did not allow her ambitions for them to be affected by her misfortune. Her children would also grow up to be powerful personalities in their own right; they all took after their parents. There was, therefore, the almost inevitable clash when they wanted to live their own lives. All the children broke away from Ella, some more than others. Three of them moved abroad and only Solly stayed absolutely true to his father's Adath, although Daniel did, too, but to a slighter lesser extent.

It was certainly Ella who chose Solly, rather than Moses, to take over from his father. What Moses felt about this we do not know, but he remained devoted to Solly and close to his mother, whom he helped to support financially as soon as he was able to do so. Solly also remained very close. When he came back with his doctorate and his semicha, he moved back in again with his mother.

Ella was universally recognized as a very forceful character: 'When you knew the mother, you knew where Solomon Schonfeld came from'.[8] In later life Moses, Solly, Kibo and Danny did become considerable public figures but Ella continued to want to influence her children. She was dogmatic and always positive that she was right. To her critics she was a battle-axe.

It is difficult to pin down why Ella so often got her own way. One of the synagogue officials was the beadle, Isaac Richer. He had served in the army in the First World War and was fearless in the face of authority. He absolutely refused to work on the Sabbath and was court martialled for the offence. He got six months imprisonment, though he was let out after fourteen days. Yet, as his son recalls, 'my father was afraid of no one – except Mrs. Schonfeld'![9]

When Victor died Ella had the house in Lordship Park but the community could not afford to give her a pension. She had to bring up the five children who were still at home on £11.12p a week and she could not manage. By October 1930 she had to take in boarders for four guineas (£4.20p) a week and with that help she scraped by. She had great difficulty in paying the teachers' salaries and dealing with the school's annual overdraft, which she told the Chief Rabbi was £1,000 a year. The occasion was the death of a founder and trustee of the school who had left money for educational purposes in his will. The problem for Ella was that its distribution had been left to the London Beth Din. In November 1931 she wrote to Chief Rabbi Hertz asking if some could be given to the JSS.

It was a difficult time economically for the whole country; the early days of the Depression. Hertz replied unsympathetically that he had his own problems; the Bayswater Jewish Schools owed £10,000 and the bank was pressing for repayment. No, there would be nothing for the JSS. He did congratulate her though in February 1932 on the 'excellent reports from H.M's inspectors', but offered no material help.[10]

It is generally agreed that Ella thought that money grew on trees in later life and she certainly passed on that belief to Solly; the trees in his case were potential donors and, if all else failed, it was fervently believed by both mother and son that the Almighty would fill the gap.[11] Ella was not hands on; she had followers who did the donkey work. The Schonfeld household over which she presided was, however, the engine room. It is remembered as genial chaos, with the sons all rushing around and relatives from Hungary occupying spare rooms. When Moses, Senath, Solly and Kibo were together, the standard of intellectual discussion reached a high level.

In late 1931 Dr Smith left the school and was replaced by the former headmaster of Highbury Secondary School, W.E. Spragg. Rabbi Munk was joint headmaster and would have taken responsibility for the Jewish studies programme. Within the Adath, Munk had built up his own supporters, but in July 1933, with Solly's return imminent, the Adath Honorary Officers said goodbye and voted him a lump sum of £100 and a year's salary at £5 a week to tide him over till the end of September 1934. By that time it was expected that he would have managed to find another congregation.

While this showed that Munk was held in high regard, his income for the year would only be half what he had been getting. He was 33 years old and had a new wife; they both had cause for concern. When he decided to move to Golders Green it was not easy to get an ultra-Orthodox community started, but during 1934 a number of refugees arrived from Germany and they provided the nucleus of worshippers he needed.

It was planned that Solly would be ready to take over as rabbi of the community and religious head of the UOHC in time for the High Holy Days in the autumn of 1933. According to some senior members now though, the same post had been offered to Rabbi Munk, which would have left Solly with just the Adath synagogue congregation. As with most religious communities, there was plenty of internal politics. There always would be. In spite of the fact that Harry Goodman and Bernard Homa regarded Munk highly, it was Kestenbaum who dominated the UOHC Council and made sure the seat was kept warm for Solly. Moses wrote to Solly at the yeshiva as early as November 1930: 'From the beginning

Kestenbaum has taken up an attitude of hostility towards Munk'. Rabbi Munk moved on, as it was now publicly said had been arranged from the outset. Harry Goodman angrily denied that this was the arrangement. At all events, Munk was to prove an inspiring spiritual leader in his own right.

When Solly left for the Continent in early 1930 to obtain his rabbinical qualification, he studied in Nitra and then moved to Slobodka Yeshiva near Kovno in Lithuania and also enrolled in the University of Koenigsberg to gain a doctorate. He studied English Literature, Pedagogics and Oriental Languages, and his thesis was on 'The Creation, the Fall and the English'. One of the JSS pupils also remembers that Solly was engaged and disengaged during those years,[12] so it was not all hard work. Financial support came from a number of sources, including Moses who sent him £1.50 from his wages at a chemical company. As a result of all this activity, less than three years later, Rabbi Dr Solomon Schonfeld came back to London.

When Schonfeld left for Nitra he only had a good school certificate – the 1930s equivalent of five GCSEs. It would have been a very long academic trail winding from GCSE to a British PhD, lasting at least eight years and probably ten. Dr Schonfeld managed to complete his studies in Europe in three years - at the same time studying for his semicha, which also involves mastering a seriously lengthy curriculum. It has to throw some doubt on the rigour of the examination for a PhD at a Continental university between the wars but it was not an unusual situation at the time. Perhaps it was the Continental equivalent of a Masters degree which also entitled the holder to the title of Doctor. It seemed something of a team effort; in his thesis he acknowledged the help he had received from a good friend, Dr Judith Grunfeld, who had a similar Continental doctorate and who was to work with him closely in the future, and from Senath on philological research, the study of the language used.

The semicha was a different matter. Schonfeld would have had the benefit of his father's tuition at home for many years and he was supervised at Nitra by two great rabbis: the head of Nitra Yeshivah, Rabbi Samuel David Ungar and his son-in-law, Rabbi Michoel Ber Weissmandl, a distant Sternberg cousin. He had also spent time at yeshiva with Weissmandl before his father died and he had certainly worked hard. There is no doubt he earned his semicha but there are different grades of qualification. The minimum examination is on the first of four parts of the Shulchan Aruch. Did he only master that or did he cover all four parts of the work, which would be the equivalent of first class honours? He certainly studied the second part because his notes on it survive.

In later life Schonfeld never pretended to be a great Talmudic expert. He looked to more widely read scholars to solve knotty points of Jewish law for the UOHC. Where his father had not accepted the legal decisions of the Beth Din of the United Synagogue, his son soon had the perfect excuse for doing so. In 1934, Yechezkel Abramsky, a great Talmudic sage, arrived in London. Abramsky was a rabbi in Russia by the age of 17 in 1903, but he had always been at odds with the atheistic communists. In 1929 he was sentenced to five years imprisonment in Siberia, but he was helped by senior British politicians, like George Lansbury, the head of the Labour Party, to get this quashed and emigrate to England. The Chief Rabbi was delighted to be able to make him the day-to-day head of the rabbinic court.

There was an occasion during his tenure of office when Abramsky was giving evidence in a British case and the judge asked him who was the greatest expert on Jewish law in England. 'I am', said Abramsky. The judge was unused to such bald claims and said to Abramsky, 'Rabbi, weren't you taught to be modest?' From the depths of one of the largest and unruliest beards in captivity, Abramsky said, 'Yes, M'Lord, but I'm on oath!'

As far as Schonfeld was concerned, he now had far more knowledge than the vast majority of his congregation and the rest could be safely left to Abramsky, who had been to his own alma mater, Slobodka, among other yeshivahs. There were other good Talmudic minds in the ranks of the UOHC community rabbis as well. Where did Schonfeld stand in matters of law? Jacob, Solly's brother, who himself spent five years in yeshivahs, describes his sibling as a Heter Rabbi – a Permission Rabbi. When a congregant has a problem and needs a generous interpretation of Talmudic commandments, a Heter Rabbi would be likely to give one. Some rabbis stick strictly to the letter of the law, while some try to find a way round intractable problems. For example, in the case of suicide, the Talmudic law is perfectly clear in considering it a monumental sin, because it is up to the Almighty to decide the time of death. Suicide is punished in Jewish law by denying the person the right to be buried in a Jewish cemetery. However, if the person committed suicide while mentally ill they would not be held responsible for their actions. So it was effectively agreed by many rabbis that anybody who commits suicide must have been mentally ill at the time they made their terrible decision. It still remains a sin today but, using this loophole, the mourners can give the body a Jewish burial. Heter rabbis would approve of the thought process, and Jewish law does not condemn looking for the loophole, in the same way as in secular law, where it is illegal to evade tax but it is perfectly legal to avoid it, if it can be done legitimately.

Schonfeld would have said that he always tried to apply a balanced view. Finding a way, though, fitted in with his attitude towards any problem he would come up against for the rest of his life. If there was an obstacle to his plans, it was there to be removed or circumvented. He believed that problems were to be eliminated by hard work, by deep thought, by persuasion, impassioned appeal, logical argument and an insightful psychological approach. And if none of those worked to eliminate the problem, then a way round it would still have to be found.

That was Schonfeld's approach, though he would have quoted the rule that one can neither subtract nor add to the Torah. There were many instances where Jewish law is absolutely clear and then Schonfeld would apply it rigorously. For example, a scroll of the law can only be moved from one house to another if it is going to be used there three times. Schonfeld always insisted that this rule be applied.

The JSS had made progress in his absence. In 1932 it had been possible to dedicate two new classrooms at Alexandra Villas, plus the Fink library and a science laboratory donated by Pincus Paul, the inventor of many internationally recognized fur dyes. Like everybody else, Jews would like to be remembered after their death. All sorts of buildings are financed and named after parents, as charitable donations, by Christians and Jews alike, such as the Burrell Collection, Robinson College Cambridge and the Fink library.

Ella spoke cautiously at the dedication of the library and classrooms: 'After a long and bitter struggle the school might be said to be turning the corner.'[13] All they now needed, she spelt out, were books, apparatus, donations, subscriptions and, above all, more pupils. She was critical that 'Adath members who had revered Victor, still sent their sons to non-Jewish schools. If they would only visit the JSS she was sure they would be converted from this habit.' She had been equally critical of the reaction of her own children to her financial problems, writing to Solly in 1931 that, 'I am sorry to say the children do not bother about it at all'.[14] As only Moses was over 20 years of age and Senath and David had hardly left school, this was a little hard. Teenagers often expect parents to deal with all the financial problems.

Many of Victor's supporters were indeed anxious to help expand the school roll. Bernard Homa, his doctor, sent his son Ramsay to the school. But it was only two weeks before he pulled him out again; the teaching was simply not up to standard. Aaron Winegarten lasted three years but later considered them totally wasted. The problem he felt was that the staff were always changing and, at 14, he escaped to the Regent Street Polytechnic.

Solly returned to London late in 1933. When he first entered the synagogue for the Friday night service, everybody stood up, even those who were Munk supporters. The English base to which Solly returned was very different from the world we live in today. The state took a far greater interest in public morality than it does now. The Hays Office in America set standards for what could and could not be shown in films. The Lord Chancellor in Britain censored plays. Lord Reith, in charge at the BBC, was a strict moralist and was quite capable of banning a comedian who used smutty material. Solly would say 'dammit', but much to the dislike of the ladies in the family. Top shelf magazines were, of course, far less explicit than they are today. The pill had not been invented. Abortion was illegal. At Universities like Oxford and Cambridge there were only single-sex colleges. Women had to have left the precincts at Jesus College, Cambridge by 10 o'clock at night and by midnight at Trinity College. If Jesus men did not regard the distinction as psychologically valid, the prohibition was still rigorously enforced. The Lord's Day Observance Society had widespread support in maintaining the solemnity of the Sabbath day. Shops closed on Sunday and in Wales the pubs did as well. There was no television and so no erotic films available in the home. There was no drug problem for the great majority of the population.

In that milieu the moral attitude of the country as a whole could be compared in some respects with the standards set down for a community that lived by the laws of *Torah im derech eretz*. It might be felt that the majority of the community drank too much but that was not unknown among Jews either. The need for the Charedim to build walls of Talmudic observance around the community to keep out low standards of popular morality was not considered an urgent problem. That situation would change over the years.

When Schonfeld returned in 1933, he was thrown in at the deep end. There had always been a great need for money for the school; what Solly immediately brought to the fund-raising party was style and chutzpah. Here was a poor group of small synagogues in an unfashionable part of London. They had a little school in a converted house and hardly any equipment. Only a tiny percentage of the Jewish community believed in the concept or indeed the desirability of a Charedi school, and the effects of the Depression on public generosity had inevitably been severely adverse. So if a fund-raising dinner was to be held for this minute enterprise, which local hall might be appropriate? Solly booked Claridges! Only the finest hotel in the West End was good enough. What was more he persuaded Sir Robert Waley Cohen, the supreme power in the United Synagogue, to take the chair and to be Chairman of the Appeal Committee. The list of patrons Schonfeld collected would have done credit to any fashionable Jewish charity today; the Chief Rabbi, Haham Gaster, Dayanim Feldman and Lazarus, Barnett Janner MP, Sir George Jones MP, powerful industrialists like Oscar Philipp, Henry van den Bergh, Gustave Tuck and many others.

The rationale was that nobody in the public Jewish eye would want for one moment to be seen to be against Jewish education. No matter whether they thought a successful Charedi school was pie in the sky, no matter how lukewarm might be their private support for such a concept, no matter how they yearned to send their sons to Eton, no Orthodox Jew in any kind of authority could say publicly that more and higher levels of Jewish education was a bad idea.

Waley Cohen, who came from a mixed Orthodox/Reform background, said in his speech at the dinner that, 'he had had his doubts as to whether separate Jewish schools were the best way in which we could further the work of Jewish education, but I am now convinced that this work is going to be of enormous importance to the future of Judaism in this country'. That was the public stance, but the reality was very different. If they could afford it, the children of the Jewish well-to-do would definitely not be put down at birth for the JSS. The growth of Jewish schools would only come from unremitting hard work by dedicated supporters in pursuit of the goal. As Barnett Janner said in his speech at the dinner: 'In the years that have passed, Mrs. Schonfeld has, day in and day out also advocated the same cause.' Compliments for Ella were a theme of the evening.

That night Solly had arrived. Resplendent in full evening dress – though with a rabbinic frock coat – and a neat reddish-blond beard, he looked like a British counterpart of the Jewish Hollywood star, Paul Muni. Confidently, he took his place with the good and the great. It was a remarkable performance: a young rabbi, with the ink hardly dry on his semicha, addressing the distinguished company to the manner born, on what he intended to do with the school movement his father had started. It was this new 22-year-old rabbi, *Dr* Schonfeld, who laid down his marker when he spoke at the dinner. He said his job was to 'teach the boys their Judaism and their Englishism'.[15] They were, he said, both parts of one homogeneous whole. The school would teach science, literature, Judaism, languages, history, sport and art. *Torah im derech eretz* would indeed remain the cornerstone philosophy of his schools throughout his life.

The aim was to raise £10,000 to rehouse the school in a building which would get the approval of the Ministry of Education. First things, first; the school was teaching up to Matric ('GCSE' level). The teachers might not be so good but the pupils were – as they always would be

– excellent material to work on. The JSS could, however, still be closed down if the Ministry found the school's infrastructure unacceptable. One of the industrialists present pointed out, quite correctly, that a decent school could not be built for £10,000. He offered £2.50 for every £100 raised. In all that night, £3,000 (equivalent to about £142,000 today) was raised.

Solly's full evening dress was symbolic of his approach. He was, by nature, a great showman. Some said he would have made a great actor and he was certainly able to play many roles when he set out to achieve his objectives. Very often there would be little substance behind the facade; the full evening dress might well have covered an inability to pay pressing school creditors. On the other hand, who could fail to be impressed? Where young United Synagogue ministers would have appeared in a dinner jacket with a vicar's clerical collar, Solly would have fitted in seamlessly at a diplomatic levée. He was to become a negotiating magician and even if it was all done with mirrors, it was no less effective for that.

One of Schonfeld's closest colleagues over the years marvelled at the control he had over his audiences in his prime. One youngster remembers the rabbi conducting the Neilah service at the end of Yom Kippur, the great fast. With his considerable height, his blue eyes and neat beard, he was a formidable figure. Schonfeld's singing voice was not distinguished but when he prayed that the gates of heaven would remain open for the community, the boy never doubted that there was no power in the celestial world who would refuse his entreaty. He had a great effect on his audience, though even in those early days he could be confrontational. Addressing the same boy on his bar mitzvah, he ticked him off for looking round when reading his portion of the Torah, to see that Solly was following the prayers. He could admonish members of the congregation in the pulpit, by name, on occasions as well. He was not a typical rabbi.

Most saw Solly's ability to change roles at a moment's notice as remarkable; the Charedi rabbi, the poor schnorrer (beggar) for his schools, the Moses leading the people to a better educational land, the steely dictator and the charming PhD were all in the magic box, to be produced to order. It has to be recognized, however, that it is only possible to make such differing characters credible if each attribute actually exists within your personality. Schonfeld was, quite genuinely, multifaceted; he enjoyed mixing in different worlds and felt comfortable in all of them, in part because of his monumental self-confidence.

Schonfeld recognized that one of his main tasks was to spell out the advantages of a Jewish education to a sceptical Jewish community. He was newsworthy when he came from Slobodka and took the opportunity offered by *The Jewish Chronicle* to make his case. In the article he made many crucial points, the most important of which was that a young person should not decide to be an observant Jew because it would please other people; he had to do it for himself. He held that it would be easier to come to that conclusion if he was properly educated in the tenets of the religion.

Like his father before him, Solly looked for support from the widest area possible. He felt it was no longer enough to just recruit paying guests for a dinner. It became his custom to invite the great and the good to become Patrons of the Jewish Secondary School Movement. It was not surprising that Sir Robert Waley Cohen (1933), Lord Nathan (1934) (from Schonfeld's articled days), and Moses Gaster (1937) should agree. Future eminent names, however, would include R.A. Butler (1943), Edmund de Rothschild (1947) and Clement Attlee (1956). Then there was the film maker, Sir Michael Balcon (1949), philanthropist Sir Louis Sterling (1955) and Sir Michael Sobell (1959), the father of Lord Weinstock of GEC. Chief Rabbis, cabinet ministers and business leaders, all were roped in to lend their distinguished status to the good cause. It was PR at its most professional.

Money was one thing, but good teachers were still hard to find and Schonfeld wanted an inspirational, properly qualified, *Torah im derech eretz*-supporting, highly experienced woman to run his projected girls school. And one he could afford. He had, in fact, found her when his mother invited a fund-raiser from Poland to join them for Friday night dinner. Their guest was a Frankfurt-trained teacher, Judith Grunfeld, who had worked with Sarah Schenirer in Poland. Schenirer was the moving spirit in providing a proper Orthodox Jewish education for girls in Poland and her inspiration spawned a large number of schools, many of which are alive and well to this day. When Grunfeld had first come to London to raise money for the Schenirer schools she had been welcomed by Chief Rabbi Hertz and thrown in the deep end at a small dinner he arranged for her with some of the Jewish movers and shakers.

When the time came for her to speak Grunfeld started by painting the picture of the spiritual deprivation of the girls in Europe and the Talmudic solution. To her surprise, at this very early point in her address, she was interrupted by Hertz, who thanked her for her unfinished contribution and started to talk of the necessary budgets and outgoings with which Schenirer had to deal. As he explained to Grunfeld in private later, the aesthetic and moral approach was not the best way to reach the pockets of the senior members of the United Synagogue!

Grunfeld was now 31 years old, compared to Solly's 21 years, and she and her German lawyer husband, Isidor Grunfeld, had recently had a baby. For the educational talent scout, however, Judith Grunfeld was the perfect candidate. An experienced fund-raiser, she was also a forceful personality and strikingly good looking, which did no harm when trying to raise money. Schonfeld immediately asked her during the dinner if she'd like to teach at the school.

Grunfeld demurred because she had to care for the baby, but Schonfeld was persistent and soon successful. Like Schonfeld, Grunfeld felt the Almighty had always guided her footsteps. As she said, 'Sometimes in life one feels the moving hand of the Divine, and this is a great privilege'. Also, like Schonfeld, she believed that it was always possible to win, no matter the odds against her. One of her favourite sayings was, 'All the darkness cannot extinguish one tiny light, but one tiny light can extinguish all the darkness'. Grunfeld agreed that her parents could look after her baby while she taught at the JSS. She was soon appointed Head Mistress of a JSS girls school which was opened in 1936 in Stamford Hill, and for the rest of Schonfeld's life she was to be one of his greatest supports.

The need for money for the schools constituted a continuing crisis but it doesn't cost anything to dream. Schonfeld saw the school system he wanted to create in absolutely clear terms. The JSS would not be developed as what would become a secondary modern school for the children of the poor. He looked round the small classrooms, officiated at the morning assembly in a disused garage, and still determined that his would be a public school. The masters would wear gowns, there would be prefects and a house system, the children would have a uniform, a Speech Day and a Sports Day. It was this vision which somewhat differentiated the JSS from the JFS. The Jews' Free School would set its sights lower than the great public schools when it came to the height of its ambitions for its pupils. Schonfeld deferred to nobody.

Schonfeld, like his father before him, contemplated taking non-Jewish children as well, though this never happened. He felt it would be good for them to see how well they were treated in a Jewish school, compared to the bullying which was often the fate of Jewish children in a Christian school. As for the non-observant Jews, the policy would be not to take children from the Reform and Liberal movements, always assuming that any of their parents wanted to be involved in a Charedi school in the first place. Most of the pupils would come from Charedi families, but he would take 9 per cent of his intake from the ranks of less observant families within the whole Jewish Orthodox community. His choice of 9 per cent as the figure was taken from the contents of incense, as laid down in the Talmud Tractate Kerithoth 6a.

Incense is made up of many elements and one of the essential parts is Galbanum. This is a foul smelling ingredient but without it, the other parts do not mix happily together to produce the desired result. The percentage of Galbanum in the mixture is 9 per cent.

NOTES

1. *The Jewish Chronicle*, 3 July 1930.
2. David Kranzler, *Holocaust Hero* (Jersey City, NJ: Ktav Publications, 2004).
3. Ibid.
4. *The Jewish Chronicle*, 19 February 1937.
5. David H. Kranzler, 'Schonfeld, Solomon (1912–1984)', *Oxford Dictionary of National Biography* (Oxford: Oxford University Press, 2004).
6. Schonfeld archive at the University of Southampton.
7. Derek Taylor, *British Chief Rabbis: 1664–2006* (London and Portland, OR: Vallentine Mitchell, 2006).
8. Councillor Joe Lobenstein in conversation with the author.
9. Rabbi Richer's son, Herbert, in conversation with the author.
10. London Metropolitan Archives, Hertz papers.
11. Jacob Schonfeld in conversation with the author, 2006.
12. Aaron Winegarten in conversation with the author, 2007.
13. *The Jewish Chronicle*, 15 July 1932, p.5.
14. Schonfeld archive at the University of Southampton.
15. Ibid.

# 3   1933–1938: Life Gets More Difficult

As the 1930s wore on, arguments about religious differences almost paled into insignificance compared to the major Jewish problem: the threat posed by the anti-Semitic fervour of the new German Chancellor, Adolf Hitler. Thankfully, in 1933, Hitler could only attack German Jews and this, at least, gave the British community the chance to concentrate on the problem. Initially, only a small number of realists appreciated the necessity of getting all the German Jews to emigrate before it was too late. Eventually 85 per cent did leave the country before the war, but the task of finding them an alternative home was difficult in the extreme.

The Jewish organizations around the world tried to create havens for refugees. Not for the first time, one of these needed to be Britain and the Board of Deputies called on the government soon after Hitler came to power to discuss what could be done. Both sides realised the gravity of the situation but diplomacy was of the essence in arriving at a satisfactory approach to the problem.

From the British point of view immigration was a hot potato in a country striving to come out of the Slump and with millions of its own citizens unemployed. It was feared that simply to allow unfettered Jewish immigration would be politically unpopular, and would not cast the Jewish community in a good light. In the 1890s Jewish immigrants had been accused of undercutting the wages of the British-born, in industries such as tailoring. It could happen again.

Furthermore, the country was in a difficult financial position. With the large numbers of unemployed, tax revenues had suffered and outgoings on dole payments had increased. Exports, too, had been badly affected by the Slump and yet there were demands for more money to be made available for rearmament. Accepting additional financial burdens by supporting an unlimited number of immigrants – even if they could be classed as refugees – was really not an option. The Americans, like many other countries, refused to alter their quota system for immigrants. The British would block another possible exit route by limiting Jewish immigration into Palestine where they were the de facto power, given a mandate by the League of Nations.

The Jewish leadership in Britain recognized the justice of the government's economic arguments and came up with a truly noble solution: they would guarantee that if the immigrant visas were granted, they would, themselves, ensure that the state was not called upon for any financial support – now or in the future. Negotiations were conducted with a senior Jewish delegation. For 150 years the representative body discussing Jewish concerns with the government of the day had been the Board of Deputies. Its current president, Neville Laski, was a highly regarded barrister and a member of the delegation. There was also the Chairman of the newly formed German-Jewish Aid Committee, Otto Schiff, who had been instrumental in getting the Jewish community out of Belgium in the First World War. The Home Office were also happy to accept his word for the massive commitment involved. In the end it was agreed that visas would be provided for the total of between 1,000 and 5,000 refugees that both sides considered would be in need of them; the final figure, however, would be 50,000.

The years that followed were to see vastly greater demands made on the charitable efforts of the Jewish community than had been initially envisaged. From 1933 to 1939 an astonishing three million pounds was raised to help the German Jewish community. That means that about 400,000 people – men, women and children – produced the equivalent of £144 million today (about £350 a head).[1]

There were, however, hidden agendas. One of them was an objective of the increasingly powerful Zionist lobby. They wanted to marry the terrible danger facing German Jews to their aim to get larger quotas for Jews wanting to emigrate to Palestine. To the Zionists, ultimately, the fate of the Continental Jews had to be incidental in pursuit of that ambition; they simply regarded them as casualties in the war to make the future state of Israel a reality.

Chaim Weizmann, the future first president of Israel, would make the Zionist position crystal clear at the 20th Zionist conference in 1937. 'I want to save two million of youth ... the old ones will pass, they will bear their fate or they will not. They are dust, economic and moral dust in a cruel world ... only a remnant shall survive ... we have to accept it.' In December 1938 David Ben Gurion, who would be the first prime minister of Israel, went on record on the same subject:

> If I knew it would be possible to save all the children in Germany by bringing them over to England and only half of them by transporting them to Eretz Israel, then I would opt for the second alternative. For we must weigh not only the life of the children, but also the history of the people of Israel.[2]

The viewpoint of the die-hard Zionist could have catastrophic consequences. For example, the Swedish government also became concerned about the threat to the German Jews. They passed a law in the Swedish parliament to suspend their immigration policies in favour of German Jewish refugees. The religious head of the Swedish Jews, Rabbi Marcus Ehrenpreisz, was, however, a fanatical Zionist. To save the German Jews would reduce the pressure on the British government's Palestine quota system. He helped to persuade the Swedish government to withdraw the law. Many of the Jews who died in gas chambers could have been saved otherwise. This was the same Rabbi Ehrenpreisz who, as Chief Rabbi of Bulgaria before the First World War, decreed 'that anyone who refused to donate to Zionist causes would be forbidden to have his sons circumcised'. This was an appalling misuse of power and quite without justification in Jewish law.

To a humanitarian like Schonfeld, the official Zionist attitude was totally unacceptable. Jewish law clearly laid down that saving life was the greatest positive commandment that could be performed and Schonfeld was never about to second guess the Almighty. He would never forgive or forget the Zionist approach at that time.

So, for the Zionists, the most welcome refugees would be the able bodied who could go on to Palestine and help build the country. Old Talmudic sages and physically inactive yeshiva students were not top of their visa pecking order. As the Zionists were well organized and often dominated committees dealing with government authorities on the subject of visas, this weighted the odds against potential Orthodox refugees. For the Charedim, like Solomon Schonfeld, this distinction was simply against Jewish law. Indeed, according to the Talmud, the wise have preference even over the women and children. The great Talmudist, Moses Maimonides, had also made it clear many centuries before: 'whoever is greater in wisdom takes precedence over his colleagues'. The Zionists were not, however, going to allow their aims and objectives to be undermined by ancient Jewish laws.

The Jewish community in Britain was keen on rescuing its brethren, but less keen on keeping them in Britain. Most of the native-born would have preferred Britain to be a form of transit camp refuge before the German Jews moved on. The problem here was not just that the migrants were foreign but that they were often poor and most were considered common; society was far more class conscious in those days than it is today. Still worse, some refugees, once in Britain, remained staunchly patriotic about the Fatherland. They were quite prepared to criticize anything in England which failed to measure up to the standards of German efficiency at home. This was naturally very unpopular and the Jewish Refugee committees felt it necessary to provide them with leaflets in German asking them to stop forthwith, to no avail. Not unreasonably, British Jews thought the German refugees were biting the hand that fed them. They were concerned that both the refugees' appearance and behaviour would be likely to let the side down.

There was also a perceived problem because the Orthodox refugees often came from the determinedly unassimilated segments of the German Jewish community. It was feared they might undermine the patriotic and inclusive image which the Jewish leaders in Britain had been trying to promote for at least the past 250 years. In pursuing this goal British Jews deserved an 'A' for effort, though they had often failed to convince all the Establishment.

For mainstream Jewry the right image was the ultimate prize. It even involved religious appurtenances. Take the *tallit*. A *tallit* is a prayer shawl worn by men at morning services in synagogue. The shawl must have fringes at its four corners, knotted in a specific way; there are no other specifications. For centuries Jews wore white woollen *talleisim* with black stripes, even though it is permissible to have a *tallit* in any colour and almost any size as long as it has four corners. For most of the Charedim the garment is all-enveloping. United Synagogue members decided the old *talleisim* had overtones of the ghetto and that wool was a downmarket material. Smaller silk *talleisim* with light blue stripes became the fashion. The ultra-Orthodox continued to stick to wool and black. It was a question of image v tradition.

The early 1930s also saw an obvious crisis building up in Austria where the Nazis were very popular. Solly went there in March, May and August 1935 and twice in 1936. At the end of that year he met a Romanian Jewess called Bertha Halpern in a hotel in Vienna. She was 22 at the time and is remembered by the Schonfeld family as a very nice girl. On 12 March 1937 there was an announcement in *The Jewish Chronicle* of their engagement, with a reception at Lordship Park. One week later, on 17 March they were married at Stoke Newington Registry Office.[3]

Today eyebrows would hit the ceiling; a week's engagement and a registry office wedding were highly inappropriate behaviour for a rabbi. In 1937, however, everybody realized that Jews on the Continent faced appalling difficulties. By then there was any amount of anti-Semitic legislation and in Vienna the prospect of a German invasion was very real and extremely frightening. What Bertha Halpern needed more than anything else was a safe harbour and Solly, by marrying her, provided her with a British passport. According to her own testimony, when they divorced five months later in Vienna, the marriage had never been consummated.[4]

Domestically, Schonfeld was temporarily married – all rabbis are expected to be so permanently – and carrying out his pastoral duties. In February 1937 when Moses Gaster was 80 years old, a JSS delegation headed by Schonfeld called on the old Haham to present him with an illuminated address to their 'spiritual father, Dr. Gaster'. It was a nice compliment from the Charedim to the only Ashkenazi who has ever served as Haham to the Sephardi community.

In August, Solly and Bertha parted amicably. Bertha gave Solly a statement confirming that the marriage had been a way of getting her a British passport and that neither she nor Solly had considered themselves married on the basis of the civil ceremony, as there had been no religious ceremony. They had, however, presumably needed to live together at times during the marriage. Bertha married again in Switzerland in 1939 and, hopefully, lived happily ever after.

Solly had taken an enormous risk. From the finest of motives he had safeguarded the life of a young woman, even if the whole of Jewish London could now know that he was a married man. Far fewer, of course, would learn that a few months later he was a divorcee. At all events, it was never held against him. Where he would have difficulty later was in proving that the Austrian divorce was valid. In 1937 Catholics could not get a divorce in Austria, though Jews could, through the *bezirksgericht*, the local court. The situation could be confusing. Years after the marriage ended, Bertha still visited the Schonfeld home in London on occasions and she was always welcomed.

That it was a marriage of convenience is also pretty well proved by some rather unorthodox evidence. Solly had just returned to London following the divorce proceedings when he received a letter from Lipton & Jeffries in October.[5] This was a firm of lawyers who had been retained by a Miss Grolman to pursue her claim against Solly for breach of promise. He had, apparently, sent her letters which might be construed as an offer of marriage. The relationship had been going on for some months during the time he had officially been married to Bertha. Naturally, for the case to have come to court would have been an unmitigated disaster. Any Beth Din would also have considered it a serious allegation. Jewish law concerning broken engagements is far fairer to the woman than was the case with many other ancient cultures. If the engagement is broken off without the approval of one or the other partner, substantial compensation is mandatory.

Solly denied that he had ever proposed marriage. He wrote to the lawyers 'I explained ... that I have not promised for sure to marry you.' As he wrote to his own legal advisers though, he did not want to defend himself in court as 'such a step would involve the probability of far greater financial and moral loss than any fight can compensate'. In later life it was a pity that he did not always consider the validity of that argument. It was agreed by November 1937 to settle out of court for the full £700 (£10,000 in today's money) that Ms Grolman wanted.

The letters of the two parties were returned to the writers and Ms Grolman gave an undertaking that, if she was asked, she would deny that any settlement had been necessary or made. Ms Grolman then disappeared from the picture, never to be seen again, except on a document in the Schonfeld archive. The question of where £700 came from in the cash-strapped Schonfeld family is lost in the mists of time, but Solly must have been very much indebted to some friend who agreed to bail him out. The size of the calamity averted could hardly be exaggerated. It was, perhaps, one of the first instances in his life when 'whenever there was an emergency, his supporters would gather round him and did what was necessary'.[6] Certainly, his supporters at the Adath who had originally recommended him for the job, would not have wanted a potential scandal of this kind.

The family were starting to spread their wings. Moses had been in Palestine, acting as the Honorary Secretary of the Palestinian Crown Colony Association. Now he was off to America to hold a series of meetings on the Association's behalf. Solly's responsibilities were many. As the rabbinic head of the UOHC, he was deeply involved in its kashrut, educational endeavours, the provision of mikva'ot (ritual baths) and the maintenance of the Chevra Kadishah, volunteers who ensured that the dead were interred in the traditional manner. He was active in encouraging other congregations to join the UOHC and in visiting them to give sermons.

He was also at the coal face in dealing with the relationship between his organization and the Chief Rabbi's United Synagogue. This was prickly, to say the least. For example, Hertz had come to the consecration of Rabbi Munk's Golders Green Beth Hamedrash in 1935 and had taken the opportunity to attack Charedi Jews who 'haven't sufficient Judaism to love their fellow Jews' and to cooperate with them. The other side of the coin was that the UOHC had been pressing since 1929 for an improvement in the expertise of the Dayanim of the London Beth Din.

The UOHC's position was that some members of the body's Dayanim were not sufficiently knowledgeable of the Talmud to carry out their functions. This criticism of the predominant and self-important United Synagogue by a tiny community of the Charedim was widely resented and matters did not improve when Schonfeld soon created his own Kedassia kosher label. The idea was that manufacturers making products acceptable to the UOHC would be able to use the label and that they would have to set an even higher standard of kashrut than that approved by the Beth Din. The Adath had always had approved shops and this was an exercise in brand building. Even so, immediately, this became a new cause of conflict. It was considered *lèse-majesté* by the United Synagogue for the UOHC to suggest for a moment that the US were not setting sufficiently high standards.

A concrete instance arose in the summer of 1936. The Home Office gave a visa to a German butcher. The Beth Din then gave him a licence to run his business. When, however, he tried to use the UOHC Kedassia label, he was told by the US Beth Din that he could not do so. The licence was solely for products approved by them. Schonfeld wrote to complain to Hertz: 'I shall try and ascertain from you *personally*'. Hertz was not at all intimidated, and wrote back tersely reiterating the position of his Beth Din. That was the end of it. As far as the United Synagogue were concerned, the flea on the back of the elephant was being swatted away again. There were justifiable arguments on both sides, but if there had been a basic accord between them the problem would have been settled amicably. To an extent the UOHC was holier than thou but, equally, the United Synagogue Honorary Officers could be unnecessarily lax in their religious practices. These arguments were, however, typical of innumerable discussions between Orthodox Jewish bodies over the centuries. Normally, however, if there was an argument with outside organizations, they would sink their differences.

Where the Chief Rabbi and Schonfeld were fully in agreement was on the subject of Jewish education. Hertz wanted the Jewish children to have intensified Jewish studies and Schonfeld was one of the few equally anxious to allocate far more time than was to be found in Sunday School classes.

In 1937 the dinner to raise money for the schools had once again been held at Claridges. During that year new classrooms were erected as a result of increased efforts to obtain the necessary financial support, and were named after such Jewish luminaries as Solomon Wolfson, Sarah Klausner, Pesye Konigsburg and Charles Goldrei. The Council of the UOHC endowed two free places at the JSS in 1938 but, of course, in addition, they continued to make a substantial annual contribution towards subsidizing the schools' overheads through the profits of the Burial Society.

In 1938 with the approaching celebration of the Chief Rabbi's Silver Jubilee in office, it was agreed to mark the occasion by raising a fund which could be devoted to Jewish educational causes. One beneficiary would be the Stepney Jewish schools, to which Hertz had given preference when Ella had asked for financial support a few years before. The other would be the JSS. One of the advisers influencing Hertz could well have been Isidor Grunfeld, Judith's husband. The refugee lawyer had taken semicha and been appointed Registrar to the United Synagogue Beth Din. He would be appointed a Dayan in 1939. Grunfeld had a fine legal brain and this complemented the exceptional Talmudic knowledge of Yechezkel Abramsky, head of the Beth Din. Grunfeld would undoubtedly have spoken up for Schonfeld if his wife had asked him to. Thus the foundation for a more harmonious relationship between the Chief Rabbi and the religious head of the UOHC was first laid on that common educational ground.

Over 2,000 donors supported the fund which raised £1,500. At the Grosvenor House dinner to mark the milestone in the Chief Rabbi's ministry, with all the available Jewish luminaries present, it was still the 26-year-old Schonfeld who presented him with a scroll of honour containing the names of the donors. Schonfeld's feel for photo opportunities was already exceptional. The fund-raising was successful but was always going to be insufficient to deal with the running costs of the schools and their constant need to expand their infrastructure. The strain of trying to keep the school going stretched Solly's nerves. Time and again he would appeal for donations and come away empty handed. He wrote to *The Jewish Chronicle* in the depths of the winter of 1937 and lamented the situation.[7] As he pointed out, he had the full support of the Chief Rabbi and Moses Gaster for his efforts, but 'if I compare this with the negative attitude which I am unfortunately encountering, I fear there is something seriously wrong'. He agreed that the school was continuing, but 'not in a befitting way'. The educational authorities were pressing him for proper endowment and equipment. He said he could understand refusals but he was getting too many 'impolite rebuffs' and he felt that the community did not want to progress. He concluded, 'Will Anglo-Jewry do its duty?'

Those impolite rebuffs were not forgotten. In future years, when Schonfeld gave as good as he got on a wide range of subjects, he was criticized for his aggressive posture. The position was adopted by too many that it was acceptable to fob off and ignore the rabbi, but *they* had to be treated with the utmost respect. Schonfeld would increasingly not see it that way.

What Schonfeld was striving for was a school roll covering 10–18 year olds. He often said that real Jewish schooling only took place in the secondary stage of education between these ages. Where the Jewish community was losing its boys was after their bar mitzvahs. Up to that time they followed the example of their parents and studied for the great day when they came of age. After their bar mitzvah they began, as adolescents, to develop their own view on life and, without Jewish studies, their commitment too often withered on the vine. It was for those crucial years that Schonfeld wanted the responsibility of keeping them on the straight and narrow.

Anglo-Jewry certainly would do its duty if it believed in the cause. Apart from the money for the German refugees, the community collected money for a whole range of other good causes. The Jews are generally accepted to be in the medals in the world championship for fund-raisers for charity. Even British political parties have looked to experienced Jewish experts to help with their financial problems. The problem for Schonfeld was that the community in the 1930s did not see Jewish schools as a priority. As far as the vast majority were concerned, Sunday School would suffice. Another problem was that there were two kinds of appeal for donations within the Jewish community. On the one hand, there was the major fund-raising function, supported by the A and B lists, often in the ballroom of a top hotel, with all the guests dressed up to the nines, and which offered the chance to mingle with the mighty, including guests of honour such as top politicians, show business stars or even royalty. The worthy objective would be to help good causes like the Jewish Blind, organizations looking after the Jewish handicapped, or Jewish old age homes. Within Synagogue Ladies Guilds and Boards of Management up and down the country there would be similar functions arranged on a smaller scale.

In stark social contrast, there would more frequently come a knock on the door, usually on a Sunday morning. Outside their portals would be a man in a dark, shabby suit, with a large hat and a long beard, and usually speaking very little English. He would ask for money, showing them a piece of paper or a card on which there was a description of the charitable cause. This was often not known to the home owner, the card could be in Hebrew which they did not understand and any money they gave they wrote off as having gone to an indeterminate good cause. These visitors were known to the Jewish public at large as 'frummers' – which meant the Charedim – or 'schnorrers' – which meant they were beggars. Sometimes they were just that, begging from their wealthier brethren for their own personal needs.

The vast majority of this door-to-door fund-raising was for genuinely good causes though. The real problem with the Charedi efforts was that they were too often perceived as foreign and downmarket by those who were approached. The rich often condemn the poor as common, in many cases because the rich were born poor and hate to be dismissed by the 'old money' as nouveau riche. There was also always the suspicion that the money was being collected under false pretences or wasted, which some of it certainly could have been. The difficulty in reaching a judgement here is that people who raise money for charity are very good hearted, but, not necessarily, financial wizards. They can pile up high administrative expenses which eat up a large percentage of the money raised. They can make horrific errors in their investments, as even the Church of England did some years ago. The money can be raised for one purpose and spent on another.

This last accusation would often be levelled behind closed doors at Schonfeld. Did he raise money for the school and then give some of it to a desperately poor widow trying to avoid her children being taken into care by the local authority because she could not manage. Or did he pay a bill for a doctor for medicine which a congregant badly needed, because before there was an NHS, there was nobody to provide it free. It was never suggested that Schonfeld took a penny for himself. though he would have been totally justified in being reimbursed for his expenses. When he had money, there was a suspicion that it might go to pay the most pressing bill. Certainly, when he badly needed something for the schools and did not have the money in the bank, he might spend it anyway and worry about how to pay for the item later.

Solomon Schonfeld's schools would have been seen as part of these Charedi efforts to raise money. Gathering funds was extremely hard work and could be depressing, as it involved the level of rejection which every professional salesman takes in his stride. Schonfeld had one advantage though, not possessed by the average salesman. He could tell the potential donors that it was their duty to give him what he needed, which he believed it was. This would be another recurrent theme. A cadre of supporters, some for only a short time, some for many years, a few for his lifetime, but all for good, would back him up with hard cash.

In the wider world, senior politicians were becoming seriously concerned at the way the Jews were being treated in Germany. Stanley Baldwin, the former prime minister, made an appeal for the Jews on 8 December 1937 and the public contributed more than £500,000. It was not just Germany though. The virus of anti-Semitism was spreading: in Poland, for example, anti-Shechita (ritual slaughter) laws had been passed. Just as discriminatory, if a Jew said publicly that he thought a court sentence was unjust, he could be imprisoned for up to two years. The Romanian government was very anti-Semitic. The situation was deteriorating rapidly for the Jews in many parts of the Continent and much worse was to come.

By 1938 the Chief Rabbi was 66 years old and had held the office for twenty-five years. His wife had died and he sadly missed her support. He was at an age when most men retired. Instead, he faced two daunting challenges. The first was a long-term problem: his leading Honorary Officer, Sir Robert Waley Cohen, was the effective head of the United Synagogue. This body had reluctantly elected Hertz in 1913 as Lord Rothschild had been the President of the US at the time and had threatened to resign his communal position if Hertz *was not* elected. The United Synagogue Honorary Officers caved in, but Hertz was never the kind of man Waley Cohen would have chosen if he had had his way originally.

To begin with, Hertz was born a Slovakian and brought up in America. He was a staunchly Orthodox Jew who was determined to keep the United Synagogue in the Orthodox camp. Sir Robert wished to be more English than the English and wanted the United Synagogue to find a modus vivendi with the Reform movement, in which his mother was prominent and among whose adherents he had many friends. The Reform movement had started as a breakaway Orthodox community in the 1840s and had stayed that way for the best part of 100 years. In the 1930s, however, led by an American rabbi whose views were far to the left of the Orthodox, they had started to abandon fundamental Orthodox practices. Their views, and the views of the Liberal Synagogue movement, which was even further divorced from Orthodox beliefs, led to thunderous denunciations by Hertz, even though he was heavily criticized for the multilayered heaps of his contumely by many in his own camp. The battles between Waley Cohen and Hertz raged intermittently throughout the incumbency of both men. It reached a stage towards the end where they often could only communicate through intermediaries.

Hertz was certainly isolated because the Honorary Officers of the United Synagogue acted as Waley Cohen decided. Waley Cohen was a very senior Shell executive and a businessmen of that rank is not accustomed to being thwarted. He was also prepared to put in the hours, which is the root of power in a voluntary organization. Fortunately for the future of the Orthodox community, the 1870 constitution of the United Synagogue laid down very clearly that in all matters of religion, the Chief Rabbi had the final say. Even so, Hertz had been under immense pressure from Waley Cohen for many years to allow changes to be made, changes which would weaken the Orthodox position.

For example, the Chief Rabbi was the sole authority for recommending to the government that a synagogue be authorized to conduct marriages. At the time Solly came into his life, he had recently agreed to give permission for a Liberal Synagogue in the North of England to issue such documents. These certificates, however, were often for weddings in which one or other partner was not, by Orthodox standards, Jewish at all. Hertz would never have agreed to solemnize the marriages within the United Synagogue, but he allowed the Liberal Synagogue to do so, even though he subsequently regretted it. His rationale was that the 1930s were not the time to split the community further. Even so, the community, outside the Charedim, was already by no means of one mind.

Hertz's second problem was considerably more serious: Adolf Hitler and war loomed in the immediate future. In 1938 Hitler was still content just to get rid of the Jewish segment of the German population. As they were prohibited from taking most of their possessions with them, the opportunities were immense for what, effectively, was officially approved looting of their assets. The government gorged itself on Jewish bank balances. Thankful for great mercies, a final total of about 50,000 Jews came to Britain – a tremendous and wonderful effort by all concerned.

By comparison with the overall achievement of rescuing most of the German Jewish population, Schonfeld's personal contribution would not be all that large. It is particularly ironic that Otto Schiff, as Chairman of the renamed Jewish Refugee Committee responsible for most of the 50,000 rescued, is either forgotten or denigrated, whereas Schonfeld has correctly received the plaudits he so richly deserved. Schiff is accused of not doing enough while Schonfeld is praised for doing anything at all.

That was the historical lesson that Schonfeld would repeatedly illustrate: that if a man is sufficiently determined, even without a major power base, it might just be possible to achieve miracles. It was no longer Schonfeld's way at this time to *ask* for support. He was far more likely to demand it within the community. He learned the approach from his role model, Michoel ber Weissmandl, the son-in-law of the head of the Nitra Yeshiva. When the Hungarian rabbi, his old study partner from Tyrnau and Nitra, wrote to Schonfeld in 1938 to persuade him to demand action, as the danger facing the Austrian Jews worsened, he accused Schonfeld – and if the cap fitted, anybody else around him – of indifference to the developing calamity. In his letter he wrote in capital letters: 'ARE YOU MADE OF STONE THAT YOU DON'T MELT?' It was not that Weissmandl was putting on an act; the situation was as desperate as he painted it. It was the only possible approach; not supplicatory, not coaxing, not appealing. Weissmandl demanded and Schonfeld learned the lesson. His fund-raising took on another dimension.

This forceful approach would be added to Schonfeld's total armoury of persuasive tactics. In non-financial negotiation with authority, for example, the young Schonfeld was more flexible than the Jewish leadership as a whole, although as he grew older he would lose that skill. Schonfeld recognized better than the Jewish leaders that politics is the art of the possible. The leadership would meet in conferences and resolve to ask the government for major policy changes to help with the refugee problem. Conference speakers have a habit of trying to outdo each other in the extravagance of their demands. Schonfeld, unrestricted by any conference resolution, could be more pragmatic in his approach. He knew he had no power when dealing with government departments, other than the force of persuasion. By contrast, the Jewish leadership tried to act as a pressure group on the national stage in order to impress their community that they were doing their best. Unfortunately, they were trying to achieve unrealistic objectives when the whole country was facing disaster.

The British government faced its own overwhelming dilemmas. The Balfour Declaration, promising that the government would look with favour upon a National Home for the Jews in Palestine, had been issued in 1917. The government had made contradictory promises to the Arabs at the same time to persuade them not to support Britain's enemies in the First World War. This naturally led to both sides remonstrating when the British tried to improve matters in the 1920s and 1930s. As another war with Germany loomed, Britain was seriously unprepared for such a conflict. The more the 1930s wore on, the greater the importance of Arab oil and stability in the Middle East became to the national government, which had a massive majority in the House of Commons. British interests had to come first; no other approach made any sense.

So in reality the interests of the Jews carried very little weight. The British government, seeking to neutralize the Arab nations, would introduce a White Paper in May 1939 which reduced Jewish immigration into Palestine to a tiny fraction of what was – and would be even more – needed by the Jewish communities contemplating fleeing Europe. The situation was complicated still further by the need to reduce support for Hitler within Britain. The British Union of Fascists never exceeded a membership of 50,000. They never had an MP elected on a fascist ticket. The British people would not support extremism. Nevertheless, the government did not want to give the fascists a weapon of their own making: publicly supporting almost unlimited Jewish immigration to a Britain with high unemployment would have been a public relations gift to the fascists. Media favourable to them would have been in their element.

There was already a degree of anti-Semitism, based on supposed worldwide international conspiracies, described in the best-seller produced by the Czarist secret police many years before, *The Protocols of the Elders of Zion*. For those who hated the Jews, no accusation was too far fetched, and the government worried that the public might be gullible and believe such rubbish. They, therefore, considered they had to be very careful how they dealt with Hitler's fanatic hatred of the Jews and with the worsening anti-Semitic legislation within Germany.

There was another consideration. The purpose of British diplomacy was, very rightly, to try to stave off war. In such circumstances, interference with the internal affairs of another major European country would be very likely to lead to an aggravation of the ongoing crisis, without necessarily helping the German Jews in any way. Moreover, such interference was not accepted practice in diplomatic circles at that time. The League of Nations did not act as it did when the Muslims were threatened in Bosnia three quarters of a century later.

So it was impossible, officially, to get sufficient visas for refugees, and the Jewish authorities in Britain were respectable citizens who would expect to go through authorised channels to do their best for those who wanted to leave Germany, and eventually Austria, Czechoslovakia and Poland. In addition, of course, a lot of German Jews over-optimistically hoped that the Nazi excesses would be a passing phase and stayed put, hoping for the best.

Hertz was desperate to help any Jew threatened by Hitler, but he did not have the support he needed. He had two able Dayanim to settle legal questions, but they were both refugees and it was not their job to take the lead in the purely secular area of public relations within the wider community, or to help Hertz in his negotiations with a Britain which, to them, would have recently been a foreign government. It would have been helpful if Hertz had had some powerful clergy to support him, but the United Synagogue ministers were firmly under the thumb of the lay leaders of their congregations. They were pointed in the direction of synagogue administration. They were good for comforting the mourners, lecturing to bar mitzvah boys and visiting the sick; they had not been appointed to office to give their communities leadership. With a few exceptions, that role was strictly reserved for their synagogue's Honorary Officers. Only Hertz could provide Orthodox leadership and he was being worn down by Waley Cohen and those who thought like him. He could not even hope for support from a colleague in the Sephardi camp. After the Sephardim had fired Haham Gaster in 1917, they did not appoint another spiritual leader for more than thirty years.

Even in these perilous times, the different Jewish bodies trying to help refugees still could not stop quarrelling and vying with each other for supremacy. In July 1938 the Orthodox Agudas Yisroel had opened an Emigration Advisory Service in London to deal with emigration enquiries. It was immediately criticized by Otto Schiff and the Jewish Refugee Committee. Schiff said he was 'heartily sick of Agudas Israel and their machinations'. He told the Hilfsverein, the Jewish organization in Germany dealing with emigration: 'its committee is absolutely condemned by all the leading organisations'.[8] The Jewish organizations were fiddling while so many central European countries burned with anti-Semitic oppression.

A few months earlier, in March 1938, the Germans had marched into Austria and annexed the country. Jacob Rosenheim, the international president of the Agudas Yisroel turned to Hertz for support. They both agreed that a special fund was needed immediately to help German Jewry even more and to raise the funds to help Jews in other countries threatened by the Nazis. Hertz agreed to be the chairman. It was Schonfeld, a well-known fund-raiser, who was suggested for the role of Director of the Chief Rabbi's Religious Emergency Fund, which, in November, became the Chief Rabbi's Religious Emergency Council (CRREC). Hertz and Schonfeld may have clashed in the past, but in the present emergency they found it easy enough to set aside their differences.

In building their relationship, however, there must have been another consideration for the Chief Rabbi and it was of an intensely personal nature. Two years before, in August 1936, he had been dealt a devastating blow when his son, Daniel, committed suicide whilst still living at home. Daniel was a doctor and a research chemist. The death certificate says he took Nembutal and 'killed himself while of unsound mind'. The Coroner said that 'from a note he left behind it is quite clear that his state of mind was such that he had apparently lost faith in himself'.[9] The codicil of 'unsound mind' ensured that Daniel was buried in Willesden cemetery in London. Daniel was by far the brightest of Hertz's offspring and the Chief Rabbi and his children would have been bereft. If anyone appeared in the future to fill the yawning gap, it might help with the pain.

So less than two years after the loss of his son, Hertz enthusiastically greeted the arrival of the 26-year-old Schonfeld as Rosenheim's nominee and Weissmandl's spokesman. Here was a proper rabbi, not a reverend. Here was the young man Daniel might have been, and one who not only approved of Hertz's orthodoxy but, by his own behaviour, suggested that there could be a little more stringency added to even the Chief Rabbi's approach. For example, in the 1920s Hertz had been noted attending a non-Jewish education conference without covering his head. The ultra-Orthodox would have wondered how a man with such standards could have achieved the high position he held, though covering the head was not the rule at that time, as it is with so many today. Hertz would have blessed his good luck that, just when he needed a Schonfeld, one turned up.

The first meeting of the CRREC was on 21 July 1938 and the only people present were the Chief Rabbi, Harry Goodman, Jacob Rosenheim and Solly. Others would join later, but it was from that small nucleus that the body started. Thirteen thousand appeal letters were sent out and support was solicited from such community luminaries as Lionel de Rothschild, who Hertz called upon in person, taking Rabbi Dr Schonfeld with him. There were five meetings of the CRREC in 1938, but there would only be three in 1939 and only one in 1940 according to the Minute Book.[10] Once Schonfeld had settled in, he was much happier to work alone without interference. This was very much in line with his normal approach in the future: Solly did not really like committees.

For the Jewish Establishment, the most aggravating thing about Rabbi Dr Schonfeld was that he could not be controlled by the United Synagogue lay leaders. He was not employed by them and his organization was totally independent of them. Disastrously, from the point of view of the Board of Deputies, he was also not bound by any community agreement on the right way to approach the government. For 150 years that had been the role of the Jewish Board of Deputies. They were democratically elected, represented the majority of the community and were full of Jewish leaders. By contrast with this august assembly, Schonfeld was the epitome of the loose cannon and he was regarded with deep suspicion by the main body of the Jewish leadership. Waley Cohen's aim for years had been to gain total religious control by grinding down the Chief Rabbi. The last thing he wanted was to see him suddenly supported by a young, vigorous, independent, charismatic assistant with the same views as his religious chairman – or even more extreme, as it seemed.

From the point of view of the United Synagogue leadership, even more outrageous was the fact that the young rabbi was quite prepared to confront them. If they wanted a battle, Schonfeld was always prepared to give as good as he got. Waley Cohen must have felt that his support at the 1934 fund-raiser had done little to pacify his Charedi critics. The head of the Board of Deputies was still Neville Laski, the son-in-law of Moses Gaster, the old Haham. He knew the power of the lay authorities and he also knew that it was the Charedi rabbis who often ruled the roost in their own communities. He had witnessed the arrival of the Rabbi of Ger at a railway station on the Continent:

> Hundreds of thousands of, to me, Mediaeval looking Jews wearing strange hats and kaftans crowded on to the platform ... Excitement reigned supreme. I stood on a railway truck against a fence to obtain a better view, but soon repented, as a surging crowd, marching step by step with the Rabbi, nearly turned me and the truck into the roadway.[11]

Schonfeld came from a community which could, in the future, have the same regard for its rabbinic leader. In fact, Schonfeld would never have agreed with this level of devotion. He was not a Chassid and derided such leader-worship.

Although Schonfeld's appointment as Director of the CRREC could be portrayed as an administrative role, both men knew that Schonfeld would not be satisfied to let situations develop. In that November of 1938 Schonfeld took his first step on the international stage. He was invited to lecture to the Jewish provincial synagogues in Eire and he managed at the same time to meet Eamonn de Valera, the country's president, and talked to him about the plight of the Jews on the continent. De Valera promised to help, but jobs were hard to find in Ireland as well and a flood of immigrants was eventually considered likely to make matters worse.

The problem to which Schonfeld gave top priority was the danger facing the rabbinic leaders and synagogue officials in Germany. When the Adath had solemnly considered the problem, they had agreed to take care of ten refugees. Schonfeld recognized this number was derisory by comparison with the size of the problem. He had in mind 500, and the first problem was the necessary visas. The Chief Rabbi had no difficulty in arranging an appointment with the Home Office, but the pressure on the job market was uppermost in that ministry's mind. They asked Schonfeld why Britain needed these specific 500 ultra-Orthodox officials? What special skills did they possess which were unavailable in a country with millions unemployed. Among other suggestions, Schonfeld provided an answer the Home Office were generously prepared to accept. We have seen that a high proportion of Orthodox Jewish men wear an undergarment called a *tsitsit*. Schonfeld told the Home Office that all the proposed refugees could make *tsitsiyot*![12] The country was, in fact, as short of *tsitsit* knotters as it was of flint knappers! Nevertheless, the Home Office nodded gravely and provided the visas. In addition Schonfeld managed to persuade the

Dutch to accept forty-three rabbis, the French twenty-eight and the Belgians seven.

Schonfeld's explanation would never have occurred to Otto Schiff and, if it had, he would have rejected it as untrue and ludicrously far fetched. Schonfeld knew better; the Home Office just wanted an excuse to accept refugees because they were decent men. Schonfeld provided the fig leaf and it covered the nakedness of the argument.

### NOTES

1. Pamela Shatzkes, *Holocaust & Rescue* (New York: Palgrave, 2002).
2. Benny Morris, *Righteous Victims: A History of the Zionist-Arab Conflict, 1881–2001* (New York: Random House, 2001).
3. *The Star*, 11 March 1937.
4. Schonfeld archives, University of Southampton.
5. Ibid.
6. Jack Lunzer in conversation with the author, 2007.
7. *The Jewish Chronicle*, 19 February 1937.
8. Shatzkes, *Holocaust & Rescue*.
9. *The Times*, 1 September 1936.
10. CRREC Minute Book, Southampton University Archives.
11. Harry Rabinowicz, *A World Apart* (London and Portland, OR: Vallentine Mitchell, 1996).
12. Jacob Schonfeld in conversation with the author, 2006.

# 4  The Storm before the Storm

In September 1938 the Munich agreement between Hitler and Neville Chamberlain led to Czechoslovakia having to give up part of its country to Hitler. For the Jews in the area it was a disaster. In November of that year there were also very serious anti-Jewish riots in Germany, including the infamous Kristallnacht, when there was widespread destruction of Jewish synagogues, homes and property. As the situation worsened throughout Eastern Europe, a growing number of people believed that war could not be delayed for much longer.

If a crisis is a time-sensitive problem, the Jewish community in Britain recognized that there was now an imminent crisis. For Schonfeld the challenges ending up on his desk at the CRREC were absolutely massive. This was not a question of making arrangements for a maiden aunt to come for the weekend. Over 9,000 youngsters would arrive in the course of a relatively few months in 1939 in every state of indigence. Many different organizations would look after them. They would need bedding, clothes, schooling, feeding and money for every kind of necessity. A large number would be housed in non-Jewish homes through the generosity of volunteers, but the children had to be spread over the country and often were placed in non-Jewish areas as well. One of the results is that it has been estimated that, overall, only about 35 per cent remained actively Jewish.

For Schonfeld, it was not just a question of rescuing the children. It was also essential to make every effort to ensure that they grew up to remain true to the Orthodox faith of their parents. When their families had to be left behind in Europe and eventually became victims of the Holocaust, Schonfeld felt that this became an even more sacred trust, but the problem was that his was a tiny organization and his religious views were not widely shared.

Some children arrived just before Passover and Solly went to see Hugo Lunzer, one of the most senior members of the Adath community. He told him, 'Thirty-four children are arriving on erev [the evening before] Pesach and you must find room for them' (at the Seder services held at home on the first nights of the festival). Solly added jocularly 'If you don't have places for them by 11 tonight, I'll have them marching barefoot with placards saying "Hugo doesn't want us for Pesach".' Places were found for them.[1]

To the majority of the other relief organizations, the question of a strictly Orthodox upbringing was not a high priority. They were mainly concerned with housing, feeding and maintaining a positive flood of refugees. After all, while the main relief organization had spent £233,000 in the six years between 1933 and 1938, in the first half of 1939 alone it spent £183,000. At the peak, over 3,000 refugee families received weekly financial help.

A large number of Jewish children were converted or left the religion through neglect by Jewish adults, many of whom could have done more. There were also children who were proactively recruited by missionary organizations associated with the Church of England. For example, the nineteenth-century Barbican Mission to the Jews had been founded to convert Jews to Christianity. It also worked overseas with the same agenda, particularly in the rich hunting grounds of Eastern Europe. In 1938 the mission obtained twenty-five desperately needed visas for Czechoslovak children. For parents trying to save their children, in order to obtain one of the visas they had to agree that their offspring would be converted when they reached England. Harry Goodman was just one Jewish public figure who protested vigorously but nothing could be done. The Barbican Mission had broken no laws. Solly was infuriated at what he called a 'children's estranging movement'.

For Schonfeld, and those who felt like him, the way the children's religious needs were being dealt with was a catastrophe. He was not alone by any means, but others usually did their best on a smaller scale than the Director of the CRREC. The Golders Green Beth Hamedrash, under Eli Munk, raised sufficient funds to start a hostel at Tylers Green near High Wycombe where the religious education of the children remained a paramount consideration, but the hostel could only take a maximum of twenty-five boys when it opened in 1940.[2] A subsidiary aspect of the crippling effect of the Nazi attacks on the Jews continued to be the separation and alienation of so many victims from the religion.

The work at the CRREC increased in intensity throughout 1939. The need to get as many Jews out of Germany, Austria and Czechoslovakia before war broke out was imperative. The CRREC offices were inundated with requests for help and the paperwork was mountainous. Twenty-hour days were not unusual. Solly made do with a bowl of corn flakes for breakfast and grabbed meals as and when he could. It would get to be a habit with him.

The prime concern of the CRREC was to get visas from the Home

Office to allow the refugees to enter the country. This effort was not helped by the Council for German Jewry (CGJ) warning the Home Office that the CRREC's financial guarantees to support the immigrants were unreliable. Hertz had to tell the Home Office that his organization did not depend on the CGJ. Such squabbling between influential Jewish organizations gave out entirely the wrong message to the government. After Kristallnacht in late 1938, though, the Home Office did everything they could to be helpful. Effectively, if visas were asked for, they were provided. British consular offices in Germany and Austria issued large numbers of them. The government may have decided to close the immigration gates in Palestine, but they were now prepared to provide sanctuary in Britain if only the refugees could reach their shores.

It was at this time that Schonfeld cemented his reputation for all time. If a man is to achieve lasting fame, it will usually be for a single achievement: Nelson for Trafalgar, Wellington for Waterloo and Montgomery for El Alamein. For Schonfeld it was his part in the Kindertransport, the rescue of many hundreds of children from the death camps, in which millions of those less fortunate would be gassed to death in the coming years. There may have been hundreds of thousands left behind, but it was still a stunning victory. Schonfeld fully deserved permanent fame for not only doing more than his share of the work and bringing out adults as well, but being determined enough to do it himself, rather than to rely on others. Schonfeld was not the kind of man to be content with letters to the press, complaining that others were not doing enough.

As far as he was concerned, the buck stopped at the door of the CRREC. Michoel ber Weissmandl had demanded to know if he had a heart of stone to just watch the disaster develop. There is nothing like challenging a personality like Schonfeld's to get the best results. And the more impossible the task, the more challenging the proposition. It was not the dull daily routine of a rabbi's job in a small community in North London. It was the chance to act, not just on the national stage, but on the world stage. It was at this time that Schonfeld's approach was cemented for the next twenty-five years. 'He had no time for committees or budgets or precedents or permissions or red tapes. "May we?" or "Would it be possible?" were not in his language. He demanded and he got.'[3] His voice in the pulpit or addressing a meeting was also very distinctive. It was said to be 'Like Moses might have heard out of the burning bush. Metallic, sonorous, seigniorial, compels attention and expects obedience.'[4]

Over the years the spotlight on Schonfeld's efforts has been very unfair to Otto Schiff – to name but one leader of the Jewish Establishment who achieved far more. In the five years from November 1933 to Kristallnacht in 1938, 17,000 refugees had come to Britain and 6,000 of them had re-emigrated to other countries. In the five months after Kristallnacht a further 25,000 refugees arrived, of whom 17,000 went on to other countries. There was much more to it, however, than the issuing of visas. There were in fact many tens of thousands of visas issued by the Home Office which were never used. Only half the recipients used the permits issued between January and June 1939. The reason was partly that so many Continental Jews kept the visas like insurance policies against the worst case scenario, and when the worst duly arrived, they could not use them. When war was declared and it was too late, tens of thousands of visa holders were stranded and the vast majority did not survive. Too many Jews on the Continent would not believe until too late that the vitriol in *Mein Kampf* was not just a politician barnstorming.

There were occasional minor triumphs. Thirty Polish rabbis and their families managed to get to Siberia before Germany invaded Poland. With a lot of hard work by the CRREC, they were given permission by the Russian and British governments to go on to Palestine via Teheran. It was a drop saved from an ocean of catastrophe.

It was also the inevitable bureaucracy which delayed the rescue efforts; the selection of the fortunate minority from the hundreds of thousands of applicants begging for the precious pieces of paper. There were photographs to be supplied, forms to be filled in, lists to be sent to foreign governments, permission to go from the countries they were leaving and the intricacies of transportation. Continental governments, allied or favourable to Germany, were usually unhelpful and there were long delays. The whole situation was a nightmare as 400 volunteers in the CRREC alone struggled to deal with a positive tsunami of work.

Although all made distinguished contributions, the work of one young refugee, who became the CRREC's secretary, was typically noteworthy. This was Marcus Retter, who would be an unwavering supporter of Schonfeld as long as the rabbi lived. He did a vast amount of administrative work after arriving from the Continent as a refugee with Schonfeld's help. Many others heeded the call. For example, in March 1939 a specific Refugee Children's Department and a Children's Relief Fund were inaugurated by the CRREC, and Judith Hertz, the Chief Rabbi's daughter, came to play a major part in that.

So between Kristallnacht and the summer of 1939 thousands of Jews arrived from Germany, Austria and Czechoslovakia. Schonfeld was responsible for about 1,500 of them, including 750 children. Every one of those he rescued was a terrific achievement, but the leaders of the community, like Schiff, did rescue much larger numbers, with the unfair result that the Jewish Refugee Committee has been heavily criticized in many quarters for not rescuing even more. The Kindertransport were by no means exclusively arranged by Schonfeld. They were an effort by many parts of the community to rescue as many children as possible. The word has sometimes become synonymous with Schonfeld's efforts, which were wonderful but not unique. The fate of these other immensely hard workers and dedicated humanitarians was to be forgotten in the small print of history; Schonfeld became famous for the rest of his life. Otto Schiff could have been excused for saying there was no justice.

By comparison with Schonfeld's approach, the Jewish officials in the major relief organizations were simply unable to apply the mixture of innovation, chutzpah, energy and intellect that Solly could bring to bear if push came to shove. He would conduct negotiations with the authorities with respect and courtesy, but also with firmness. Norman Bentwich had been the first Attorney General in Palestine. At the time he met Solly he was the Professor of International Relations at the Hebrew University and well respected in refugee relief circles. Bentwich summed up Solly: 'Indeed Machiavellian. I soon realised that I was no match for him and that I could not follow the twists and turns of his agile, if erratic, mind.'[5]

The truth was that Solly could run rings round the bureaucrats. As one historian concluded after careful consideration: 'His achievements were largely due to superior astuteness in negotiating within and around the perimeters of government policy.'[6] Of course, this skill had been a necessary requirement for Jewish survival over many continents and 2,000 years.

The arrangements for the first Schonfeld Kindertransport were finally completed and the rolling stock was available to move the children on 10 December 1938, but this was a Saturday. Schonfeld went to Germany and delayed its departure till the Sunday after the Sabbath ended. Back in London Waley Cohen thought this quite unnecessary but in Germany support for Schonfeld's action came from one of the greatest Reform scholars, Rabbi Leo Baeck. For his part, Schonfeld never restricted membership of the Kindertransport to solely Orthodox children. Jewish organizations on the Continent may have failed to give equal treatment to the ultra-Orthodox in the provision of visas, but Schonfeld would not sink to their level. Schonfeld was actually advised by the Foreign Office that it was dangerous for him to go to Germany to help get the children out. He risked arrest or assassination. Schonfeld ignored the advice and was in Germany within twenty-four hours.[7]

Early in January Schonfeld brought another 250 children to England from Vienna. They were put up at Northfields, the girls' school in Stamford Hill, and in other houses in the neighbourhood. The creation of the girls' school had been a typical Schonfeld effort. Judith Grunfeld had come to him with the news that she was pregnant. In her condition it would have been considered inappropriate for her to continue to teach at an Orthodox Jewish boys' school, so she told Solly that she was resigning. Solly immediately bought a school building and started the girls' school in order to retain her services.

Schonfeld needed as much space as he could get for the refugees. He would knock on the doors of the Adath community and ask how many refugees each household would take. Now it is no small sacrifice to share your home with often penniless refugees, but it was hard, if not impossible, to refuse the Rav. While Solly was always prepared to coax and cajole, he was also capable of fierce denunciation when he felt a congregant was not doing his duty of giving succour to his coreligionists, and he would spread the word in no uncertain terms.

For their part, the Home Office wanted reassurance that the children had relatives in Britain. Where such family members did not exist, Schonfeld would search the lists of congregants of the Adath for someone with the same surname as the child. He would then inform them that he had found a long lost relative and would they kindly confirm, if they were asked by the authorities, that this was the case! Schonfeld ignored the illegality of such procedures. Solomon Lebrecht was a senior member of the Adath community and found himself roped in one Friday night to forge documents, writing the names of spurious relatives on dozens of forms, even though it is forbidden to write on the Sabbath. As the hours went by, Lebrecht asked whether he could, perhaps, smoke a cigarette but was firmly refused permission by Solly, on the grounds that Orthodox Jews are forbidden to smoke on the Sabbath! It is permissible to break any Jewish law in order to save lives, so working on Shabbat could be excused, but smoking could not. Solly had once kept the school children filling in visa applications for refugees long after the beginning of the Sabbath. He then delivered them to the Home Office in his car, left it in town and walked home. It is permissible to break the laws of the Sabbath to save life, but not otherwise.

Schonfeld also arranged to send refugees on to other centres. The same day the children arrived from Vienna, sixteen of them were sent to Sunderland. An appeal for funds raised an immediate £500 (£23,000 today.) Schonfeld took care to announce that the accommodation was being provided through the good offices of the JSS (Jewish Secondary School). He did not want to suggest that this was solely a Charedi effort because he still wanted the support of the wider community. Of course, again, Schonfeld's efforts were only a tiny part of the whole. In Hampstead Garden Suburb – with a far smaller Jewish population than it has today – there were 100 offers of private homes where the families were prepared to accommodate refugees.

In February another 150 teachers and scholars, plus 120 Yeshiva students reached Britain safety through CRREC auspices. Solly was pleased with the achievement but he knew very well that the need for sanctuary far exceeded what any one government could offer. So he began to work on other governments as well. As a result, another 260 rabbis and their families were eventually able to leave countries under Nazi domination. Solly reported to the Home Office: 'As a direct result of British behaviour, many other governments followed her example by granting permits.' It was perfectly true, but many a hardworking executive would have missed the public relation's opportunity to flatter the government. It made a strong contrast to the criticism which rained down on the department from other Jewish organizations who felt it was not doing enough.

Among the groups the Home Office accepted in March were ninety-nine teachers and seventy-three students. Solly had struggled to find ways of legitimizing the influx. He had, for example, found a bankrupt yeshiva in Manchester, staffed it with refugee German Talmudists, and then applied for temporary student visas. It was announced that the young refugees would take up their places for the beginning of what was now to be called the next academic term. He founded another yeshiva in three houses in Stamford Hill and called it Yeshiva Ohr Yisroel. He obtained sixty permits for prospective students, and the Yeshiva would continue in existence until the end of the war.

One problem was that the students had to be under 18 years old and many did not qualify. So Solly again doctored the records without any compunction. In his eyes the task of saving lives would always take precedence over awkward regulations. As far as he was concerned the ends justified the means. It was, after all, literally a matter of life and death for the youngsters. Solly would readily risk criminal prosecution on their behalf. There is no doubt about it, deliberately falsifying a large number of visa applications is strictly illegal. Helping just one individual to get a passport would, in the future, cost a cabinet minister his job. Behind the cloak and dagger romance of a Scarlet Pimpernel was the reality of the possible consequences of breaking the law.

Otto Schiff, as one of the most influential Jewish voices, was often called upon to justify Solly's serious bureaucratic shortcomings when it came to relations with the government. Wringing his hands, Schiff told Solly that 'he did wonderful things but always in the wrong way'.[8] He complained that 'he always had to clear up the mess afterwards'.[9] And Schiff would have known nothing about the deliberate falsification of records. One of his most awkward problems came about when the Home Office stated categorically that it would not issue any more visas unless Schiff's organization took financial responsibility for the students. Where was the money to come from? To make matters even worse for the CRREC, Schonfeld lost one of his strongest supporters in March when David Gestetner died. Only in the early years of the war did the government agree to pay for the minimum needs of the newcomers.

All the refugee organizations had run out of money trying to deal with the flood of refugees entering the country and the orderly, bureaucratic Schiff mind was often in turmoil. In fairness, Solly did not make his life any easier. When one considers, however, that by November 1939 £15,000 *a week* (£670,000 today) was needed to support the refugees, it was not surprising that it was a nightmare trying to feed an uncontrolled number of additional mouths.

The Schonfelds had their own personal problems. Ella had cousins in Vienna whom she naturally wanted to rescue. Schiff too wanted to accept the enormous burden of the now seriously endangered Austrian Jews. The fact was, however, that there simply was not the money available to keep to the guarantee that, if admitted, the refugees would not become a burden on the state. A proportion of the German Jews had been able to bring at least some of their assets with them when they emigrated. By contrast, the Austrian Jews after Kristallnacht had all their valuables confiscated by the Nazis and those who arrived were practically destitute. A considerable number of the Charedim had started off destitute anyway, but the consistent and unique Schonfeld response was to blithely ignore the problem. If he could get the visas, he could get the refugees out. He'd worry about how to keep them fed afterwards. In later life he would often follow the same rule book.

Between January and June 1939 22,000 refugees reached safety in Britain. Among them were Solly's Kindertransport children and, if Schonfeld's name lives on, it was because he had the great advantage of rescuing the children in the most publicly visible way. The sight of tiny tots arriving at London railway stations, bereft of their parents, hanging on to hardly larger siblings, often in tears, would melt the hardest news editor's heart. The cut-off age was 16. On one occasion there was no transport to take them to the hostels which Solly had created in North London by putting beds into his schools and even moving into the attic of his own home, so that forty children could sleep in the house. So he commandeered a fleet of taxis and every driver, not all of whom were Jewish, refused to accept any money for the journey. There was much additional generosity; for example, when the refugee children arrived in Britain, Marks and Spencer gave every one of them free shoes.

Home Office officials would inspect the arrangements made to house Solly's refugees. They measured out the available floor space to ensure that the precious visas would not outnumber the ability to put a child into a bed. On every possible occasion Solly would overestimate the numbers he could look after and one of his congregants felt it his duty to tell the Home Office of his misgivings on this point. When Solly heard of this, he rounded on the wretched man in the pulpit in front of the whole congregation. 'Mosser' he roared in Yiddish, which means 'informer'. Ostracism within the Right Wing community was a very powerful weapon. To be rejected by the congregation, when membership was the basis of someone's self-esteem and lifestyle, made this a severe punishment indeed. It remains today the ultimate Charedi stick, just as the rewards of conformity are the carrots.

Schonfeld's problems did not stop when the children were housed and enrolled in the JSS schools. Many were seriously disturbed by their ordeals. They would cling to the teachings of their absent parents, so that there was unrest on such subjects as how soon after eating meat they could eat a dairy dish. Chaim Bermant, the future great *Jewish Chronicle* columnist, recalled his time as a schoolmaster at the school and the necessity to go to the aid of weaker teachers in their classrooms, when they were trying unsuccessfully to keep order; most of them had not been trained to look after unruly kids. Some of the class might not understand the language in which the lessons were given. The teachers often found it difficult to make ends meet domestically and they were almost all distracted by frantic worry about the family members they had left behind on the Continent. If the children tried them too hard, there were teachers who would hit out in frustration, slapping faces or cuffing heads. Educationally, it was chaos and the outside world had to be kept in the dark because there were still a vast number of other children who needed to be saved.

Non-Jewish organizations were also moved by the plight of the refugees. The Lord Mayor of London started a Czechoslovakia Refugees Fund and raised £263,000 (about £11 million today). March saw a second conference called by the CRREC of rabbis and ministers.

Over 1,000 former synagogue officials and their dependants were now being cared for by the Council. There was a full-scale effort to find them jobs and homes all over the world. Rabbis, teachers, chazanim and shochetim were sent to the Dominions and South America.

In the middle of this impossibly busy schedule Solly still managed to carry out his rabbinic duties. Never was the old adage truer that if you want something done, ask a busy man. In April he was to be found delivering a memorial lecture for his congregant, Saul Fleischman. The columns of *The Jewish Chronicle* regularly included information on where he would be speaking on Shabbat around the UOHC congregations. He thought nothing of walking miles to them from his home in Stamford Hill.

In May there was a bittersweet moment when Moses got married in New York. He had met his wife when he was working as Lord Josiah Wedgwood's secretary in Palestine. Ruth Betinsky came from Far Rockaway, an affluent part of Long Island, and the wedding was at the prestigious Ambassador Hotel on Park Avenue. Moses and his new bride decided to set up home in America and he was the first of the Schonfeld children to settle down abroad. It was a wrench; Moses and Solly had always been close. They remained in touch through their correspondence thereafter, but they only saw each other about once a year with the Atlantic dividing them. Daniel also married that year; his bride was his cousin Edith Asenath Nitzevet Feldmann, who was five years older than him, but destined to outlive her husband by many years.

Solly's role in the CRREC involved him in close contact with the ageing Chief Rabbi. In Glasgow in June Hertz met with representatives of the Home Office and thanked them for their help. Solly went with him and also spoke. It must have looked strange to the officials for Hertz to be accompanied by a rabbi whose community did not even recognize the Chief Rabbi's authority, or indeed to be accompanied by a rabbi at all, as United Synagogue ministers, of course, did not normally have semicha.

More and more money was needed to keep the schools afloat as the number of pupils swelled. At the end of June, Ashe Lincoln, KC, President of the JSS Endowment Committee, welcomed the famous film star, Conrad Veidt, as guest of honour at a fund-raising garden party. Veidt, most famous today for being the Nazi officer shot by Humphrey Bogart at the end of *Casablanca*, spoke about a railway porter who had collected 2½p each from his mates at an entry port. It was to pay the duty for a girl who wanted to bring her sewing machine into the country; there was not a dry eye in the house. By this time Solly was able to announce that he now had 400 children in his schools, from a roll of no more than thirty just a few years before.

When war threatens, what is most important is the safety of the children. This was particularly the case in 1939 as the damage caused by air raids on civilian towns during the recent Spanish Civil War had highlighted the dangers of this new threat. Mass evacuation for children to the countryside was now the government's policy, and Billeting Officers were appointed in rural areas to requisition space for temporary homes for the children until the war was over or it was safe to go home. The religion of the families in those homes was not an overriding factor and now, naturally, most Jewish children found themselves in non-Jewish homes. Their Jewish religious education was inevitably neglected as a consequence. The Jewish community in Britain lost thousands more future congregants by disaffection.

Jewish schools in London had been declining for years before the war. Most of them had been located in the East End and the drift of the community to the suburbs had made them more difficult to reach. They were coming to the end of their useful days. The roll of the Jews' Free School had declined from its Victorian peak of 4,000 to only 1,000 pupils. The Solomon Wolfson School in Bayswater could take 500 children but only had 100. Most Jewish children, if they had any Jewish education at all – half did not – only got it at Sunday School. When the children were evacuated even this was likely to stop and it would be unlikely that many full-time schools would find it viable to reopen after the war.

The JSS schools were an anomaly, but where they might have a very large increase in the number of pupils, the organization was still fighting for recognition and acceptance. The vocal opposition continued to insist that their pupils would be removed artificially from mixing in society and that, as a consequence, they would be at a disadvantage later in life. Solly described his struggle in 'the face of a wave of prejudice and ill-founded fear'.[10]

When war was imminent it became necessary to evacuate the JSS children too and Solly was instructed to take them to five villages in Bedfordshire. The centre for the migration was Shefford. Judith Grunfeld would be in charge, although she had to look after her own children who were now aged 6, 4 and 1. From Monday 28 August 1939 till Friday morning, 1 September, at six in the morning, the JSS children reported to the school playground in case the order came. Solly told them in English and German what was going to happen and that, when they were billeted in their new homes, they could eat anything but meat. At last, on the Friday, 500 children said Tefilat Haderech, the prayer for those who are travelling, and moved off. At the front of the procession were two sifrei torah. Of course, this was not just religious symbolism. The children were going through experiences which could easily have led to mass psychological problems. Solly had to replace their parents and their homes. He did it by reassuring the children that the Almighty was still there looking after them. Like the Children of Israel in the biblical wilderness, he saw to it that the sefer torah – the modern representation of the Ark – still led them onwards.

He also set out to replace the parents, personally, as did all the adults. Any child he found who needed a hug, got one from Solly. He used to ask them if they had pocket money and, if they had not, he would find a half crown (12.5p) for them, the equivalent of over £5 today. If it gave them some small comfort in terrible times, it was money well spent, though where it came from is anybody's guess. A typical example of his intense compassion was that, late one evening, he found a child crying and, to take her mind off the horrors she was experiencing, he took her for a drive round London in his car. In these days when teachers are forbidden to even touch a child, for fear of paedophiles, a hug would be unthinkable. Luckily for the children it was 1939 and good people were prepared to provide the affection they desperately needed. Solly loved children, he even remembered their names many years later when they met again, and he fully recognized that these small mites were, temporarily, his responsibility, to bring up as though he were their father. The grateful thanks of those he saved, both physically and mentally, have echoed down the years, and those bearing witness commend him from all those parts of the world where the children finally ended up. Schonfeld had a number of finest hours, but this was certainly high up on the list of the best. Among the children would be a number of his strongest supporters over the coming decades; boys like Joe Lobenstein, who would become a power in local politics in North London for many years. Others became powerful businessmen and their gratitude and generosity would support him through the toughest times.

It was indeed in these terrible days that Solly made many of the friends who were to support his efforts throughout his lifetime. One such was Bernard Kahn whose story only emphasizes just how much can be owed to one man. The 14-year-old Kahn was warned in Germany of his likely arrest and deportation to the concentration camp at Dachau. He fled to Holland and stowed away on a boat docking in Liverpool. He then, literally, jumped ship and swam to the shore where he was arrested and imprisoned. When he was released he went to the yeshiva in Gateshead. There he was recommended to Schonfeld and the rabbi procured for him no less than thirty visas for the rest of his family to leave Germany. To add to the indebtedness, Schonfeld also intervened when Kahn's sister-in-law, Joyce, had a problem during the war. The difficulty was that she did not want to work on the Sabbath. A tribunal considered her case and, for all the work piled up on his desk, Schonfeld still found the time to attend the court and support her views. The tribunal found against her but she was transferred to another factory where the management were more understanding. Bernard Kahn never forgot Schonfeld's monumental kindness and support when he was in great need of it. When he became a successful businessman and could repay the debt, he always did so in hard cash. He was one of many.

The children's train arrived at Biggleswade on that 1 September and Solly hurriedly followed to the new base in Shefford in his little Ford 8, loaded with Vienna sausages, four large mess saucepans and a hamper with plates and cutlery. Solly was one of those people who have a perfectly good insurance record but are considered terrible drivers by their friends. Certainly that was his cousin, Sir Sigmund Sternberg's opinion. Solly was said to be the first British rabbi to own a car, which was said to be akin to a rabbi today owning a helicopter, another example of his unconventional lifestyle. When he saw the children settled he rushed back to London to be in time for the Sabbath, while the children started to settle down in rural Bedfordshire. To some extent, the villagers did not know what had hit them. The local St Michael's Hall had been set aside for the school headquarters and some of the older boys immediately started practising the reading of the appropriate portion of the Pentateuch (the first five books of the Bible), for the morning service on the following day. Not the adults, but the children. In their homes on the Continent many had been steeped in Torah knowledge and needed little help. Meanwhile the teachers spread out to explain the children's dietary requirements to as many of the village families as they could reach.

A considerable number of the locals may never have seen a Jew in their lives. An even larger percentage would never have come across the intensity of religious observance which permeated the children's behaviour. Many of the villagers who had cooked handsome dinners for their new guests were offended when the children refused to have anything but dry bread. If they only spoke German it was even less easy to explain what the problem was. On the next day, the Sabbath, the children had their service, and afterwards there was enough for each of them to have one sausage and one piece of bread for lunch. From there on it was only possible for things to improve.

Many of the villagers were unhappy initially with their charges and complained to the local vicar. They asked the billeting officer whether they could have different children. They all agreed that the kids were well behaved and were obviously unhappy at giving offence, but they were clearly unsuited to their placements. The vicar, on the other hand, was delighted to have some genuine Children of Israel in his midst and went to work to get the villagers to understand the background. The billeting officer was far too busy to make changes anyway and told the villagers they'd just have to cope.

The children would stay in the villages for six years. Many lifelong friendships were eventually forged between the local families and their evacuees and there were innumerable examples of the kindness of the villagers. Typically, one mother explained to her friends that she could not attend the weekly whist drive early one summer. On the day in question her Jewish house guest had to be taken to have his hair cut. Why on that day? The Christian mother patiently explained that it was Lag b'Omer, the only day between the festivals of Passover and Shavuot when a haircut was permitted. Compare this with the enthusiasm with which so many people – not just in Germany and Austria, but in countries like Poland, France, Greece and Rumania – helped the Nazis to round up and deport their Jewish fellow citizens to concentration camps and death. The British are a remarkable people.

The standard of education provided by the teachers soon won accolades from the school inspector from the Ministry. A great deal of the responsibility for the children rested, of course, with Judith Grunfeld and she was never found wanting. She was supported by a very strong and dedicated team, which included Dr Abraham Levene, the Head Teacher and Solly's sister, Senath, who was now Mrs Petrie.

After the war broke out in September Solly had the additional task of looking after the religious needs of the children at Shefford. Judith Grunfeld did a tremendous job winning over the locals, but she needed many religious appurtenances which were not readily available in Bedfordshire, such as *tsitsit* and kosher wine, *tephillin* and *talleisim*. Solly was her personal parcel post, even though he continued to be totally overworked.

To help keep the rescue launch afloat in 1939, many more volunteered to help. Solly worked them terribly hard and no one put in more time than his devoted secretary, Ruth Lunzer, his PA, Marcus Retter and Judith Hertz. As she and Solly went on to work long hours together when he was in London, it was easy for a friendship to develop, which eventually led to love and to Solly asking Judith to marry him. Judith accepted the proposal, which was announced in *The Times* on 5 October. It would be no surprise that, on the day he married her, early in

1940, his secretary, the devoted Ruth Lunzer, had to take him out to buy a new shirt and tie. Even this happy event was used by Schonfeld's critics to attack him: some would suggest behind his back that he had married Judith as a good career move. However, even some of those who have studied the Schonfeld archive have pointed out that there was greater warmth in Judith's letters to Solly than those he sent her. This latter point is easily explained. First, Judith had more time for correspondence and was able to express herself at greater length. Second, Judith was very literary; she learned a great deal of poetry by heart and was particularly knowledgeable about the correspondence of Keats. Third, Solly would not have forgotten the trouble his letters to Miss Grolman had got him into only a couple of years before and would have been wary of making the same mistake again.

Solly was always going to be a difficult husband. Controlling as powerful a personality as his was a major challenge for even as intelligent and devoted a wife as Judith. However she was fully prepared for the challenge: she had written to him in October 1939 when they got engaged 'to the most impossible person I know – and the only one I want to know'. Judith needed Solly's warm and strong personality. Years later, he was talking to the adolescent daughter of a friend as they walked home from her house after a Sabbath lunch. The young woman said that she hoped she would grow up to be a genius. She recalls that Solly told her to wish for no such thing. He said that Hertz was a genius but, as a result, Judith was 'a deeply unhappy woman'. Genius often comes at a high price for those who have to live with it. There were other reasons for her unhappiness. The Hertz household had been without its mother since 1930. The Chief Rabbi was under great public pressure while his children grew up, and their needs could well have been one burden too many to carry. One relative recalls that in those years there was little warmth in the Hertz household.

It would be generally agreed among their closest friends in the future that Judith was the only one who could handle Solly. Lady Hazel Sternberg, whose in-laws were cousins of Ella, said that Judith was 'clever and nice. She was calm and accepting.'[11] She had always known that it would not be a normal married life, because she was going to be married to a public figure, and public figures constantly have other demands on their time besides their families. Nevertheless, they shared an enjoyment of the theatre and the cinema and Judith would provide the harbour to come home to when Solly had finished being buffeted by the gales of his many responsibilities.

It was suggested by some – and still is – that Solly saw his marriage as a way to improve his chances of becoming Chief Rabbi. The position had gone from father to son on three occasions in the past – the Niettos, Lyon/Hirschell and the Adlers, but never from father to son-in-law. A pragmatist like Solly was, however, very unlikely to have harboured any such hopes. He belonged to the Adath and the power in the land when it came to voting for a new Chief Rabbi lay with the United Synagogue. He must have known that his chances, with them in control were, at best, negligible.

It could not be said that the path of true love was likely to be unencumbered with obstacles. Hertz wrote to his sister, Sadie, in March 1940 from Haifa, where he was recuperating from illness, to explain what had happened:

> Thursday after Yom Kippur, Judith announced to me, 'Father, I promised to marry Dr. Schonfeld!' My reply was 'If you have promised, you must keep your promise.' And she did. They were married on January 16th at 103 Hamilton Terrace, the undersigned officiating. They flew to Palestine for their honeymoon and by accident I ran across them in Rome on their return. Dr. Schonfeld is a Hungarian, by descent that is, for he was born in London. His father led the opposition against the Rabbinate as long as he lived. The son studied at Slobodka Yeshivah and got his Ph.D ... The crisis came some two and a half years ago in connection with the German refugee children and the problems that followed in their wake. I found that of all the clergy, he possessed most personality, common-sense and fearlessness towards the assimilated aristocrats. His help proved invaluable. I could never have ventured to rescue 250 German rabbis and families without him as my shammas, representative and 'cossack'. Add to this he is an exceptionally handsome man, six feet high, blue eyed, a renowned schnorrer [fund-raiser], persuasive and affable; it is understandable that he could win Judith. They are _very_ happy ... Ever your loving, Joe.[12]

The fact that he knew the young rabbi had been divorced – the engagement and marriage to Bertha had hardly been a secret – proved no obstacle in those perilous days. Marrying a Jewish damsel in distress in order to provide her with a probably lifesaving passport was heroic, rather than questionable, behaviour. Even when the second marriage was to a Chief Rabbi's daughter, the first could be easily explained away.

The man likely to obstruct the marriage was not Hertz; it was the Registrar General. His office refused initially to accept the validity of the divorce from Bertha, awarded in Vienna after only six months of marriage. How could a British subject marry in England and get a legitimate divorce so soon in Austria? Solly's lawyers came up with an acceptable explanation. As his father had been Austrian until 1927, Solly, they insisted, was Austrian by birth. He had lived there as well when his father was on his way to Palestine in 1919 and on their return a few years later. He had been there again when he was attending yeshiva in 1927 and in 1928 before his father died. It was now contended that he had taken a home in Vienna in the summer of 1937 with the intention of setting up in business and settling down in Austria. Agreed, this last intention seems more than questionable. The argument continued that, as a Jew, he could legally get a divorce in Austria; ironically, as we've seen, if he had been a Catholic at the time, he would not have been able to do so. The Registrar General accepted the explanation.

Officialdom being satisfied, the next problem was just as delicate. A Jewish marriage certificate, a ketubah, does not specify the bridegroom's marital history. A British civil marriage certificate does. As both are normally completed where the wedding takes place, the fact of the first marriage would have to be noted at that time. This was hardly desirable. So, on 7 December 1939, a civil wedding ceremony took place in Edinburgh between Judith, the daughter of a Rabbi Hertz, and Sol Schonfeld, a 'divorced author'. No newspaper ever picked it up.[13] It was now possible for the religious wedding to take place at the Chief Rabbi's home in London in January 1940 without filling in another civil wedding certificate. It was a small wedding, as a lavish event would have been inappropriate in wartime. The Chief Rabbi gave a charming address to his daughter and his new son-in-law and totally ignored the past. As he said, 'nothing fills me with greater joy than such a soul resolve on the part of the man into whose hands I now place an infinite trust – the happiness of my child'. Solly and Judith honeymooned in Palestine, going via Rome during the period of the 'phoney war' before France was invaded and Mussolini came in on Hitler's side.

After the war Solly and Judith would move to 73 Shepherds Hill in Highgate and the Adath community would come to see Judith as not very approachable. She was detached from the congregation and there was no doubt that an agreement existed between husband and wife that she would not have to act the role of rebbetzen. There is a letter from Judith to Solly before they were married in 1939, talking of an obstacle to their future happiness. The problem is not identified but it could well have been the future relationship between Judith and the community.

It seems unlikely anyway that Judith would have considered the lower-middle-class district of Stoke Newington and Stamford Hill appropriate for the Chief Rabbi's daughter, and Solly recognized that a considerable proportion of his community would soon spread into North West London anyway. In the future he would continue to walk long distances on Shabbat to visit the different synagogues, and Highgate was about as central as he could get. At the same time, Highgate would never be a major centre for the Charedim so, by living there, he was distancing himself from the heart of the community. It was part of the compromise which enabled him to have a foot in both the Orthodox and Charedi camps.

Hertz grew to be very fond of Solly. He treated him more like a son than a son-in-law.[14] In 1940 when Jacob Schonfeld was bar mitzvah he went to the Chief Rabbi's house to receive an autographed copy of a book the Chief Rabbi admired. 'Hertz said to me in his typical rasping voice "You're going to be a great man – just like your brother"'.[15] Hertz loved Solly's English accent. It was incongruous in a Charedi community which had its roots firmly on the Continent, but it was absolutely genuine. He gave Solly the nickname, Bill, which stuck to him with many of his friends for a number of years. It was a backhanded compliment, but it demonstrated that his son-in-law was a one-off. Judith and her friends used it privately as an in-joke.

The two rabbis did not always agree by any means and there would be occasions when Hertz had to distance himself publicly from Solly's pronouncements. The bond of affection remained, however. As Hertz said on one occasion when Solly was away: 'With all his faults, I miss him.'

### NOTES

1. Jeremy Schonfeld, in conversation with the author, 2007.
2. Bernard Koschland, 'Tylers Green Hostel', *Jewish Historical Society of England* (June 2006).
3. Chaim Bermant, *The Jewish Chronicle*, 19 February 1982.
4. Ibid.
5. Pamela Shatzkes, *Holocaust & Rescue* (New York: Palgrave, 2002).
6. Ibid.
7. Jeremy Schonfeld, in conversation with the author.
8. Shatzkes, *Holocaust & Rescue*.
9. Ibid.
10. Schonfeld archive, University of Southampton.
11. Lady Hazel Sternberg, in conversation with the author, 2007.
12. London Metropolitan Archives, Hertz papers.
13. The wedding certificate is in the Schonfeld archive at the University of Southampton.
14. Jacob Schonfeld, in conversation with the author, 2007.
15. Ibid.

# 5  Wartime

Once the war started, the chances of getting the Jews out of occupied Europe almost evaporated. The only two Jewish communities in countries under Nazi control which were not virtually wiped out in the Holocaust were the Germans and the Danes. The Germans because there was enough advance notice after Hitler came to power in 1933 to get 85 per cent of them out of the country by 1939. The Danes because, one dark night in 1943, the Danish government spirited the vast majority of them to Sweden in a magnificent clandestine operation.

Obviously, nobody could know at the outbreak of the war that every attempt to avoid the Final Solution would prove a failure, though a few recognized the inevitable. It was the pragmatic Harry Goodman who said, 'All we can do is save a few souls'. As six million Jews died, the arguments raged during and after the war about whether at least some part of the appalling tragedy could have been avoided. The fact is that no Jewish community in the free world was successful in achieving this; if Schonfeld lamented his failures, so did everybody else grieve for theirs around the Jewish world.

Many initiatives had to be abandoned. There had been a last minute effort in April 1939 by Weissmandl and Schonfeld on behalf of 200 Jews in Nitra, where Solly had first studied for his semicha. The idea was to move them to Canada and America but visas and transport were needed. Negotiations dragged on and they were still unresolved when the war started. Most of the 200 died in the concentration camp at Auschwitz.

By 1940 Britain stood alone against the all-conquering Nazi armies. In late May the British Expeditionary Force had been evacuated from Dunkirk but most of its equipment had had to be left behind. Between July and December 1940 over 70,000 British civilians were killed in the Blitz. Nazi submarines sank British shipping at an alarming rate in the North Atlantic, threatening the country with starvation and insufficient armaments to continue the struggle. Any chance that the British government at the time would use any of its sparse resources to help foreign nationals – after all the European Jews were not British – was remote. The survival of Britain as a free country was, quite correctly, the only item on the government's agenda. It's obviously true that there would have been a few anti-Semitic civil servants and politicians who were actually opposed to helping, but the right approach was self-evident; the country had to be totally geared up to winning the war. Everything else was less important than that. There would be pleas in the future, for example, to bomb railway lines leading to the concentration camps but, here again, there were considered to be other more pressing war priorities for the use of the aircraft.

There was much work for the CRREC to do as the bombs rained down on London during the Blitz. The Committee had created an American office which initially consisted of Solly's brother Moses. In truth, the grandiose name was covering up the cracks in the edifice again. Moses worked hard for the cause and wrote *The Mark of the Swastika* in 1941 as part of the effort to get the United States to enter the war on the allied side. Back home Solly was in greater danger. He would drive round Stamford Hill during the air raids to be on the spot if he was needed. Green Lanes was bombed and he collected some of the victims in his own house for shelter, hot drinks and discussions on what to do next. When he was told he should take shelter as incendiary bombs and land mines rained down, rather than drive around, he said that there was less traffic on the roads during the raids!

Through the generosity of one of the Adath members, Solly had been able to set up his office in Westminster, near to the government buildings. The cost of his telephone and typist were taken care of as well. As a minister of religion he had not been called up for the armed forces in view of the work he was doing. He was, therefore, able to labour furiously for the CRREC, sending out for his favourite semolina pudding rather than taking a break for meals. Sir Robert Waley Cohen at the United Synagogue took the opportunity to make jokes about the welcome he would get if he volunteered to be a Chaplain to the Forces. It was a sniping assault on Schonfeld's courage and was totally unjustified, if his heroic exploits on the Continent before the war were taken into account. When he was a thorn in the flesh of the Nazis, it was impossible to anticipate what they might do to prevent his activities. If, however, Schonfeld had become a chaplain, it would have removed one of the few people who would stand up to Waley Cohen, and that would not have escaped the notice of the United Synagogue Honorary Officers. In any event, the director of the CRREC was doing much more valuable work at home.

Winning the war would require many talents. For instance, in addition to being a distinguished rabbi, Weissmandl was a keen scientist.

He had, for example, a long-term interest in producing a perpetual motion machine. It was probably his example which led Solly to have his own views on how to achieve victory. He wrote to the Air Ministry to offer them his advice. For example, why not attach parachutes to the rears of aircraft with engine failure, to enable them to land safely. He would have been amused to see the American Space Shuttle at the end of the century, landing with a parachute billowing from its tail section. When the V1s came later in the war he wrote again to suggest that the flying bombs be harpooned to bring them down. Patriot surface-to-air missiles lay a long way in the future, but if the technology had existed, it was a good idea. The Air Ministry politely acknowledged his recommendations.

Weissmandl had remained in Czechoslovakia and actually survived the war, though his family did not. He kept in touch with Solly through a mutual friend in Switzerland. He passed on useful information about what was going on. As far as the British authorities were concerned, this correspondence was illegal, as nobody was allowed to communicate with an address in enemy territory except through official channels. Nevertheless, nobody tried to stop Schonfeld and Weissmandl from writing to each other. Solly was still sailing close to the wind.

On the home front one of the first essentials was to deal with the 1,500 foreign national Jews who had been interned on the Isle of Man and elsewhere. The roundup had been more in the nature of a trawl than a matter of careful selection. Large numbers of known fascists were also interned and, with the threat of invasion looming, it was better to be safe than sorry when it came to deciding who to get out of the way.

For Solly at the CRREC, the first task with the internees was to find some way to feed the families if the breadwinner had been imprisoned. That meant more fund raising. Then it was necessary to reassure countless partners that their other half was safe and well. At the outset of internment it was easy to confuse the concept of an internment camp with that of a concentration camp; after all, the first concentration camps had been created by the British in South Africa at the time of the Boer War and had, indeed, been internment camps. Then it was necessary to ensure that conditions in the camps were as good as possible, and to get those internees who were ill, released. It was a case of déjà vu for Ella Schonfeld, as her brother-in-law had been interned in Alexandra Palace in North London during the First World War and the family had visited him there.

Schonfeld persuaded the War Office to give him a pass so that he could visit every internment camp. During the first few months after they were set up, he did four tours to cover them all. Solly, who could charm the birds off the trees, got on extremely well with the camp commandants and was able to explain, in impeccable English tones, the absolute necessity for a whole range of Talmudic observances. Kosher kitchens and synagogues were established in all the camps, paid for by the CRREC, and rabbis were selected to minister to the flock. As Schonfeld reported later:

> overcrowding was rectified, occupations and entertainment schemes were organised, unsuitable camps were replaced with better ones and there were arrangements for services and the instruction of children. Kosher food purchased by the Council was sent to improve diet. The Council was responsible for the release of about 1,000 internees.[1]

There were some extraordinary situations in the camps. In Port Erin on the Isle of Man there was a New Year service held in the local cinema. There were 200 in the congregation, but no minyan. A minyan is ten male Jews whose presence is necessary for certain prayers to be said. The 200 were all women who had been separated from their menfolk. This, Solly could do nothing about.

Logic, common sense and humanitarian instincts were all valuable weapons in Schonfeld's arsenal in discussion with authority. In addition he used bluff, because if you can't outgun the opposition, that's often the only alternative. It was a question of impressive note paper, the careful dropping of important names, the suggestion of powers back at Head Office who were fully in agreement with him and the occasional white lie, all in a good cause. Schonfeld was still representing the severely disadvantaged and he was not going to let the bureaucratic niceties stand in the way of getting a result. The bluffs often worked, but the problem would be that they became standard equipment in Schonfeld's armoury. To paraphrase somewhat, the power of bluff corrupts and the absolute power of bluff corrupts absolutely. In his later years, when he fine-tuned his bluffs less effectively, they would fail to win the day on too many occasions. They would also become more brazen and, therefore, more easily seen for what they often became: empty rhetoric. That, though, was a long way in the future.

Solly, leading the way, encouraging, supporting, positive and optimistic, naturally generated hero worship among his younger helpers. In later years, when his strength faltered and when his behaviour became more erratic, they would remember him in his prime, finding the solutions to any number of individual cases of hardship and putting in more hours than anybody else. Just one of those who toured the camps on behalf of the CRREC was Maurice Unterman, who would become the influential rabbi at the Marble Arch synagogue in London in the 1970s. Such men would never forget the debt that so many owed to Schonfeld.

The war did not start to turn in the allies' favour until Hitler invaded Russia, the Americans came in after Pearl Harbour in December 1941 and the battle of El Alamein was won in 1942. For the British there was still the upcoming need to invade Europe and to destroy the rest of the Nazi war machine. Faced with this mammoth reality, the Jewish efforts in Britain, on behalf of their Continental brethren, remained fragmented. The Zionists still wanted to link the plight of the Jews with the restrictions on Jewish immigration into Palestine. That hidden – or not so hidden – agenda took precedence for them over everything else. Most of the other official Jewish bodies muddied the water with large and impractical ideas. For example, Selig Brodetsky, the new President of the Board of Deputies, wanted all the Jews in Europe to be designated British-protected, a decision which would have been immediately ignored by the Nazis. Worse, it would have prejudiced the safety of those on the Continent who were genuinely British subjects. There would be another proposal in early 1943 that: 'The German government should be told, through some appropriate channel, that Jews, especially women and children, should be allowed to leave all countries under German control.'[2] Exactly which appropriate channel they could use was conveniently left open to the government to decide, along with the task of how to get Hitler to pay any attention to such an instruction. It was also considered the government's responsibility to work out how to provide the vast tonnage of shipping the Jewish pressure groups would need if they were able to move the Jews in danger to safety.

Different ideas came from different organizations. In 1942 the Board of Deputies created a Consultative Committee to try to coordinate all the interested parties and to make a common approach to the government. It met regularly for six months but, as everybody continued to try to influence the authorities individually as well, it fell apart in recriminations. It was not that anyone's intentions were less than admirable. It was just that the recommendations were grandiose and unrealistic. The Jewish academics and businessmen in authority were dealing with situations for which nothing could have prepared them. It is easy with hindsight to come up with policy ideas that might have been more practical than those adopted. By the end of 1940, however, nothing could have stopped the Nazis perpetrating the Holocaust.

If Schonfeld was as unsuccessful as anybody else during the war, he was a much better strategist. He recognized, for example, that the British government would not change its Palestine immigration policy except in very special circumstances. Not doing anything to upset the Arab world, with its control of vital oil supplies, was sound foreign policy in wartime. Proof of the government's position, if proof were needed, was provided by the fate of the 1,600 illegal Jewish immigrants who reached Haifa in Palestine on a passenger ship in the early days of the war. *Pour encourager les autres*, 900 of them were deported to Mauritius. They were imprisoned in the Beau Bassin camp for the rest of the war and 128 of them died from various illnesses. While there was, naturally, a need to distinguish between internees – friendly aliens – and detainees – enemy aliens – overall the British treatment of both was humane. The administration in Mauritius was, however, defective, and there was much suffering.

The deportations aroused much adverse publicity, particularly in America. The situation worsened when more were to be sent to the island in late 1940 and the ship was blown up by the Jews to prevent it from sailing. Nearly 300 on board died. The British government needed its image on the deportations improved, and quickly. Schonfeld rushed to the rescue. Why not issue visas for Mauritius for Jewish refugees who managed to get out of occupied Europe? Wouldn't that make Mauritius seem more like a refuge than a prison? The Foreign Office liked that idea very much and issued 340 visas.

For many months efforts were made to get Jews out of semi-neutral countries, like Hungary and Bulgaria, on the basis that they held the necessary Mauritius papers. None of the Jews with Mauritius visas ever reached the island but it is likely that some Jews used the documents to stave off deportation to concentration camps and, thereby, survived the war. That was typical Schonfeld. Look for the customer benefits for the government, not just why it would be good for the Jews; a standard marketing approach.

There were other small successes but each one was highly significant to the people who benefited. Many neutral diplomats on the continent had issued visas for Jews which their countries refused to honour. The CRREC took up the cases with the South American and other governments concerned and many hundreds were successfully rescued. In addition, five hundred refugee Talmudic students from Europe, stranded in Shanghai, were moved on Swedish ships to the Americas. There were other individual cases. At one point, much later, Schonfeld found a supporter to help him buy an island called Strangers Cay, near Nassau in the Bahamas. The idea was to issue visas for entry to the island, but it did not work out in the end. The wartime results did not amount to much but, given the overall situation when so much was impossible, anything was worth trying.

The CRREC had been involved in heroic activity with the Kindertransport before the war. It would be doing equally high profile work when the war was over. In the meantime Schonfeld was buried in a multitude of activities which, though they did not make the headlines, did a great deal of good. Part of his time was devoted to the children at Shefford. He could safely leave the day-to-day administration to Judith Grunfeld, and Dr Levene was an excellent Headmaster. Nevertheless, Solly liked the children to know that he was still there for them in the background. They needed a father figure, they loved to see him and, even with everything else he had to remember, he still rarely forgot a name. The British Council had provided the nucleus of a library for the school, which had around 150 pupils. Even clothing was provided for needy children. In early 1941 they were able to celebrate the first anniversary of the founding of the only evacuee Yeshiva. Beth Jacob was supported by the Keren Hatorah organization in London and an advanced Jewish studies curriculum was offered to both girls and boys.

In fact, everything at Shefford was mixed and as the older children could not be supervised in the way they were at boarding school, there were concerns that juvenile love affairs could lead to unfortunate results. That did not happen once in all the years the children were in the Bedfordshire countryside. Certainly, there were a few marriages and subsequent births, but nothing untoward happened, and that was as much down to the children as the teachers. The academic results were good too. If all the adults would have preferred a degree of separation, nobody suffered from the fact that it was not feasible in wartime.

Judith Schonfeld was a town girl, educated at South Hampstead High School and Somerville, Oxford. Now she and Solly found a home near Harlow in Essex which had the bucolic address of Walnut Tree Cottage, Loyters Green, Matching Tye. It was twenty-two miles from London and about fifty miles from Shefford and Solly took to the country life with great enthusiasm. The cottage had four acres of land, including a field, orchard, kitchen garden and the overgrown sites of six cottages for which Solly was repeatedly refused planning permission. The cottage had three bedrooms and had been renovated to add a bathroom and even a mikvah. Judith originally cooked on a primus stove and the well water was impure. For Solly it was still a paradise and Judith transformed it into a cosy English cottage while she lived there. Judith was on site full-time and Solly would join the family as often as he could get away. After the war Solly would continue to use the cottage but Judith had not enjoyed her wartime experiences and preferred not to go again. The cottage must have been lonely and isolated at nighttime. In London Solly stayed with Ella during the war in Lordship Park when Judith was in the country.

From the beginning of the marriage Judith did not wear a sheitl, preferring a scarf to the wig, but she was the Chief Rabbi's daughter and Solly's wife, so to that extent she was beyond public criticism, whatever might be said behind her back in Charedi homes. With the future home base in Highgate, the level of religious observance of the Rabbi's wife could be tactfully ignored by the Adath communities in other parts of London. Few United Synagogue wives at the time did wear a sheitl. If there was any question of why Judith was not by his side in community matters, Solly would ask 'Do you take your wife when you go out on business?' Attack, he normally believed, was the best form of defence.

The question of Jewish education for the Jewish evacuees around the country was a great problem. Simply to get the children together with the teachers was often, geographically, impossible. Nationally, there was a Joint Emergency Committee for Jewish Education but Schonfeld had not joined it. He did not want to risk being committed to decisions of which he did not approve. The influence of Sir Robert Waley Cohen, the head of the United Synagogue, continued to be focused on a reconciliation between the Orthodox and the Reform movements. He had asked Norman Bentwich and Lily Montagu to co-chair a conference on Jewish education which Schonfeld condemned as: 'intended to throw all Jewish education into the hands of these people, excluding all Orthodox Jews'.[3] Hertz vetoed the meeting very quickly. Schonfeld made his position clear again on the occasion of the centenary of the Reform movement in this country in 1942: 'Its course has been marked by ever wider breaks with traditional practices and still more with the traditional spirit, which it is doubtful whether the founders would ever have sanctioned.'[4] On this point he was quite correct.

There were not enough Jewish teachers in the country to educate the children either, but when Schonfeld offered thirty refugee rabbis, he was told that their English was not good enough. This was probably true, but it was a problem that could have been overcome with goodwill on both sides. The question of cooperation between the UOHC and the Emergency Committee had been raised at the Union's AGM in the summer. Schonfeld had told the meeting that it was: 'unfortunate that they had to face such a farcical situation as that in which questions of kashrut, the Din and chinuch [education] were administered by people who were not only indifferent but opposed to them'.[5] There were instances which proved his point. For example, Waley Cohen had been very antagonistic towards a move to try to provide matzos for evacuee children at Passover. His view was that, in times of rationing, it was wrong for the Jewish community to ask for special treatment.

The fact was, though, that bread was only rationed after the war, when flour was costing too much in precious foreign exchange.

Hertz often took Schonfeld's side against Waley Cohen:

> As Chief Rabbi I am supposed to care for religious teachers, Rabbis, scholars and clergy. Rabbi Schonfeld's activities come under this heading. This is not a communal matter, but a religious matter, and when it comes to religious matters, no communal organisation has the right to dictate to the Chief Rabbi.[6]

The best, however, that could be achieved for a lot of children was the production of leaflets, which would have done little good. A large number of Jewish children effectively had no Jewish education, which was one of the reasons for the lack of religious commitment which became a growing feature of that generation after the war. By contrast the Sabbath services at Shefford were run by the pupils. It was like the synagogue at Cambridge during the war when a front row of illustrious rabbinical refugees from Europe sat back contentedly as the students conducted their own services.

Schonfeld was still, of course, the pastoral rabbi at the Adath, though it was understood that his other heavy responsibilities might prevent him being at every wedding, every funeral, every bris (circumcision). Forty-six synagogues were now affiliated to the Union and during Festivals Solly would continue to walk miles to visit them. During Passover in 1942 he was at Stamford Hill for the first days, Hampstead for the Sabbath, and on the 8th day he was at Hendon in the morning and Edgware in the evening, which is a long way to travel on foot. He also found time to write a eulogy when Fanny Lunzer died in June 1941. The mother figure in the Adath community, Fanny had come to Britain in 1888, borne ten children, had thirty-two grandchildren, was ever-present and would be pleased that many of her great grandchildren remain prominent today in the community.

Schonfeld also remained the religious head of the UOHC. He presided at a meeting of the thirty-three rabbis affiliated to the Union in December 1941. Among the subjects under discussion, as the Blitz petered out, were doubtful ingredients in branded food products, the times when *tephilin* should be put on and the problems in wartime in observing the laws of *shatnes* (these concern the materials which can be used in clothes. The rules are laid down in great detail and forbid the mixing of wool and linen).

The obituary for Fanny Lunzer, a speech to mark an anniversary, a discussion on shatnes; the minutiae of normal life in Britain, could not assuage the torments which racked the minds of the refugees when they thought of what was happening to their families in Europe. The word would eventually reach Solly of the fate of his friends in Slobodka, those who had welcomed him when he came to study for his *semicha* ten years before. In one day in October 1941, out of a Jewish population of 25,000, the Nazis executed 10,000. In one day. Perhaps, in such circumstances, it is the performance of the minutiae which keeps people sane. In the case of an occasionally Orthodox Jew going into battle, it was a help to morale to have a set of *tephilin* to put on in order to pray in the correct manner in the morning, even if it was not their normal practice; the CRREC made this possible. From March 1941 every observant Jew in the forces was sent a fortnightly kosher food parcel, with the blessing of the Ministry of Food. The CRREC arranged supplies for Passover to the troops; in 1944 they sent out 25,000 lbs of matzo, 500 lbs of meat, 15,000 pints of wine and 5,000 hagadas. They sent out thousands of other prayer books too, as well as the Chief Rabbi's popular *Book of Jewish Thoughts* which was reprinted many times.

In the middle of all his other responsibilities, Schonfeld still found time to write his educational curriculum for Jewish youngsters, *Jewish Religious Education*, which was published in 1943. It was a determined attempt to sell Jewish religious education to Jewish parents. Schonfeld held that in a Jewish school nobody was embarrassed by being Jewish. The children's self assurance was strengthened by standing up as a Jew. He pointed out that JSSM children were not ghetto minded. They did not feel inferior. He suggested that the alternative was to send them to a non-Jewish school where they would be exposed to teasing and intimidation and only the committed fittest would survive, a course of action which Schonfeld believed to be cruel as it would impair their personalities. The likelihood was that the child would respond to ridicule or ostracism by giving up and conforming. It did indeed happen all the time. By contrast: 'The JDS (Jewish Day School) gives them the protection and nourishment in their years of helplessness'.[7] Schonfeld seldom passed up a polysyllabic word, even if several monosyllabic ones were readily available. His messages suffered from this, though Jewish day schools certainly did enable the pupils to learn their faith when they were young and easily led, in the right surroundings. As always with Schonfeld the argument was not intended to just encourage its readers to consider the intellectual implications of accepting or rejecting it. He stormed: 'British Jewry! What are you going to do about it? You have resources for furs, diamonds and pleasures. What about the well-being of your children and the future of your people?'[8]

Schonfeld was a committed Orthodox author but, unfortunately, the commitment of an author is not enough to keep a reader engrossed. Schonfeld's literary output would in the future sometimes be difficult to understand (*Why Judaism?*), sometimes too elementary in content (*Message to Jewry*) and sometimes too peripheral to the needs of the community (*The Daily Prayer Book*). The latter would be an attempt to provide a more ultra-Orthodox alternative to the Singer Prayer Book but failed to penetrate the market, in part because the Charedim did not feel the need for any English translation of the Hebrew. Schonfeld's copious marginal references were also intellectually beyond many potential users.

There continued to be a serious need to raise money. Over the years half a million pounds was raised and spent by the CRREC on 'rescue, relief and rehabilitation, on welfare among children, Servicemen, internees and others in need' (£20 million today).[9] Many methods were adopted but Solly preferred to call on possible donors in person rather than write them letters. He was very persuasive and very successful. A lot of non-Charedi fund raising also took place at dinner dances, but there he was in competition with Jewish charities with much longer track records. Apart from the fact that mixed dancing was forbidden in Charedi circles, Solly thought that a good alternative might be to have a concert. A member of the Adath congregation had a son called Solomon Cutner who was a professional musician. With very little arm twisting it was agreed that the great pianist, whose stage name was Solomon, would give a performance in aid of the schools. It would be held at the Whitehall Theatre which was readily given free for the good cause. Now all Solly needed was someone to organize it. He remembered that one of the Ben Zakkai youth club regulars, a Hungarian youngster, liked classical music. With a little more persuasion, the youngster agreed to organize the event and sell the guinea tickets (£42 today). They sold like hot cakes and the young man decided that this might be a promising career. So it turned out to be, and Victor Hochhauser became one of the finest international concert promoters of the next sixty years. The concert was a great success, though the interval was somewhat protracted as Solly borrowed a room during it and conducted both afternoon and evening services. When it was pointed out that the soloist would be ready to start again before the prayers were concluded, Solly said cheerfully: 'He'll wait'. Indeed Solomon offered to join the congregation.

One of the most admirable things about Schonfeld was always his indifference to the status of the job that needed doing. He really did not mind whether he could do good by mingling with the mighty, making representations to Ministers of the Crown, or dealing with the problem of one poor Jew in financial trouble. If it crossed his desk, he was there to sort it out. And if he had to deal with it personally, he would do that too. If Schonfeld had the greatest difficulty in working within committees, the other side of the coin was that he was always prepared to do the work himself.

The Nazis constantly tried to propagate the idea that the war was the fault of the Jews. The consequent temptation for the community to maintain a low profile was widely accepted. The evidence, however, that the unthinkable Final Solution was a reality mounted throughout 1942. The Polish government in exile received incontrovertible information from their homeland of its implementation and in December the fledgling United Nations organization roundly condemned the Nazis for murdering the Jews. The demands for action to halt the slaughter came from all over Britain but when it came to practical action there was really nothing that could be done to ameliorate the horrific situation. The British Foreign Office promised that everything would be tried 'compatible with the requirements of military operations', which enabled it to avoid doing anything at all. It was, however, asked to address far-fetched and naive solutions, such as, for example, that it consider the possibility of aiming to get two million Jews out of Europe (as suggested by the WJC and Jewish Agency), or the JA invited it to 'forget legalities and make Palestine into a Jewish sanctuary'.

It was a ghastly dilemma but the British still desperately needed to keep the Arab nations from joining the Axis. Their nightmare was that the oil supplies needed to fight the war might be curtailed. Allowing an unlimited number of Jews to enter Palestine was not going to help keep the Arabs happy. The Axis powers would have been delighted at such a diplomatic blunder. Nevertheless, the atrocities could not just be ignored. As Richard Law, the civil servant at the Foreign Office handling the response, remarked, 'We would be in an appalling position if these stories should prove to have been true and we have done nothing whatever about them'.[10] So the Allies needed to stall and they had little difficulty in dragging out discussions until interest among the general public waned. They were, admittedly, somewhat embarrassed by the United Nations' condemnation which was read out in the House of Commons. Sir Henry (Chips) Channon MP recorded the moment in his diaries:

> Jimmy de Rothschild (Liberal MP for the Isle of Ely) rose and with immense dignity, and with his voice vibrating with emotion, spoke for five minutes in moving tones on the plight of these peoples. There were tears in his eyes and I feared that he might break down; the House caught his mood and was deeply moved. Some-

body suggested that we stand in silence to pay our respects to those suffering peoples, and the House as a whole rose and stood for a few frozen seconds. It was a fine moment.[11]

The government then returned to realities and the fine moment only led to a conference to consider the whole question of refugees in the Spring of 1943 in Bermuda. This did not achieve much, though Jewish refugees who had reached Spain could henceforth go to safe havens in North Africa through the Gibraltar frontier. Back in Britain, however, Herbert Morrison, the Home Secretary, did issue 900 visas for refugees, including 183 for Jewish children in Vichy France who could join relatives in Britain. At the end of the war the generally agreed figure for French Jews killed in the Holocaust was 90,000.

Schonfeld was realistic. He understood the government's position and tried to square the circle. If no declaration had a chance of passing if it included offering specific refuge in Palestine, then how about Britain promising 'temporary refuge in its own territories or in territories under its control'? There was support from no less than 277 MPs for a motion in the House to that effect, but the Board of Deputies would not agree to it. Brodetsky, as a fervent Zionist, would not support any motion which left out Palestine. He had been specifically asked by the American Zionist organization to get the measure stifled. Brodetsky had another reason for opposing the motion. He continued to dislike intensely any attempt to influence the government except through the medium of the Board of Deputies. They had been the official conduit between the British Jews and parliament since George III's accession, and Brodetsky felt he had to hold the line. As the Schonfeld supporters worked for the motion, the Board of Deputies lobbied against it. The supporters were now, naturally, confused and started to withdraw their support. The motion failed and Schonfeld, correctly, blamed the Board of Deputies: 'The sabotage by Jews of our effort to help Jews, met with success'. Indeed, to put personal prestige ahead of the remotest chance of rescuing Jews on the Continent was inexcusable. Of course, the internal squabbling also made it easier for the government to reject approaches it did not like, on the grounds that it was not clear whether they represented the views of a majority of the Jewish community. The fact was, though, that the motion would have failed anyway because the government felt that a statement on the subject by Clement Attlee in January 1943 covered the ground more fully than Schonfeld's draft.

The recognition that Schonfeld was prepared to challenge the Jewish Establishment over the declaration provided additional fuel to the blaze of their anger at his position. They were soon to get a chance to fight back when Hertz and Schonfeld visited the Home Office on behalf of the North London Yeshiva. The Home Office sent a copy of the minutes of the meeting to Hertz at the United Synagogue, which was not his office, and when the letter was opened by the officials, they discovered that the Home Office had referred to Schonfeld as the Deputy Chief Rabbi. The United Synagogue immediately wrote back saying there was no Deputy Chief Rabbi: 'We think it important that you should be made aware that Dr. Schonfeld holds no office under the United Synagogue and is not connected with any synagogal organisation which participates in the maintenance of the Chief Rabbi or recognizes its authority.'[12] A copy of the letter was sent to *The Jewish Chronicle* which commented that someone in the organization had it in for Schonfeld. That particular someone was almost guaranteed to be Sir Robert Waley Cohen. Nobody else would have had the power to authorize the sending of such a letter. *The Jewish Chronicle* was equally heavy handed in rebuttal: 'If every official mistake is demolished with such a crude and thunderous barrage of contradiction and with such complete absence of tact, good feeling and savoir faire', it was not going to help the cause.

The religious fate of Jewish children not under his care continued to worry Schonfeld throughout the war and he fought hard for the Guardianship Act which was passed in 1944. This act established that Lord Gorell would chair a committee who would have guardianship rights over all refugee children in Britain. Thus while the danger of their being baptised was much reduced, it was too late for many.

As the war drew to a close, the allies started to liberate the concentration camps. Immediately Schonfeld organized mobile synagogue ambulances. These would be fitted out with kosher food, medical supplies, prayer books, a sefer torah and a kitchen. The first one was consecrated by Hertz in November 1944. As the Chief Rabbi quoted felicitously: 'and when he (Jacob) saw the wagons that Joseph had sent to carry him, the spirit of Jacob, their father, revived' (Genesis 45.27). Eventually there would be more than a dozen such ambulances sent to different parts of Europe. Schonfeld had no difficulty in getting the financial support he needed to go to Europe to try to help those who had survived the horrors of the camps. 'He was not sure of his rank but he entered as Chief of the Imperial General Staff. He would commandeer transport fleets. He found them [some of the refugees] homes and jobs and lent them money.'[13]

In April 1945 the British 21st Army Group entered Belsen in Lower Saxony and what happened next illustrated the contrasting viewpoints of both the Jewish and non-Jewish organizations who tried to deal with the appalling situations they found on the Continent. Belsen was a comparatively small camp for holding prisoners and there were no gas chambers. Nevertheless, 50,000 prisoners had died from disease in the two years it had been run by the Gestapo and a current typhus epidemic was continuing to claim hundreds of victims every day. The Senior Jewish Chaplain with 21st Army Group was Rev. Isaac Levy and when he saw the condition of those who had survived, he sent to London for more help. Schonfeld dispatched Rabbis Munk, Baumgarten and Vilensky, three ultra-Orthodox rabbis. It was decided to burn the camp to deal with the typhus. The liberated prisoners were taken to an army camp in Bergen-Belsen nearby. Slowly the daily death toll diminished. The army correctly saw its job as saving as many lives as possible, restoring the victims to health and sending them home to their own countries to rejoin their families. The problem was it could not work with the Jewish survivors. Too often all their families had been killed and the last thing they wanted to do was return to the countries whose officials had often cooperated with the Nazis in their arrest and deportation. Most wanted to go to Palestine but that country was still closed to them. So most of the Jewish survivors chose to remain in the army camp.

The needs of the victims differed, of course. The needs of the ultra-Orthodox were not the same as those of survivors who were less Orthodox or not Orthodox at all. Rabbi Munk tried to help the Charedim to follow the *mitzvot* again; the CRREC sent kosher food, *tephillin*, prayer books, *talleisim* and *sifrei torah*. Rabbi Baumgarten listened to the appeals of the ultra-Orthodox and obtained permission from the army authorities to build a mikvah. It was an essential element of an Orthodox wedding and married life and even in the appalling world of the camps, some couples had fallen in love and survived. It says a lot about the commitment of the Charedim that, lacking warm clothing, medicines, suitable buildings and innumerable other necessities of life, what they asked for was a mikvah.

Not all the clergy were helpful. Rabbi Vilensky, for example, pretended to be the plenipotentiary of the Chief Rabbi. Levy said Vilensky never visited the hospitals where so many of the patients were dying and he was accused of bribery and stirring up trouble. In the end he was put under house arrest for his own safety before being shipped out of the camp. There was no question of controlling the rabbis from a London headquarters. Schonfeld confirmed to Levy that the rabbis were to report to him, as the Senior Jewish Chaplain, on all administrative matters.

The row that developed between Schonfeld and Levy was over material sent by the CRREC to the camp. Schonfeld gave instructions that it was to be devoted 'only to what he called the "kehillah" or "gemeinde" by which he meant the religious element'.[14] When this was discovered, the Board of Deputies disassociated themselves from the instruction, and Israel Brodie, the Senior Jewish Chaplain to the forces, approved the cancellation of the order. 'All supplies, such as books, food, clothing etc., should be addressed to the Committee for fair distribution.' Schonfeld refused to accept the ruling. He made a feeble excuse that the non-Orthodox could forage for food in the vicinity of the camp but the religious 'were engaged in more "Godly" activities.' It appeared to be Schonfeld at his worst, making arrogant and offensive gestures in public and alienating the less Orthodox community. The alternative, however, would have been to tell the truth and that could have done even more damage. The truth was that Schonfeld did not trust anybody else to look after the Charedi survivors. He had very bad memories of what had happened when he relied on other people. Before the war the Austrian Jewish Establishment had kept the exit visas for the young and fit, whether Orthodox or not. The Zionists had scuppered his efforts to get the bill through parliament, condemning the Final Solution, only a couple of years before. The army authorities were treating all the survivors alike, even though the Jews were, genuinely, a special case, and the Charedi had needs which did not apply to their co-religionists. From Schonfeld's point of view some positive discrimination was justified, but to make that case would have been to sow dissension between the groups at exactly the time when everybody needed to work together. Schonfeld preferred to draw the criticism onto his own head and to leave intact the relations between the relief groups as much as possible. It was not the first time, nor would it be the last time that Schonfeld provided the hammer with which the non-Orthodox could hit him over the head. But, of course, in the middle of an unspeakably appalling situation, nobody had much time to take into account the practices of the Charedim. What's more, many did not understand the importance of the *mitzvot* to the people concerned, and many had agendas that were antagonistic to the practices of that section of the community anyway.

The different viewpoints of the secular Zionists and the ultra-Orthodox continued, even when the subject was the Jewish children who had survived in the camps. They needed a refuge which the Zionists insisted should be Palestine. For the Charedim the Holy Land was only the natural setting when the Messiah came, as that was what was ordained in the Bible. Schonfeld attacked both views in *The Jewish Chronicle* in June 1945: 'They err equally who refuse to build Eretz

Yisroel till the coming of Mashiach, as who attempt to ignore Zion's dispersed children until the coming of the Jewish state.'[15]

In August 1945 the war in Europe was over and the unbelievable violence of the atom bomb explosion on 6 August, totally destroying Hiroshima, presaged an early end to the conflict in the Far East. Everybody breathed a vast sigh of relief and prepared to get back to normal.

Just before the JSSM school returned to London, Judith Grunfeld made a memorable speech to a large gathering in Shefford and the surrounding villages:

> The guests are leaving now and they are leaving with a blessing. You all know the famous saying in the Bible when G-d says to Abraham 'Those that bless thee shall be blessed'. No doubt this can be applied to these children of Israel that were under your care and the way you have made them welcome here. We pray that the kindness you have shown to them will be repaid to you from above and that the Divine blessing may come upon you abundantly so that your own children may be strong and your families happy ... when teachers at school want to drive home a lesson about how to live up to a great challenge, they will bring up the example of what happened during the Second World War in Shefford, the little village in Bedfordshire.

It was Judith Grunfeld at her most impressive. It seems unlikely that those villagers would ever again experience the level of religious oberservance among ordinary human beings which motivated the children and teachers they had had in their midst. With that tradition of tolerance which had epitomized the British attitude to the Jews in their midst over the previous three centuries, the Bedfordshire villagers kept the faith.

If the war had been difficult, though, the peace was going to bring a return to the hard grind of trying to keep the JSSM schools going. The government support for the children at Shefford was not going to continue. The JSSM schools were still not state-aided. Schonfeld could see stretching before him yet more years of going, cap in hand, to ask for money to keep the ship afloat. Metaphorically, he shrugged his shoulders and prepared to soldier on.

At least by now he was a famous figure throughout the Jewish community. Wherever he appeared, the audience would be attracted as if to a modern-day pop concert. In 1945 one of his parliamentary supporters, the conservative Sir George Jones, was trying to retain his seat in the House of Commons and Solly agreed to speak on his behalf at the Astoria cinema one Sunday. Political meetings for a backbench MP are seldom well attended nowadays, but on this occasion the theatre was completely full and overflowing. He was still only 33 years old.

NOTES

1. Solomon Schonfeld, *Message to Jewry* (London: JSS Books, 1958).
2. Pamela Shatzkes, *Holocaust and Rescue* (New York: Palgrave, 2002).
3. Schonfeld archives, University of Southampton.
4. Ibid.
5. Ibid.
6. London Metropolitan Archives, Hertz papers.
7. Schonfeld archives, University of Southampton.
8. Solomon Schonfeld, *Jewish Religious Education* (London: JSS Books, 1943).
9. Schonfeld, *Message to Jewry*.
10. Shatzkes, *Holocaust and Rescue*.
11. Bernard Wasserstein, *Britain and the Jews of Europe 1939–1945* (London: Institute of Jewish Affairs, 1979).
12. *The Jewish Chronicle*, 26 February 1943.
13. Chaim Bermant, *The Jewish Chronicle*, 19 February 1982.
14. Isaac Levy, *Witness to Evil* (London: Peter Halban, 1995).
15. *The Jewish Chronicle*, 26 June 1945.

1. Rabbi Victor Schonfeld, c. 1905, before his wedding.

2. The Schonfelds in April or May 1914. Left to right: Betti and Jacob (Victor's parents) with Daniel, Ella, Samu (Victor's brother), Solomon and Victor. This was photographed probably in Grosswardein, Transylvania, where the older Schonfelds had moved.

3. The Schonfelds, 1922. Left to right: Moses, Solomon (standing), Akiba, Daniel, Ella, Asenath, David, Victor.

4. Solomon Schonfeld, September 1927, probably before leaving for Trnava Yeshivah.

5. Rabbi Dr Victor Schonfeld, late 1920s.

6. The Adath Yisroel Synagogue, Green Lanes, London.

7. The funeral of Rabbi Dr Victor Schonfeld, outside his synagogue, January 1930.

8. Rabbi Dr Joseph Herman Hertz, c. 1935.

9. The Schonfelds, 1938. Left to right: Moses, David, Ella (seated), Asenath, Daniel, Jacob, Akiba, Solomon.

10. Judith Hertz, September 1939, shortly before her wedding.

11. The wedding in the Hertz's drawing room, 104 Hamilton Terrace, January 1940. Left to right, seated: Kato Weisz (Ella's sister), Ella, Judith, Dr Hertz. Standing: Asenath, Akiba, Dr Solomon Schonfeld, Daniel, Ruth Hertz, David, Josephine Hertz, Ernest Petrie (Asenath's husband), Edith (Daniel's wife), Joir Weisz (Kato's husband), George Weisz.

12. Solomon Schonfeld's self-designed cap-badge. (Photo by kind permission of Ruthie Morris.)

13. Solomon Schonfeld at the inaugural meeting of the Va'ad Hakehilot (Central Committee of Polish Congregations) in Krakow, February 1946.

14. Dedicating the first Synagogue Ambulance. One of few photographs showing Dr Solomon Schonfeld together with Dr Hertz.

15. Dr Schonfeld in uniform at London Docks, discussing the distribution of newly arrived children to waiting adults.

16. Dr Schonfeld with Rabbi Eli Munk and Mr Stanton at a Hasmonean School sports day, Parliament Hill Fields, c. 1950.

17. With Jeremy at the cottage, c. 1953.

18. At a wedding, early 1950s.

19. Dr Schonfeld at the opening of the Northwold Road Synagogue, 1955. (Photo by kind permission of *The Jewish Chronicle*.)

20. A school speech day, showing Schonfeld to the left, H.A. Goodman speaking, Dr Judith Grunfeld in the white hat, and Ella Schonfeld and Joe Loebenstein on the extreme right.

21. Dr Schonfeld in 1964, with Julius Loebenstein (father of Joe) and Dayan Hanoch Padwa.

22. Dr Schonfeld with young visitors on Purim 1978.

# 6  The Problems of Peacetime

Schonfeld travelled to Poland and the Displaced Persons Camps in November 1945, soon after the war ended. The problems were monumental and heart-rending. Many Jews were stateless, having been deprived of their citizenship. The German survivors were offered a stark alternative in July 1945. They could either go back to living in concentration camps, the scene of unspeakable horrors, or they could join the general German population and be treated accordingly. Schonfeld wrote despairingly to *The Times* at the end of the month but to no avail and that remained the choice for years. He was back in Europe in March 1946. He found that many of the Jewish survivors were being attacked and murdered by the Poles and 'I, too, was marked down for assassination and was spared only as a result of providential circumstances'.[1] He was referring to a last minute change of route which avoided an ambush. Schonfeld was asked once whether this had not put him off. He replied: 'No, I did not return home. If the Almighty needs me, he will guard me. If he does not need me, why should I run for my life.' He had already risked assassination when organizing the Kindertransport before the war. He still, on occasions, travelled alongside two soldiers with Thompson machine guns in the back seat of his car.

The extent of anti-Semitism among the Poles at the time may seem unbelievable when the horrors of the concentration camps had only just been revealed to an appalled world. Nevertheless, in July 1946, for example, a Christian boy in the town of Kielce accused the 200 surviving Jews of killing a friend to obtain his blood. It was the ancient Blood Libel again and the Polish police, army units and secret police stormed the building where the Jews were sheltering. They killed 39 of them and wounded 82. At the trial which followed the massacre, all the members of the government's forces were found not guilty. To that extent Poland was still a war zone. Schonfeld may not have been a chaplain to the forces but, as a Jew, his experiences in Poland could certainly be described as being on active service.

Desperate survivors besieged his Polish hotel room and clamoured to see him. He visited many towns, which would have exposed him to harrowing problems: 'On Wednesday, I visited the few surviving Jews of Debica, Sandomierz and Ostrowiec. The Jews of Sandomierz are particularly interested in receiving funds for the reburial of the Jews shot on the way to the death trains.'[2] Back in Warsaw he managed to obtain more visas from the Belgian and Italian embassies and dealt with American and French authorities. In spite of the now obvious results of the Holocaust, the bureaucratic wheels continued to grind very slowly.

There was still a tremendous amount of work to do in Europe. The pathetic remnants of the Jewish communities needed help to stand on their own feet again. There were countless cases of survivors who had no idea whether their relatives were alive or not and, if they were, where they might be found. The CRREC was a port of call which offered some hope and it dealt with tens of thousands of enquiries.

The need was, as always, for funds to finance the work. Schonfeld had spent a number of years before the war practically begging for financial support for the schools. It was demeaning and he often faced rejection and derision. When he was raising money for refugees from Europe, however, he felt no necessity to beg; he felt it was the duty of anybody who was able to help to do so immediately. After the war Joyce Cohen, the sister-in-law of Bernard Kahn who had escaped Germany by stowing away on a ship bound for Liverpool and then swimming ashore, worked for textile magnate, Louis Mintz. She recalled a visit from Schonfeld who told her eminent boss: 'I want £2,000 from you. I want 200 blankets and I want them today' (£2,000 is the equivalent of £60,000 today). Everybody knew that Schonfeld would never take a penny of the contributions for himself. Where charities have administration costs, permanent staff to pay and offices to keep up, Schonfeld allowed no such items to come between the donations and the needy. To one person who pleaded he had many cost and cash flow difficulties, he said dismissively 'Rich man's problems' and repeated his request.

In fairness, however, he was less successful in ensuring that the recipients were always the people designated in the first place. Money might be raised for one worthy project and then a bill would arrive for something even more urgent. In such cases Schonfeld would pay the bill that was first on the list. If the donor had found out that this had happened, they could well have been annoyed. The situation would crop up on many occasions throughout Schonfeld's lifetime. He always meant to spend the money for the purpose he raised it, but that was not, by any means, always the way it worked out.

The result of his work in Poland was to rescue another 1,000 children from the Displaced Persons Camps where they languished after the war.

The Kindertransport ran again. Schonfeld organized two trips in 1946 and a third in 1947. For the first in March 1946 he managed to get a block visa from the Home Office for sixty children. He brought in 150 on a boat, telling them to pass on their visas to one of their friends when they had been seen by the customs officials. This was obviously illegal, but the alternative was to desert them and leave them to their fate. Many of the children from the camps were very sick and four ambulances were waiting at the quayside to take them to hospital as soon as the ship had docked. One child recalled: 'He didn't ask questions about whether we were religious or not. Many of the children came from assimilated or not very religious families.'

Schonfeld spoke Yiddish to those who did not speak English. On the boat he taught them to sing 'Daisy, Daisy' and reassured the frightened, isolated little refugees that they had bright futures. Many of the children ended up in JSSM schools and at Clonyn Castle in Ireland. The house had been bought for Schonfeld by a Manchester benefactor and was in a particularly useful location as there was no food rationing in Ireland and the children needed plenty of nourishment. They received a warm welcome from the locals, in spite of the fact that the local priest had announced before their arrival that they were bloodthirsty and disease ridden!

Maintaining the children was, as usual, a financial nightmare. Solly had not worked out how to pay the bills and a large number of local Irish tradespeople found their accounts in arrears for lengthy periods. Eventually the Central British Fund bailed Schonfeld out, but it was a tortuous business. On the other hand, the children thrived, which was the object of the exercise.

The agreement with the Home Office was that the children admitted would all be 'orphans'. The mother of one of them arrived a year later and the Home Office recognized that the orphan was no such thing. They carpeted Schonfeld and demanded to know how a man of the cloth could lie to them. Schonfeld was totally unabashed. He asked them 'Would you deprive one child of its mother?' There was no answer to that.

Even getting the children out of Europe had often involved enormous difficulties. Many Christian families naturally did not want to give up the children they had worked so hard to save. There was also the desire of some Catholic bodies to try to keep the Jewish children so that they could grow up in the faith to which they had become accustomed. In one monastery Schonfeld asked to see a dormitory after dark. In the gloom he said the first words of the *shema*, a key Hebrew prayer. When a number of voices completed the sentence he knew he had found Jewish children.

His schedule was frantic. On one Sabbath he found it necessary to fly from Warsaw to Berlin. He spoke to one passenger who went on to Israel eventually and recounted the story years later. He told him that his journey on Shabbat was *Pikuach Nefesh*. The principle remained that to save life it is permissible to break any other law.

The new Polish government was only prepared to deal with the members of the Committee of British Relief Societies Abroad (COBRA). So Schonfeld arranged for the CRREC to become a constituent member of the organization. Then there was the question of impressing the Poles, who would have paid little attention to the pleas of a traditional rabbi.

Fortunately, the CRREC could also become associated with UNRRA – the United Nations Relief and Rehabilitation Administration. So Solly arranged for that too and then went to his tailor to get himself a uniform which was indistinguishable from that of a British army officer. The flashes on the shoulders were UNRRA and his cap was specially designed to include the emblems of both the Ten Commandments and the Star of David. The rabbi was transformed into a United Nations representative and received the respect the organization merited. Solly was well able to play the part of a senior officer and even continued to wear his beard. The only other familiar figure in an army uniform to have a beard was the late King George V! Only the navy wear beards.

In January 1946, still as director of the CRREC, Solly went to America to report on his post-war work in Poland and Eastern Europe. He addressed 1,200 guests at a banquet held at Astor House in honour of the United States Secretary to the Treasury, Henry Morgenthau. The Mayor of New York, William O'Dwyer, was another guest. Once again the rabbi of a minute North London community of Charedi Jews was performing on an international stage. One Sabbath found Solly walking miles to attend synagogue on the Upper East Side of New York, having started from Long Island. The journey took him across the Queensboro Bridge which has no facilities for pedestrians. So the police held up the traffic to make sure the rabbi was in no danger from the cars!

To the Adath community it was incredible that such a pinnacle could be reached by their rabbi, Dr Schonfeld. Where their own concerns were parochial in the extreme, their rabbi was accepted as a distinguished member of the British committee trying to help rebuild the shattered remnants of European Jewry. Schonfeld had established himself in a position they could never hope to reach and the community bathed in the glow of his success.

From this time on, whatever the future might bring, Schonfeld would always be held in great esteem throughout the ranks of the ultra-Orthodox in Britain. He would be an icon, accepted in illustrious circles, known to the powerful, rich and famous in both the world of British Jews and in the wider British Establishment. It was an achievement which aggravated the leaders of the mainstream British Jewish community beyond measure. Rabbis were supposed to be minor functionaries. In discussions in smoke-filled rooms, they criticized the fact that Schonfeld continued to commit the cardinal sin of not knowing his place.

The JSS started up again in London. The school in Lordship Road would be called Avigdor for the next fifteen years. A second school, Hasmonean, was at The Drive in Golders Green. Its headmaster, Walter Stanton, was a good academician with history degrees from Oxford and Leeds. He was a member of the United Synagogue and had intended to pursue an academic career. In 1944, however, he had been visited by Solly who told him, flatly, that he was going to be the headmaster of Hasmonean. Stanton found himself so impressed by the charm, personality and drive of the rabbi that he agreed to take the job at the beginning of 1945. He was to prove an outstanding appointment and a brilliant teacher.

When he arrived the school was co-educational, though the plan was for two schools; the girls at The Drive and the boys to be relocated. Schonfeld continued his policy of marrying the best of Jewish education with the structure of a public school. The children were divided into houses and the long grace after meals was said every lunchtime. There were Jewish Studies classes every day, and morning assembly with the teachers in academic gowns.

The school was – and always remained – non-selective. A child with an Orthodox mother did not need to pass an exam to get in. This would make the academic results achieved by the children even more remarkable in the years to come. Time and again their exam marks equalled and exceeded those of schools who chose the brightest children they could identify in a competitive entrance exam. The boys wore *yarmulkes* which created a problem when they were playing sport as they were kept in place with a metal clip. The question of whether it was acceptable to play football and risk injury from misheading the ball would be decided in favour of wearing the *yarmulke*.

The Schonfeld family was spread widely. Sergeant David Schonfeld was with the Intelligence Training Centre in Karachi and Moses had settled down in the United States. Jacob had been at Gateshead Yeshivah in the North East of England for most of 1943 and 1944. He went on to emigrate to America where he attended Yeshiva College between 1947 and 1955. Senath was married to Dr Ernest Petrie, although the marriage was not going well. She had worked during the latter years of the war at the Mill Hill Emergency Hospital for Allied Forces in London, but she also spent time recruiting volunteers to help in the German concentration camps after they were liberated and helped Solly with the children he brought to Britain after 1945. She had developed into a woman of extraordinary presence. She was tall, angular, wore big straw hats and was strikingly good looking and highly articulate. She was always extremely English in her manner, though her Hungarian cherry soup was much esteemed. Like others in the family, Senath was widely recognized as not being averse to telling others off. All in all, a formidable character. Senath would eventually go to Harvard to join the psychology faculty where she was asked to lecture on her speciality, which was prefrontal leucotomy. This procedure was designed to help patients with depression by isolating the frontal lobes of the brain from the rest. It was held to improve the condition, but her research eventually proved it to have potentially disastrous side effects. Senath's literary output included *Personality and the Frontal Lobes* in 1952 and *Individuality in Pain and Suffering* in 1967. In later life she would write poetry, four volumes of which were widely published. David and Jacob would also become psychologists, though in different disciplines within the science. David emigrated in 1956 and eventually founded the psychology department at the University of Calgary in Canada.

Kibo had joined up as a private and served in the Royal Artillery from 1940. By 1945 he was a Major and when he was demobilized he became a distinguished economist, journalist and broadcaster, living in a large terraced house in Chelsea, materially and philosophically far from his upbringing in North London. There were rumours that his wife, Zuzanna, was not Jewish but Solly confirmed she was when he went through the records when he was in Poland after the war. Not everybody in the Schonfeld camp came through the war unscathed, though. A few years after hostilities ended, Ruth Lunzer, his devoted secretary, who had worked herself to a frazzle, had a serious nervous breakdown due to stress and strain. She never fully recovered. During the war Solly and Judith had started their family. Judith could not contribute to the work in Shefford as their eldest son, Victor, was born in 1940 and their second son, Jonathan in 1944. The third boy, Jeremy, would arrive in 1951.

It was difficult to turn from the horrors of the war in Europe to the demands of peacetime Britain. This applied to the JSSM schools as well. Head teachers have always had to contend with unruly pupils, but the JSSM teachers in 1947 were faced with problems for which nobody could have been properly trained. Within the school were children who had survived concentration camps. The numbers tattooed on their arms marked them out. Their families had been butchered, the children had been torn from their parents, they had survived in the camps in hopeless and endless squalor, with hardly anything to eat and only probable death as their constant companion. The children had every reason to be traumatized by their experiences. It was hardly better for those who had been sheltered in Christian homes, because the fear of betrayal and subsequent deportation was always with them. If a child was unruly, the head teacher would have considered this far preferable to the possibility of mental breakdown. All of the children who survived the horrors of the camps would have seen human beings behaving in a bestial manner. It is not necessary to recount the mounds of unburied corpses, the piles of gold teeth torn from the dead bodies, and the emaciation and haunted expressions of the survivors. That the children ever recovered from those traumas was amazing and much of the credit for it goes to the school teachers who were devoted to doing what they could to help.

There were, of course, any number of Adath matters which Schonfeld had to see to, and his flair for the dramatic gesture to make a point was still very evident. In 1947, for example, he was said to have discovered a bakery licenced by the Kedassia which had started baking before the end of Passover. So, he, personally, threw oil on it and it went up in flames. From the point of view of safety, this is not recommended. It is also a story attributed to other religious leaders. What is certain is that on one occasion he arrived late for a function and could not reach his seat. He was reported to have climbed or vaulted over the tables! He was, physically, in those days a very strong man.

Judith's continued reluctance to be involved in synagogue affairs could have been attributed to many different things. She might have grown tired of the many occasions since her mother's death ten years before, that she had acted as her father's hostess. Hertz had a very bad temper, he was a tough taskmaster and a large number of the troubles of the Jewish world finished up on his doorstep. It must have been a frenetic atmosphere, one that resulted in his children not developing into the adults he had hoped they might. Alternatively, she might just have found the Adath congregation too extreme in its Orthodoxy, compared to her own United Synagogue standards, or too un-English. It also might have been that she was very shy, which she was, though gifted in many ways. For whatever reason, she would come to the Adath shul on Rosh Hashanah and Yom Kippur, in common with the wives of other Adath rabbis, but was not seen in its precincts otherwise. Judith is remembered as very quiet and reserved. A lady who never opened up to the members, she did, however, have a friendly smile for those she liked. Even so, she once said to one of the Adath Honorary Officers, 'I don't want anything to do with your community'. Judith did not just dislike going to the Adath; she also did not want heated business meetings in her home. She did not want the house invaded by the almost round-the-clock activity which characterized Solly's working life at his office, with its constant comings and goings and often heated meetings. Her home was a haven from all that and she wanted the synagogue, the schools and her home kept separate. Until 1960, though, the family moved to Lordship Road every Friday afternoon to be near the synagogue and Solly would give a *shiur* (religious lecture) to the youngsters in the Chevra Ben Zakkai every Friday night.

What Judith did have was her own circle of friends, based on her childhood and university experiences. Solly enjoyed the visits and often discussed religious viewpoints with them. One pastime both Solly and Judith also had in common was gardening which they found a source of great enjoyment, though he was better at mowing the lawn than anything more horticultural. Between 1947 and 1948 they had spent £650 on terracing and landscaping the garden in Highgate. That's £17,000 today. As usual, Solly was managing to keep more activity balls in the air than a master juggler.

Apart from his work on the Continent and in America, and apart from his responsibilities to the Adath, there were also the schools. As a whole, Jewish education in London at the end of the war was in a parlous state. There had been nine Jewish schools in London before the war but only the Stepney Jewish, the Solomon Wolfson, the new ultra-Orthodox Yesodey Hatorah (founded in 1943) and the JSSM schools survived the war. The others had been bombed, their catchment area had disappeared in the Blitz, or the children had been evacuated and did not return to their old homes. Large areas of the East End, around the docks, had been comprehensively devastated by the Luftwaffe.

The JFS school buildings had been destroyed as well and what had to be resolved was what should happen now. In 1944 it was publicly suggested that JFS should be rebuilt in Central London, but Schonfeld had written to the *Jewish Chronicle* to oppose it. His reasoning was that such a school should be in a neighbourhood where there was already a substantial Jewish population.

The key to the future lay in the government's recent 1944 Education Act. Among the many provisions of this excellent and far-reaching piece of legislation was an acceptance that state-aided religious schools had their place in a post-war Britain. Hertz had had long discussions with the Ministry of Education and was assured by the Minister, R.A. Butler, that he was in favour of such schools and that the government would provide financial support.

In May 1939, faced with the prospect of the coming war, the main Jewish educational bodies had met to pool their resources. The Jewish Religious Education Board (JREB) and the Union of Hebrew and Religion Classes, together with the Talmud Torah Trust had covered most of the ground pre-war. A new body was now created – the Joint Emergency Council for Jewish Religious Education (JEC). The Sephardim, Jews' College and the United Synagogue joined up later. The attempt, however, to create a totally representative Jewish educational body hit the inevitable buffers when the Education Officer at the JREB started to conduct unofficial negotiations with the Reform and Liberal movements, to work out a way of including them in the new organization. Such a move would undoubtedly have had the approval of the United Synagogue's Waley Cohen. He remained keen on repairing the rift between the Orthodox US and the Reform till the day he died. Only Chief Rabbi Hertz had prevented him from doing so and Hertz would have discussed his tactics with his son-in-law, Schonfeld. On the other side, Lily Montagu, the head of the Liberals, said she was very willing to talk to anybody in the Orthodox camp, even Schonfeld: 'Perhaps I may convince him that he won't damage his position through having something to do with heretics. After all, he may snatch us from the burning.' Schonfeld would not have found the prospect equally amusing. He was well aware that Lily Montagu had her own very strongly felt beliefs, and they were totally contrary to his own. Beneath the banter there was a deadly war continuing to be waged over much of the Jewish world for the hearts and minds of the community. The Progressives depended on defections from the Orthodox ranks for much of their numerical growth. Schonfeld considered that the ultra-Orthodox educational tradition was only safe in his hands. Hertz was completely opposed to the admission of the Progressives to the JEC anyway. He wrote to his flock:

> There is a serious danger of Jewish religious education being deprived of its Jewish and religious character ... it is clearly my duty as Chief Rabbi ... to rescue our educational machinery from the hands of men who are inimical to Traditional Judaism and its fundamental institutions.

In the future workings of the JEC, Schonfeld could have taken the line that he was doing no more than the Chief Rabbi asked of his supporters.

There was a conference in November 1945 on the Reconstruction of Jewish Education in Great Britain to plan the way forward. The conference agreed to pool the claims of all the schools which had been lost. This was particularly generous of the trustees of the funds of the

Jews' Free School, which possessed the majority of the available assets. The school had a freehold worth £100,000, a war damages claim of £40,000 and other assets which brought its total fund to more than a quarter of a million pounds. It also had another 50 per cent of that total guaranteed in government grants, making a total of £375,000 in 1945, which is the equivalent of nearly £11 million today.

Schonfeld, while desperately in need of this money, was well aware that his own school movement had absolutely no right to a penny of the JFS money or that of any of the other defunct schools. JFS had been the flagship of the Jewish schools pre-war. If it had not managed to maintain its student roll of 4,250 at the beginning of the century, it had still been a school to be reckoned with, with 1,000 children in its classrooms in 1939. What was more, it still had the support of the Rothschilds. If Schonfeld was going to get even a part of the JFS money for the JSSM, he was going to have to persuade the government, the Chief Rabbi, the Jewish Establishment and the local authorities that this was the right way to dispose of the funds. And in 1946 his greatest ally, his father-in-law, the Chief Rabbi, Joseph Hertz, died.

There are highs and lows in every life. For Schonfeld one of the highs had come because of the war. As an obscure rabbi in a tiny community, one result of the war and the events leading up to it was his emergence onto the stage of British Jewry. He had left an indelible mark over the eight years. Whatever feathers he had ruffled, however unorthodox his methods on occasions, he had achieved an enormous amount. The reputation he had richly deserved for saving innocent lives would be in place for the rest of his life, but his power base in the larger community was destroyed for ever in 1946. Schonfeld once said to Joe Lobenstein, one of his Shefford pupils and now a distinguished London politician, that 'he wasn't a normal person. He couldn't just settle for the Rabbi's round of home, dinner and preaching. He would do what was most needed.' To a considerable extent, though, that was if he was allowed to.

When the war had been over for a few years, there was no longer a real need for the CRREC, as the main pillar of its *raison d'être* was now removed. Acting as the Chief Rabbi's representative and sheltering behind his office, Schonfeld had immediate access to a whole range of organizations, committees and influential movers and shakers. He had not always been welcome, but he had used his negotiating skills well. Now he no longer had Hertz's backing or any official place in the hierarchy of British Jews, except for his position within the small and unrepresentative UOHC.

The animosity that Otto Schiff felt towards Schonfeld continued after the war. There was a meeting of the Refugee Committee at the United Synagogue Headquarters and Schiff was blunt. He said to Schonfeld in front of everybody: 'I can't listen to your proposition since you once lied to me'. Schiff was referring to the occasion before the war when Schonfeld had asked him for visas for 200 families, involving about 1,200 people. Schiff could get them but he needed Schonfeld to have 200 guarantors for their maintenance. Solly said he had that many. The fact was that he only had ninety guarantors, though he produced thirty to forty more later. Schiff was furious at the time. Now Schonfeld could not understand the fuss. He asked Schiff if he would rather he had not saved the lives. From Schiff's point of view, there was the danger of losing credibility with the Home Office, sacrificing his honour as a gentleman, additional financial burdens which could not be absorbed and glitches in bureaucratic procedures; the system was all. For Solly there were lives to be saved that day and to hell with the system. It was not surprising that a contempt for bureaucracy became one of Schonfeld's enduring traits. His view was that, as the representative of a small organization, he could not change the rules, so he would just have to get round them.

Even on the Right Wing, the UOHC was much smaller than the Federation of Synagogues, though the Federation, in its practices, was moving closer to those of United Synagogue congregations. After the death of Hertz, the leaders of the United Synagogue were happy to close ranks and firmly exclude Schonfeld from the corridors of power from then on. They were perfectly entitled to do so and, certainly, Schonfeld made little effort to be less contentious. For example, as the search started for a new Chief Rabbi, Schonfeld gave his views to *The Jewish Chronicle* in February 1948: 'The appointment of a "puppet" Chief Rabbi, who will be shackled to the Honorary Officers of the United Synagogue must stultify the office of the Chief Rabbi.'[3] With Waley Cohen's position being entirely clear from past battles with Hertz, Schonfeld said that: 'co-operation between the United Synagogue and the right wing is being undermined from the start … We do not propose seeking the friendship of the Honorary Officers of the United Synagogue in whose allegiance to traditional Judaism and wider statesmanship we have little faith.' Did Schonfeld believe he could achieve anything from such a volley of public criticism? Where was the pragmatic approach which had stood him in such good stead in his negotiations with obdurate government ministries? It was senseless to believe the United Synagogue would change course. Schonfeld might be warning his own community of the danger of becoming involved with a less Orthodox body, but if he wanted the opportunity to extend his own influence, this was definitely not the way to go about it. What was, however, also self-evident was that a powerful group of Jewish leaders, whose Orthodoxy was certainly suspect by Charedi standards, would never be attacked for such a shortcoming from within their own ranks. If there was to be an opposition it would have to come from the ultra-Orthodox. He had also seen the relationship between the United Synagogue and his father-in-law at first hand, and would have recognized that working with them would be impossible for a man of his temperament.

*The Jewish Chronicle* had floated the idea that Schonfeld might become the Chief Rabbi in due course, but this was never going to be on the cards. Schonfeld had shown that he was always going to remain independent. His own choice anyway would have been to stay within the Charedi community out of loyalty to his father's teachings and from his personal inclinations.

In the years to come, the gradual movement of substantial parts of the Orthodox community to the right would not come from the criticism of Charedi leaders like Schonfeld. It *would* come from their example, though. Schonfeld was laying down a marker that the views of the Right Wing could not be ignored. His pungent comments always made good copy for the papers. Certainly, his approach was not constructive, but then constructive negotiations are only fruitful if both sides are prepared to compromise. As Schonfeld was not – and never could be if he was to be faithful to the Charedi approach – the case for restricting himself to discussions behind closed doors, followed by prepared statements for the masses, offered few attractions.

The successor to Hertz as Chief Rabbi was Israel Brodie and he had worked with Schonfeld in wartime. Brodie had been a chaplain to the forces in both World Wars and his religious views were much closer to Schonfeld's than to his own community. With British Chief Rabbis, that is invariably the case. Both men were English born and Brodie had always supported the Charedi Yeshiva in Gateshead, near where he was born. Brodie was equally concerned to see the improvement in Jewish education which Schonfeld was spearheading and if this Charedi rabbi could infuriate him as much as anybody else, there was never any question that they were both singing from the same prayer book.

In putting its funds into the communal pot, the JFS had made a reasonable condition that it would want enough out of it again to build the school somewhere else. The East End, everybody agreed, was not the answer. Schonfeld did not want it built anywhere, unless its religious curriculum was acceptable to the Charedim, as against a body which might, in the future, include representatives of the Progressive

Movement. Certainly, as negotiations dragged on over many years, some of the trustees and members of major committees on the JEC were indeed members of Reform and Liberal synagogues. They were good and great, but definitely outside the ultra-Orthodox pale. If JFS was abandoned, the JSSM was a logical successor but the liklihood of that was slim indeed, if Schonfeld was realistic.

In July 1948, soon after his election, Brodie and Dayan Lazarus consecrated Schonfeld's new Hasmonean building in Holders Hill Road in Hendon. The classrooms were endowed in the names of JSSM supporters N.B. Walters, Samuel Behr, Moses Broder, M.J. Cohen and Max Kleeman. The school building included the Abraham Cohen Assembly Hall and Philip Halpern performed the opening ceremony and named the Dennis Halpern House in memory of his son. The MP for North Hendon was at the garden party held to raise money for a gym, tennis courts and many other necessary aspects to a school's infrastructure if they were to seek state aid. The school would be able to take 150 boys and the staff could teach them up to what would become A Level standard.

Walter Stanton and Solomon Schonfeld were equally devoted to the cause of Jewish education. Unfortunately, if they had that core motivation in common, they disagreed fundamentally on a number of other points. Schonfeld would use his power to browbeat the Headmaster on many occasions in the future. At one governors' meeting in the 1970s it would be pointed out that the boys' school library had a copy of D.H. Lawrence's *Lady Chatterley's Lover*. There had been a case which established that the book was fit to be published in the United Kingdom. This did not, however, mean that its erotic content was acceptable to an ultra-Orthodox community. Stanton defended the literary merit of the book. Schonfeld told him in front of the governors that either the book had to go within twenty-four hours or the Headmaster would. The phrasing was exceptionally and quite unnecessarily rude, but Stanton absorbed the punishment. It would be a long time before cases for unfair dismissal resulted in substantial damages for the wronged party. In the decades to come, when the governors' meetings descended on occasions to vituperation, Stanton would eventually stand up and walk out. Schonfeld always got his way because the governors were mostly handpicked supporters, but when the London borough could appoint governors, they could not have been the only members to have felt embarrassed. Stanton, of course, as a US member, was not even a member of a Charedi community.

By August 1948 the JSSM schools included Avigdor High School, the Hasmonean Boarding House and Menorah (founded by members of Munk's synagogue), Avigdor and Hasmonean Primary Schools.

There was also a post-matric (GCSE) Yeshiva. Within the country as a whole, there had been a Jewish Boarding House at the Perse School in Cambridge but it was closed down in 1948 by the governors. It was soon replaced by an entirely new Jewish public school called Carmel College, which was to have a chequered history, though it set a high standard in both Jewish and secular education. Two famous Jewish girls' schools, Mansfield College and Whittinghame College, in Brighton were coming to the end of their lives, but the North West London Jewish Day School was alive and well in Willesden in London. There were also some excellent Jewish schools in the provinces, including a Jewish boarding house at Clifton College near Bristol. Finally, and still on the drawing board, was JFS.

The negotiations on JFS were to drag on for years and Schonfeld must have decided that his best chance of getting as much money as possible for the JSSM lay in being as great an obstacle to a final agreement as possible. He set out to create a situation where the best solution for the Jewish Establishment was to buy him off. This is the only logical explanation for the tortuous discussions, the broken promises and the bad blood which was engendered. For the membership of the JEC was as determined to keep Schonfeld at bay as Schonfeld was to get a share of the spoils. It was to be a typical Schonfeld exercise; the ends would justify the means.

If, however, some of Schonfeld's methods seemed unscrupulous, it would be wrong to ignore the hidden agenda of the JEC to try to get all Jewish educational bodies under their effective control. Even the new Chief Rabbi, Israel Brodie, would have liked to have seen good Orthodox schools, like the JSSM, strengthening the body of Jewish education. As the JEC saw it, Schonfeld, under suitable control, could have enriched the Orthodox base of a body which had to rely otherwise, primarily, on Sunday schools. But the key was to get Schonfeld tamed. It was Schonfeld v the Rest but the odds did not faze Solly in the slightest.

The Schonfeld children had, by now, all left the family nest. Moses was in America. Kibo now had his secular name, Andrew, had left the world of the Adath far behind and was now very much an economic pundit. When Senath went to Harvard, Ernest stayed in London where he started to build up a big private practice among the better London hotels and their guests. Daniel had become an estate agent and property developer. After the war Jacob spent three more years at Yeshiva, at the end of which Ella decided that his future lay in America, to which he duly emigrated. Ella was already in America and 'forgot' to tell Moses of his arrival and, just in case Ruth and her son had alternative thoughts for him, she produced Jacob at a Shabbat evening meal without warning. When Jacob became an American citizen he was, of course, called up for the army and served his new country.

By 1947 Ella had moved into a hotel near Moses in America. Not surprisingly, there were personality clashes with Moses's wife, Ruth. It could not have helped that Ella was immensely proud of Kibo's new status as a public figure and recounted his successes frequently and at great length. Moses was doing well too, but in more prosaic ways. He wrote to Solly, saying that he did not want Ella staying beyond June. Ella had been there for seven months by then. The hotel was costing Moses $25 a week and he was giving her $40 a week spending money in addition. Paying for her clothes and doctor's bills he estimated came to another $35 a week. If that was not a sufficient strain, he had the moral blackmail of her 'crying acts' to live with as well. For her part, Ella may have considered Ruth was not the easiest daughter-in-law. Ella's main objective at the time was to raise funds for Jewish children who had survived the Holocaust but who were housed for the present in nunneries and monasteries. Ella would approach the rich friends of Moses to help her and this was a further embarrassment for her son.

Back in England, although the Education Act had come down in favour of faith schools, there had to be a rational plan to put the decision into practice. For the authorities, the London County Council would be primarily involved, dealing with the Jewish community in the capital. The LCC had a mountain of problems, ranging from the effects of the Blitz and the relationship between schools and Borough councils, to the provision of adequate numbers of qualified teachers and the movement of large sections of the population from the bombed inner city to suburban areas. They were sympathetic to every religious group. Above all, though, with their workload, they wanted the separate pressure groups to decide what they wanted, so that the LCC could deal with a single committee representing that viewpoint.

For the Jewish community this was perfectly reasonable in theory and totally impossible in practice. The Delegate Chief Rabbi, Hermann Adler, had called in vain for a unified committee in 1879 but every effort to reach agreement on its formation from that day to this has foundered. There was no hope of agreement on a decision on what percentage of the school day should be devoted to Jewish studies. The JEC committee was dominated by the Jewish Establishment, but with no academics with experience of actually running schools. The most important component of the committee was the London Board of Jewish Religious Education (LBJRE) and it had appointed Nat Rubin as its secretary, a most efficient expert on all government education procedures. Rubin did not like Schonfeld. He recognized him as the one person who was likely to put up obstacles to the committee's programme. It was true that lip service would always be given to the need to support the independence of all the individual schools, such as the JSSM, but Rubin intended that all the power should remain firmly in his hands.

The big question which remained was what to do about the JFS. The old East End location was inappropriate, when the community for which it was designed had practically vanished to more salubrious neighbourhoods. Schonfeld still hoped that the JFS would finish up a respected memory, in which case a proportion of its money could possibly be spent on the JSSM schools. His official argument was that it would not attract enough pupils to a district with a very small Jewish population. His other objections to JFS were that its curriculum was not sufficiently Charedi and its image was not the one he wanted for a major Jewish school. The problem with the JFS image was that it had originally been a school for poor children. It had grown to be the largest school in the country because of the enormous influx of Jewish refugees from Eastern Europe in the nineteenth century. Even its headmaster at the time, however, dismissed the parents as 'the refuse population of the worst parts of Europe', which was pure snobbery. The children were there originally to be educated to get jobs when they left at 13, and it was hard to remove this image of JFS. This was in spite of the fact that it often produced school leavers who would become eminent men: Mark Gertler, the artist, Israel Zangwill, the writer, Barney Barnato who made a fortune in South Africa, and Samuel Gompers, the future President of the American Federation of Labour, were just a few of its distinguished alumni. Schonfeld's alternative vision was still to create grammar schools which could compete with Harrow, and win. Indeed, in the future, his boys would play a chess match every year – against Harrow.

In December 1951 Brodie did call a round-table meeting. A scheme was then published in September 1952 for dealing with the Ministry of Education. Schonfeld objected. By this time *The Jewish Chronicle* was referring to the JSSM as 'Schonfeld's schools'. Schonfeld wrote to correct them: 'Any compliments to myself implied in the appellation can well wait till after my demise.' He went on to rubbish the proposal to build a new Jews' Free School in Camden Town. He called it a 'futile but not-dead-yet half a million pound project for a comprehensive Jewish Secondary School.' The money, he argued, would be spent on an 'ersatz Jewish education'. The truth was that the proposed location at Camden Town was well chosen for all the main Jewish communities, because the transportation links were so good. The demand for places from the East End had fragmented and the community was far more widely dispersed. Schonfeld's schools covered the North West and North London congregations well, but were a long way from other parts of the metropolis.

So as soon as the new JFS was proposed, Schonfeld wrote to the Ministry of Education and the LCC to oppose it again. The internal squabbling appeared insoluble. The Chief Rabbi was the president of the London Board of Jewish Religious Education and in early 1951 it had refused to try to resolve the differences with a round table conference. On both sides the fight was for control. The LBJRE wanted to integrate the JSSM schools with its own. The ostensible case for this was that it would make it easier for the JSSM schools to get state aid. Schonfeld, for his part, wanted the council of the LBJRE to have 50 per cent of its members come from the JSSM, which was out of the question as far as the LBJRE was concerned. Nevertheless, it was the LBJRE which had the right to negotiate with the Ministry of Education. The trustees of the defunct schools had made that decision in accordance with their constitutions. Schonfeld objected to this, in conjunction with Dr J. Braude, who spoke on behalf of the Jewish Day School Trust for Greater London.

Although the LBJRE were prepared to provide some places on its governing body for the JSSM and to give them a substantial grant, Schonfeld was still not satisfied. He was told there was no question of the JSSM losing its independence or of being asked to merge. Even so, he was well aware that the less Orthodox would always be able to outvote the JSSM on the committees of the LBJRE.

Chief Rabbi Brodie had submitted proposals to the Ministry of Education in 1953 before he left for a pastoral tour. He had circulated the members of the LBJRE, asking them not to speak against his proposals in his absence. Schonfeld had agreed to this, but almost as soon as Brodie had left the country, he wrote to the Ministry and objected again. It was now possible that the whole process would have to be slowed down by a public enquiry.

The only sensible solution was to reach a compromise and this was achieved in May 1954, when a meeting was held at the Head Office of the Rothschilds and under the chairmanship of Edmund de Rothschild. Schonfeld agreed to drop all his objections to the Chief Rabbi's proposals in return for the JSSM receiving £25,000 over a three year period. In today's money that is nearly £500,000. Schonfeld had achieved his objective for the JSSM but his relationship with Brodie was inevitably strained thereafter. In later years he invited the Chief

Rabbi to a function and the Chief Rabbi responded, 'It would be a great honour to sit next to Solomon Schonfeld in the world to come. But not in this one.'[4]

NOTES

1. Solomon Schonfeld, *Message to Jewry* (London: JSS Books, 1958).
2. Ibid.
3. *The Jewish Chronicle*, 27 February 1948.
4. Rabbi Meir Roberg in conversation with the author.

# 7  Two Steps Forward, One Step Back

The JSSM expanded throughout the 1950s and Schonfeld was the unquestioned Chief Executive Officer whose word was law within the movement. He would turn up regularly at school assembly and is particularly remembered by past pupils at Avigdor for his flights of fancy when addressing them. He would refer to them as wonderful boys and girls, which they found hilarious, but at the same time he had a small black book with all their first names in it, to talk to them personally.

At the end of 1953 Schonfeld started to get complaints about the head of Avigdor. Lieutenant Colonel Jacob Crystal, an Orthodox Jew with a good Cambridge background, had been appointed in 1951 but he was now upsetting some of the parents. The problem purported to revolve around keeping order at the school and Crystal was accused of being too strict a disciplinarian and unreasonable in the way he punished some of the pupils; for example, making them sweep up the leaves in the playground. Former teachers remember Crystal with little affection and the heart attack one of them suffered was put down to the aggravation of working for him. It was alleged that the headmaster was both tactless and cruel. Disciplinary problems were cited as the reason Schonfeld decided Crystal had to go. *The Jewish Chronicle*, however, said there was concern about the quality of the teaching of Jewish studies in the school, though the department head, Maurice (Morle) Grunfeld, Dayan Grunfeld's brother, was acknowledged to be a good tutor.[1] It certainly was not an open-and-shut case. When the dismissal was proposed at the Avigdor Governors' meeting in April 1954, there was stiff opposition.

The governors consisted of eight from the ranks of the JSSM and four who were appointed by the London County Council, as the Avigdor had been state-aided since 1950. Normally everybody got on perfectly well. William Frankel, Editor of *The Jewish Chronicle*, was a nominee of the LCC and recalled that he was always treated courteously, though he got the distinct impression that he was looked upon as a necessary evil. Now, however, there came a complete split. In April the JSSM governors all supported Schonfeld and the LCC governors all backed Crystal. On an

8-4 vote, it was decided that Crystal was to be dismissed. Frankel decided to head up the opposition to the decision.

The one factor that nobody had taken sufficiently into account was that the rules stated that it was necessary to ask the permission of the London County Council Education Staff Subcommittee to take such action. The LCC had actually advised Schonfeld to apply for this and he decided that it was not necessary. It was. The issue dragged on, but Crystal was given notice in September and was due to go at the end of the Autumn term in 1954. On 15 December 1954 the LCC halted the dismissal. To make matters worse for the majority of the JSSM governors, Crystal went to court and got an injunction stopping the governors carrying out the April decision. Sir Frank Soskice, who had served as Solicitor General in the Attlee governments, was retained for the governors but the question was whether this would be enough.

Meanwhile, Solly's ambition was still to influence the wider Jewish world. It was indicative that in June 1954 a letter appeared in the *Jewish Chronicle* praising the work of Councillor Sam Fisher as Mayor of Stoke Newington. It was signed by Schonfeld, along with Harry Goodman. When it came to public affairs, the Adath continued to be led by its most famous son.

Schonfeld was, as usual, fighting on many fronts. One of the most fiercely contested was for the religious soul of the new State of Israel. The marked secularity of its leaders was now out in the open and was distressing the Charedim beyond measure. The Israeli government were allowing Sabbath laws to be disregarded in public and the contribution of Judaism to the creation of the State was often downgraded. As Schonfeld thundered at a symposium in the same December the LCC stopped Crystal's dismissal:

> It was Judaism that has made Israel and had it not been for the 'religious fanatics' like me, Jewishness would have been reduced to fund raising, flag waving and the singing of the Hatikvah [the Israeli national anthem]. Zionists want to have Israel first and a bit of yiddishkeit thrown in afterwards ... it is better to know the bible in English and obey it than to know it in Hebrew and disregard it.[2]

He was particularly incensed with the secularization of Bible studies in Israel, saying that teaching the Bible as literature, and not as a series of divine commands, was blasphemy. The disappointment was more upsetting because, in the early days of the state, the hope that Israel might yet become a demi-theocracy had been very much alive.

It was also in 1954 that Isidor Grunfeld suffered a severe heart attack. Judith immediately gave up the Hasmonean Girls' School to nurse him, though Schonfeld managed to get her to remain on board as a school governor for many years thereafter. Time and again, the minutes of the governors meetings would see Judith proposing or seconding Solly's reappointment, voting for his motions and supporting his arguments. In retirement Judith was much in demand to talk of her experiences with the Sarah Schenirer schools before the war in Poland. She addressed groups of former pupils, staff and parents of the many schools which had been created on the Schenirer model all over the Jewish world. The close friendship between Solly and Judith never wavered and she would be on his side until the end of his life. With her reputation enhanced by her leadership at Shefford, she was also an icon and was nicknamed 'The Queen' or 'Ma Grunfeld' throughout the Adath community.

Replacing her was a real problem but one of Schonfeld's greatest strengths lay in his ability to recruit supporters for the causes he believed in. In the emergency created by Judith's departure from the girls school, Schonfeld found one of his most valuable colleagues in the next fifteen years. Rabbi Ephraim Kestenbaum had been born into the Adath but his family had emigrated to America before the war. He came back to England from the United States in 1955, as passionate about Jewish education as Schonfeld himself. If anything, though, his religious standards for a Jewish school were even higher. Kestenbaum had been educated at an Orthodox school in America where the young children were taught to speak Hebrew, as if they came from bilingual families. The governors at such schools believed that the teaching of Jewish studies was much more important than the normal secular syllabus. They opined that the latter could be picked up as the children grew older, and this they considered a fully adequate academic argument for their priorities. Their concentration was on Talmudic studies.

As was to be expected, Schonfeld and Kestenbaum got on famously. The JSSM leader spoke at Kestenbaum's wedding and the two became firm friends. Kestenbaum had semicha, of course, and all the knowledge that went with it. In addition he was a successful businessman, which was not unusual because, historically, it had always been the case that rabbis had both a spiritual and a commercial career. It was not until the fifteenth century that many rabbis started to restrict themselves to looking after their communities. Like Schonfeld, Kestenbaum was also convinced that the Jewish community in Britain only had a future if its children received a proper Jewish education. He wanted to help achieve that objective and Schonfeld had just the challenge to offer him; the Girls' School.

Dedicated as Judith Grunfeld was, the Girls' School had been difficult to promote. After the war, women's education was still lagging far behind men's. The national percentage of women in higher education was disproportionate to their number and prejudice against women in the professions was still considerable. When it came to schools, the importance of educating girls according to their ability was dismissed in a great many households. So Grunfeld was fighting not just against the image of the JSSM but the national viewpoint on the education of girls.

At the beginning of the 1950s, the Girls' School had well under 100 pupils. The pay of the teachers was low and the quality was, consequently, often not high. Only two or three hours a week were devoted to the religious curriculum – and that included Modern Hebrew which was really a secular subject. If the child was capable of getting in to a better school, most Jewish parents would send them to the superior non-Jewish schools. Schonfeld set out to persuade Kestenbaum that he should give up thoughts of making his name in the community as a scholar or a great businessman. Instead he should devote his energies to the cause of Jewish education for girls. It would take some time, but Solly was nothing if not persistent.

At the Speech Day in April 1954 Rabbi Dr Isidore Epstein from Jews' College had presided and Schonfeld had been able to report that the boys' school now had 220 on the roll and eight of the sixth formers from the last school year had gone on to university. Schonfeld considered that nothing illustrated the quality of Hasmonean's secular teaching better than the boys who achieved places at university. The school remained one based on a *Torah im derech eretz* philosophy.

Schonfeld's manifold responsibilities still left him a little time for relaxation. He liked to go down to his cottage in the country, planting trees, picking apples and mowing the grass with a scythe. He would take his children and cook for them while they went horse riding with the local kids or playing round him while he was writing his books. Sometimes, visitors came. Deborah, Moses's daughter, was over on holiday one year and went there for the weekend. She still remembers that one of the boys was riding his bicycle in the garden and that she asked Solly if this was permissible on the Sabbath. He assured her that as the garden was included in the area of his home, it was alright; a lot of the Charedim would not have agreed.

In January 1955 the Crystal problem came up again when Schonfeld demanded a hearing before the LCC Educational Staff Subcommittee. The subsequent proceedings were set for June. In the meantime Schonfeld turned his attention to a Claims Conference which was taking place in Paris in February. The JSSM had put in its own claim for reparations by the German government for the actions of the Nazis, but Schonfeld was told just before Shabbat had started that it might well be rejected. The conference was due to begin in Paris on the Saturday evening at 8 o'clock and the Sabbath in London ended at 5.40. So Schonfeld needed to catch the 6 o'clock plane. He had his passport and tickets taken to the airport in advance by the Avigdor's non-Jewish school caretaker, as he was not allowed to carry them on the Sabbath, and then walked more than seventeen miles to Heathrow! He arrived at the conference in time and was successful in getting the JSSM's application granted.[3] Of course, his lengthy journey resulted in two benefits, because the story went right round the community. Nobody understood better than Schonfeld the value of a good public relations story. It was not just the victories that he had achieved that would become part of his multi-threaded legend, it was often how he had achieved them.

The June 1955 hearings with the LCC ended after three days with the Subcommittee refusing to change its mind. Part of the evidence that convinced them was that Schonfeld had offered to withdraw the charges against Crystal and pay him till December 1955 if he would then go quietly. Schonfeld had also written him a glowing recommendation to help him find another job. Schonfeld did not give up: he never gave up till every avenue was exhausted. He took the row to the Court of Appeal in March 1956 and argued his case for four days before two of the greatest legal luminaries of the time; Lord Justice Goddard, who served as Lord Chief Justice, and Lord Denning, who became Master of the Rolls.

Schonfeld always insisted that he was not a litigant by nature or choice. When, however, it is considered how many times he finished up in court during his lifetime, it is difficult to accept that this was the case. It would appear far more likely that he hankered after the career he had first chosen. If better qualified rabbanim, such as Dayan Posen, officiated on minor UOHC cases, there was a larger stage for Schonfeld to perform on in the British courts.

The Rev. Malcolm Weisman was originally trained as a barrister before he became Travelling Minister to the small Jewish congregations in Britain. He knew Schonfeld in the early days and thought Schonfeld's pulpit performances then were 'a bit outrageous, animated, but with exaggerated mannerisms. They tended to be dramatic performances.' Weisman, however, helped Schonfeld to prepare his case against Crystal, along with Joe Lobenstein. He watched him in the Court of Appeal conducting his own case. It had taken two days to persuade the judges to allow him to do so. It started with Lord Denning asking him if he was a member of the legal profession. 'Sort of', said Schonfeld, and went on from there. In Weisman's view, Schonfeld put up a magnificent performance. It was all the more remarkable as he was opposed by Quentin Hogg – who would become Lord Chancellor as Viscount Hailsham – for the LCC, and Ashe Lincoln, QC, who was also top class and represented Crystal.

Schonfeld complained that the LCC were biased. Of course, he had given them cause to be so by ignoring their original advice. He felt it unjust that the Subcommittee had accused him of being a liar and a hypocrite. He also felt that they were taking away the rights of the governors. He asked for the Subcommittee's decision to be quashed. In rejecting this, the third Appeal Judge, Lord Justice Romer, commented on Schonfeld's behaviour. He said that Schonfeld:

> had a forceful personality and character and a somewhat overbearing egotism. If he thought anything was right, then it was right and that was the end of it. Since the end of 1953 Schonfeld had decided he was right to get rid of the Headmaster.

The judges also turned down Schonfeld's request for permission to take the case to the House of Lords. Crystal was ordered to be reinstated and took up his duties again.

There was, however, another side to the personality which Lord Justice Romer criticized. Rabbi Kopul Rosen was a founder of the prestigious Jewish Carmel College boarding school in Oxfordshire. He said of Schonfeld: 'My own relationship with him has not always been smooth, but one can hardly expect a colourful and headstrong personality to be widely popular in a community that esteems mediocrity' (among its rabbis). Rosen was certainly not alone in recognizing that Schonfeld would never have rescued so many or made such progress with the JSSM if he had lacked either arrogance or bluster. Achieving one's objectives through negotiation is feasible if one has a strong power base, but if one is totally outgunned by the competition, then arrogance is needed to believe it is still possible to win, and sometimes bluster to disguise the inherent weakness of one's position.

The depressing alternative was to accept defeat as inevitable. Salmond Levin was a senior member of the United Synagogue and he spoke at a meeting of the London Board for Jewish Religious Education in April 1956. There were, he announced, 14,000 Jewish children who were at least on the Sunday School roll in London but 10,000 who were not. He explained that it was: 'quite outside the financial capacity of the community to provide day schools for 30,000 children'. Schonfeld might not be able to reach that target either, but he would set the example for how it might be possible to get near that figure in the years to come.

The costs of the Crystal case against the JSSM must have been very heavy. One figure mentioned by a source close to the Adath lay leadership at the time suggests £40,000 (some £700,000 today). But the prospect of unsustainable legal expense would never deter Schonfeld. Certainly, his solicitor at the time undertook the work on a pro bono basis but he had also been the beneficiary of a visa from Schonfeld before the war. The unofficial Schonfeld Supporters Club was probably called in again.

On the first day of the next term Crystal took up his duties again and Schonfeld addressed the school without any comment on the legal proceedings. Harmony seemed to have been restored and by July 1956, at the Avigdor Sports Day, Crystal was congratulating the participants and Schonfeld was presenting the cup. The ongoing problem was that, while the courts might decide that Crystal should be reinstated, nothing could force the Charedi parents to send their children to Avigdor, if they now had doubts about the quality of the Jewish education. This would be particularly so if the Hasmonean schools were good alternatives and based where a lot of very Orthodox families from Stamford Hill were now moving, to the Hendon and Golders Green area. There was a real danger that Avigdor would become the JSSM's poor relation.

Rows also continued to break out between the United Synagogue and Schonfeld. From the US's point of view, Schonfeld still did not know his place, had ideas above his station and refused to give the United Synagogue Honorary Officers the respect they believed to be their due. From Schonfeld's position, it was important to maintain within the Charedim the courage of their convictions, to show the United Synagogue the error of its insufficiently observant ways and to endeavour to maintain the fiction that Schonfeld was still a power in the land, even though, since the death of Hertz, he was not, although he had no intention of acknowledging the fact.

In 1955 the patience of the United Synagogue President, Ewen Montagu, snapped. He was the last of the Cousinhood – the most influential nineteenth-century Jewish families – to hold power in the US. The row was the result of a totally bureaucratic argument: since 1942 the London Board of Shechita had shared its authority with the Sephardim, the Federation, the United Synagogue and the UOHC. Each community looked after the kashrut arrangements for its own community. Now the UOHC, led by Schonfeld, had opened an abattoir in Letchworth in the Home Counties, and was selling meat to London East End butchers, who were not necessarily affiliated to the UOHC, though their customers might well be. Montagu insisted that the 1942 agreement was only a war-time measure. He now wanted the authority to revert to the original organizations, which had not included the UOHC. He stated his position in *The Jewish Chronicle*: 'lest the memory of your readers is as short as is (so conveniently) that of the rabbi'.[4]

It was just the sort of attack that Schonfeld had been subjected to on any number of subjects over many years. Montagu had had a good war in British intelligence and was responsible for misleading the Nazis on the probable landing area for an allied invasion. He was accustomed to giving instructions and having them carried out to the letter. It was not a very good apprenticeship for leading a voluntary organization dealing with other voluntary organizations. He should have rejected the cheap jibe as unworthy of the body he led. Schonfeld and the UOHC did not budge.

One way of paying the bills for expanding the schools was, of course, to raise funds for the JSSM. In January 1956, on the occasion of the 300th anniversary of the return of the Jews to Britain, a Gala Tercentenary Concert was held at the Albert Hall for this purpose. The family rallied round and Daniel agreed to chair the concert committee. He had by now become the President of the First Lodge of B'nai B'rith, a charitable organization which he was to serve for the rest of his life. It was a fine concert. The London Philharmonic performed under two great conductors, Sir Arthur Bliss and Sir Adrian Boult. To organize the programme, Schonfeld turned once again to Victor Hochhauser who was always willing to help him.

It was also in 1956 that the Hungarian uprising turned into one of the nastier examples of Russian communist repression of an independence movement. Until it was ruthlessly suppressed, however, there was a small window of opportunity for those who wanted to flee the country. The Jewish population was very small, compared to its numbers before the war, but the survivors of the death camps had struggled on. They had found, however, that replacing fascism with communism was not a major step forward on the road to religious toleration. Now, given the opportunity, a lot of them fled and a considerable number of them came to London where the British Jewish community remained the largest and most secure in Western Europe.

The ranks of the Charedi Hungarian Jews had provided German Jewry before the war with much of its Talmudic muscle. The Charedim in Germany were as strict in their observance as the Hungarians but weaker in their Jewish scholarship. The Hungarian Charedim were mostly Chassidim, spoke Yiddish and a considerable number of them devoted their lives to Talmudic study, in which the native culture played little or no part. When they arrived in London they recognized that the organization which represented them was the UOHC, who might believe in *Torah im derech eretz* communities, but whose approach to Orthodoxy was most in keeping with their own. As refugees they could not expect to impose their views on the UOHC for many years, but they had considerable numbers and were possessed of any amount of tenacity when they set out to achieve their objectives.

To this new influx, Rabbi Dr. Schonfeld was something of an enigma. Certainly, he was a hero for the wonderful work he had carried out for oppressed Jews before, during and after the war. Furthermore, everyone agreed that the progress of the UOHC was the direct result of his immensely hard work. At the same time he had not divorced himself from the native culture. He believed totally in Hirsch's principles. He was also likely to be the only UOHC rabbi who spoke English as a first language, and BBC news-reader Oxford English at that. He had enjoyed an English education, he had mixed in the wider community and was *persona grata* within whole tracts of the British Establishment, to an extent the newcomers could hardly imagine. Goodness knows, it was difficult enough for the old-time Adath members to grasp. For example, when the 25th anniversary of the founding of the JSSM was to be celebrated, the guest of honour was none other than the Rt. Hon. Clement Attlee, the former Prime Minister. Schonfeld's success in persuading Attlee to attend would only enhance his reputation as a miracle worker.

Schonfeld was never content to confine himself to the committed. He was there, he believed, to spread the word all over the Jewish and – if he could – the non-Jewish world. In May 1955 he had spoken in Oxford at a joint meeting of the Jewish Society with the Cambridge J. Soc. Where an ultra-Orthodox rabbi from continental Europe might have been looked on as more of a novelty than an inspiration, the tall, elegant and masterful figure of Schonfeld could not be dismissed in that way. He told the students that it was the job of Jews to give the world the higher standard of moral decency contained in the Torah: 'To convert an idolatrous world, not to Judaism, but to civilization through teaching the principles of Torah.'[5]

The newcomers from Hungary would have approved of his decision only a year before in 1955, to recommend Rabbi Henoch Padwa for the newly created post of Principal Rabbinic Authority (Av Beth Din) of the UOHC. As Schonfeld had said at the time: 'With the growth of our members and activities, it has become necessary to consolidate the Rabbinate of the Union through such an appointment of a world renowned Godol, particularly of the Chassidic type.' What Schonfeld had recognized was that the UOHC would only have rabbinic peace if there was an outstanding rabbinic authority who could command universal respect. As we've seen, where the United Synagogue rabbis were controlled by the Chief Rabbi and the synagogue Honorary Officers, the UOHC rabbis ran their own communities. The disputes between them might be on minutiae but they could still often benefit from an umpire to give a final decision. Padwa's appointment was a very good – and totally unselfish – move on Schonfeld's part, who had, up to then, had a major role to play in such deliberations.

Schonfeld had not consulted his lay colleagues in London on who should have this role. He had sent Dayan Posen and Rabbi Elchonon Halpern to visit Rabbi Dov Berish Weidenfeld, the Tchebiner Rov in Jerusalem, who was generally acknowledged to be one of the greatest Talmudic authorities in the world at the time. Could he recommend a suitable candidate? For the Tchebiner Rov this was a real challenge. He was being asked to find a first class brain for what appeared to be a second class job. The Tchebiner Rov eventually recommended Padwa, who was thin, 47 years old and bright as a button, with a full beard and ferociously long sidelocks. He had been born in Poland but had studied at Yeshivot in Poland, Hungary and Vienna. He was interned in Austria in 1939 but managed to get released and went to Palestine; neither achievement would have been easy. At the time the Tchebiner Rov told Schonfeld his decision, Padwa was a member of the Eda Charedit Beth Din. He was impeccably Chassidic in his outlook but of a nervous disposition. At that time in Israel the security position was so bad that a driver had to be on his guard on the road between Tel Aviv and Jerusalem if he did not want to be taken unawares by a terrorist attack on his vehicle. Padwa was keen to settle for a quieter life.

The 'call' was approved and Padwa was inducted into office in September 1955. When the appointment was first announced Schonfeld had taken care to assure the United Synagogue that there was no suggestion that the UOHC was setting up a rival to the London Beth Din. He heaped praise on the United Synagogue court. The UOHC was only against those 'who didn't adhere to the teachings for which the London Beth Din stands'.

Despite attempts to reassure the US, a row still broke out between the two organisations within months. It was over *shechita* again, the ritual slaughtering of animals. This argument had a history within the British Jewish community, going back at least 200 years. Originally it was within the Sephardi community, then between the Sephardim and the Ashkenazim, and finally between the ultra-Orthodox and the United Synagogue at the beginning of the twentieth century. It had finished up in court in 1906 and neither community came out of the dispute with any credit. It was tacitly agreed thereafter never to indulge in such public disputes again. This latest row was also patched up but relations between the two sides would remain, at best, delicate.

Schonfeld could now concentrate on running the administrative side of the UOHC, plus the Adath synagogue as its rabbi, and the JSSM as the Principal. Also, when the UOHC needed a public face, it would be Schonfeld's. As Padwa was still settling in, he was happy with those arrangements as well. Indeed, in Schonfeld's time, Padwa would always remain an almost unknown figure outside his own community.

If the comments of the United Synagogue did not overly concern the UOHC, the arrival of television across the country was a very different matter. In 1955 forty-five American and London rabbis had declared that TV was a threat to Jewish home life. The Satmarer Rebbe in the United States had said, 'Purity, chastity and torah living in Jewish houses is being undermined by television.' The rabbis sold their TV sets. A movement was then started by youngsters in Stamford Hill to get televisions removed from their homes as well. Rabbi Padwa agreed. Parental guidance on what programmes to watch was not going to be necessary in the future.

In 1958 Schonfeld had been at the helm at the UOHC for twenty-five years and a Silver Jubilee Committee was created to make plans to mark the occasion. Victor Hochhauser agreed to act as Honorary Secretary and Schonfeld's published reports and letters appeared in a book called *Message to Jewry*. Dayan Grunfeld wrote the foreword, there was a celebration dinner which attracted 650 guests to the Central Hall, Westminster, and £10,000 was raised for the rabbi (the equivalent of £150,000 today). Typically, this Schonfeld immediately gave to the JSSM. For a man with his level of income, it was a ludicrously generous gesture. In the future that money would have come in extremely useful. Grunfeld listed just some of the organizations which Schonfeld had helped create: the European Union of Orthodox Jewish Organisations, the Polish Union of Synagogal Communities, the Hertz Forest in Israel, the Jewish Servicemen's Kosher Food Service, the Board of Orthodox Jewish Education and the Committee for Proclaiming Jewish Ethics. And that was without the schools and many other activities. They all illustrated Schonfeld's ability to inspire people to work together in good causes.

There were also the calls of family life for all the Schonfelds. In October 1958 the children bought Ella a flat at 83 Sea Road, Haifa in Israel. It was agreed that when Ella died, Senath, who had separated from Ernest Petrie in 1956, would take on the flat. Moses came over from America from time to time and the family would gather again. The diminutive Ella was usually late, but when she arrived, everything centred on her, just like before. The boys towered over her – even Senath was about 5'10' – but there was no question about who would dominate the proceedings.

What was missing now for Schonfeld was new mountains to climb. He had not lost interest in the Adath – he would never do that – but the battle had been won. The UOHC was growing, it was under the control of rabbinic experts and it did not really need him any more. The schools were viable, particularly now that the Hasmonean Boys' School had finally achieved state-aided status in 1957. There was plenty of work to do still, but during the war Schonfeld had become accustomed to a pivotal role under the Chief Rabbi, dealing with senior government officials and the heads of the Jewish community. Now he was sidelined into a relative backwater and his energies were such that this could not satisfy him.

At the same time, in a very competitive family, the other children were busy making their mark: Moses and Daniel as successful businessmen, Senath, David and Jacob in the academic world and Kibo as a nationally known economic authority. From being way ahead of them as a figure of note, Solly was finding himself in danger of being left behind, even if the siblings were not publicly competitive. He looked for another challenge. One major problem on which he decided to set his sights was the question of encouraging Orthodoxy in Israel.

While the Zionist movement may have been led by secularists from the start, the Jewish inhabitants of Israel came in large numbers from Orthodox backgrounds. That section of the community always hoped that there might be a renaissance of Orthodoxy in the new country. In addition, the Israeli government knew very well that it could not afford to alienate the Orthodox section of world Jewry. The battle for the religious hearts and minds of the Israeli citizenry continued – as it still does.

The question was how to give the Orthodox segment the support they needed. Schonfeld decided that one place to start was in the new towns, which were springing up all over Israel to house the new settlers. Many of them lacked an Orthodox Synagogue. So Schonfeld set out to provide them with one. What was needed was a plot of land in each town and the necessary finance to put up a suitable building. Remembering that a synagogue was a place to meet and study, as well as a place to pray, Schonfeld decided to portray the buildings as social centres for the towns, in order to avoid any ecclesiastical controversy with secular councils. Where it might not have been easy to get a grant of land and planning permission for a synagogue from the authorities, they were more likely to be amenable to a free communal centre. And if part of the building was an Orthodox synagogue, it was only a small concession for secular Zionists to approve. After all, they were not actively against those who wanted to be observant. Naturally, most Israeli officials were delighted to accept contributions from any source, and land was easy and cheap to come by. Schonfeld now had to raise the money for the buildings and called on many of the refugees he had rescued before the war and who had flourished in the years since then. Many of these supporters preferred to make their donations anonymously and the most generous supporters came from the ranks of the Charedim.

Schonfeld naturally felt deeply about the centres and would personally visit Israel to oversee progress, but he relied a lot on Aba Dunner, the son of one of his Adath colleagues, Rabbi Josef Dunner. So in 1959, a jeep containing Schonfeld, Dunner and Ella's luggage from London, set out in Israel to visit town councils and negotiate for grants of land. As usual the microscopic entity had a grand name – The Community Centres for Israel Organization. One main source of finance came from a London solicitor whose life Schonfeld had also saved before the war by getting him out of Germany. Schonfeld continued to play down the Orthodox agenda. Many councillors thought they were dealing with a Reform rabbi when Schonfeld turned up in a shirt and kippah. The formal black suit was left behind. Negotiations proceeded smoothly and Schonfeld got all the land he needed. At which point the London solicitor arrived in Israel with the British police hot on his heels, anxious that the lawyer should return home to help them with their enquiries into a commercial fraud case. From talking to councillors about Community Centres, Schonfeld found himself negotiating with his benefactor to go back to England and face the music. As the Israeli government threatened to extradite the solicitor if he did not go back voluntarily, that was the end of the story. To make matters worse, the solicitor got a substantial prison term, ending the promotional funds from that quarter and much of the respectability of the project. The only community centre which actually went up was in Ashdod and it is still there today.

The tongues wagged again. Had Schonfeld been accepting stolen money to finance the Community Centres? Schonfeld went on record that he had received less than £10,000 from the source. He did not desert his friend either, giving evidence in court that he had always found him 'absolutely honourable'. £10,000 in 1958 would be worth at least £150,000 today.

Schonfeld was not responsible for the behaviour of his friends and financial supporters. There had been other occasions when some had got into hot water. One had been known as a black marketeer in Europe after the war: crooks come from the ranks of both the observant and non-observant. It was easy for the non-Orthodox to criticize the observant for not living up to their ethical responsibilities, but such strictures equally apply to those who have chosen to turn away from the standards of behaviour expected of the Charedim. A lower standard of religious observance does not constitute a permit for lower ethical and moral standards.

The court case was another blow and Schonfeld slowly realized he was getting too old to shoulder all the responsibilities he had. The question was which to give up and when. The community centres had given up on him, but the UOHC, the Adath, the JSSM and the family all made demands. If Schonfeld decided to end his rabbinic responsibilities, who would take over?

One area he had been able to delegate was the girls' school. A while before Schonfeld had finally persuaded Ephraim Kestenbaum to take on Hasmonean Girls' School. For the next twenty years there would be no body of governors, no management committee, just Kestenbaum. When he started, the plan was to identify the members of the Charedi community who had daughters around 8 years old, and then Kestenbaum and Rabbi Munk from the Golders Green Beth Hamedresh would visit them. The object was to persuade the parents to send the girl to the school. Kestenbaum always knew when he had been successful. The parents he met on the streets of Golders Green would either greet him if they had decided in his favour, or cross the road if they had not.

Kestenbaum recognized both the limitations of this approach and the excessive time it consumed. He decided upon a different strategy, which owed a great deal to sound marketing practices he might have absorbed in his time in the United States. He held an Open Night at the school and about 400 curious parents came to see what a Jewish girls' school actually looked like. Having inspected the premises, they were addressed by Kestenbaum who told them he was the bearer of sad tidings. Due to the excessive demand for places at the school, he was very unlikely to be able to accept all their daughters! It is known in marketing circles as the Scarcity Value Customer Benefit. As very often happens with this technique, it worked beautifully. Large numbers of parents now wanted to be among those fortunate enough to have their daughters selected.

The school roll took off. As Kestenbaum put up temporary classrooms in the new and ample Parson Street grounds, the numbers increased five fold over the next ten years. It would cost Kestenbaum a fortune, personally, because he saw to it that one of the attractions of the school was the low fees. Sometimes he did not charge at all for the first two years. This would have been impossible without the financial support of many other members of the community and the dedication of poorly paid staff. The latter's reward was that an increasing number of young Jewish women would be better equipped and committed to maintaining the sanctity of Jewish family life.

There was one good candidate for the Adath responsibility when the time came to give up the role. In 1947 Schonfeld had encouraged one of the refugees he had rescued before the war to leave his Leicester pulpit and join him in London. This was Rabbi Josef Dunner, who was only a year younger than Schonfeld and who had been appointed Chief Rabbi of East Prussia when he was only 23 years old. Schonfeld had given him one of the rabbinical visas from the Home Office after Kristallnacht in 1938. Had he not done so, there was every chance that Dunner would have finished up in Dachau like so many of his colleagues.

With Schonfeld behind him, Dunner had now set up the Beis Ya'akov seminary for girls of university age. Beis Ya'akov is the name of the Schenirer movement and before Dunner's initiative there was no post-school education available for Charedi girls in Britain. It had always been possible for boys to go to Yeshiva for a period before university, but there was nothing equivalent for girls. For the next fifty years Dunner would run Beis Ya'akov until going to 'Sem' (Seminary) became a favoured option for hundreds of young women. From now on women could study at a high level if they chose to.

By the late 1950s Schonfeld definitely wanted to stand down from the Adath treadmill. He had held the post for over twenty-five years and he felt that enough was enough. The burdens, together with the demands of the schools, were becoming too great for a man approaching 50 and he was not feeling all that well either. He was subject to very bad headaches and his friends noticed a growing eccentricity on occasions in his behaviour. So it was to Dunner that he decided to hand over his UOHC and Adath offices.

The initial Adath reaction was total opposition to his plan. The president of the Adath wrote to him on 8 February 1959:

> You are aware of the consternation which the contents of your letter have caused to us all. You and your personality are so inextricably linked with the work of the Adath Yisroel synagogue that we cannot visualise any separation now or in the future ... the unanimous decision of our committee [is] not to accept the resignation.[6]

Schonfeld got his own way. The question was, with Padwa as the head of the Beth Din and Dunner in charge of the synagogue and the day-to-day administration of the UOHC, could there still be a place left for him? Of course, he still had the schools but what of the UOHC? Were they going to drop the pilot? It was agreed to resolve the problem as commercial companies have dealt with ageing executives over very many years: retire them with a fancy title but little further power. It was the classic solution of boards of directors when they wanted to cling to their founding father, even if he was in danger of proving inadequate to their developing needs as the years passed. In commercial companies this is a point of great danger. The founders are a very different breed from the grey flannel suited – or in this case black worsted – executives who seek to fill their shoes. Many a major company has floundered when the successors to the founders have not been able to measure up to the challenge.

Certainly, without Schonfeld, the new leaders at the UOHC made little impact on the Jewish community in Britain as a whole for many years. To the extent that Schonfeld remained their policy maker and public voice, their views were heard, but their own predilection for withdrawing into their Charedi shell prevented the majority community from getting the benefit of their potential input. If anything, it was the Lubavitch who would occasionally produce initiatives which brought the Charedim to the attention of a wider public over the coming decades. Vast menorahs paraded through the streets at Chanukah, efforts to get more Jews to lay *tephillin*, or groups arriving, complete with whisky, at the rooms of Jewish University students to suggest a party at which the Charedi message could be promulgated.

Schonfeld knew both sides of the argument very well. While he was fully prepared, personally, to get involved in the affairs of the national Jewish community, he recognized the potential dangers of such an approach which concerned the Chassidim. In 1956 he had defended the accusation of withdrawal by suggesting that 'infiltrating and infusing the general community' might lessen the intensity with which the Charedim observed the dictates of the religion. He accepted that the rest of the community might see this approach as bigotry, but criticism from outside did not normally concern the Adath.

At the end of the day, Schonfeld had the title of the Presiding Rabbi of the UOHC, which sounded grand but was now, if it came to a crunch, meaningless. His authority in future would have to be based on his personality and reputation, though Rabbi Dunner would normally confine himself to administration rather than compete with his mentor. In the following years Schonfeld continued to be treated with the utmost courtesy. So many of the men coming into positions of power in the UOHC were never going to forget their debt to him and the vast majority of the UOHC admired and respected their former leader.

If more allowances for his growing eccentricities might be needed in the future, that was still a small price to pay for all he had done for them in the past. Where they differed from Schonfeld was on their relationship with other sectors of the Jewish community. Schonfeld had made his own position clear back in 1951 when he had said: 'Any estrangement of Chassidim, however extreme, or any aggressiveness towards general traditional Jewry would be a misguided direction.' Schonfeld had always wanted to keep all his options open, and one reason had to be that the financial support he desperately needed would often come from outside the ranks of the Charedim.

For what Schonfeld still wanted was to improve the standard of Jewish education throughout the country. The official bodies, like the London Board of Jewish Religious Education, were settling for far lower standards than Schonfeld considered acceptable. So, in early 1959, he suggested setting up a Council of Jewish Day Schools, so that the Ministry of Education could have a single voice to consult on subjects like government aid to denominational schools. Now the fact was that the London Jewish Educational Foundation had been set up in 1954 and the LBJRE, itself, was recognized as providing that single voice. The stumbling block to the Charedim was that it covered a lot of schools of which they disapproved. Foremost amongst these were the schools created by the Zionist Federation, whose curriculum was slanted towards Israeli, rather than Jewish, priorities. Their main concern was to encourage as many Jews as possible to emigrate to Israel, to go on aliyah. The teaching of Modern Hebrew was far more likely to be intense than the teaching of the more advanced aspects of Talmudic law. Schonfeld said that the Zionist schools 'represent an attempt by the Mapai [the Israel Labour Party which formed the government] to bluff their way into and to buy with Israeli appeal money, a controlling share in Anglo-Jewish education'. The Zionist schools did not stand the test of time. Their problem was that without the religious element of a Jewish school, it was a straight fight with a non-Jewish education, which usually offered better facilities and better government support.

Schonfeld wanted to change the thrust of mainstream Jewish education from within, because he certainly could not change it from outside. The proposed council might be the answer but, of course, the Zionist Federation immediately condemned Schonfeld's suggestion as mischievous. The LBJRE also opposed the idea, saying it should continue to be the only body the government consulted. It said, remembering the row which had only ended with Rothschild's intervention in 1954: 'It would be disastrous if Rabbi Schonfeld were again to cause confusion on the subject of Jewish education.'

Nevertheless, in March 1959 a meeting was held to bring the Council of Jewish Day Schools into being. Harry Goodman was present but wanted a deferment so that Chief Rabbi Brodie could arbitrate, though Schonfeld in fighting mood did accuse both the Zionist Federation and the LBJRE of trying to sabotage Orthodox schools as part of their ongoing policy. Had not both bodies voted against the Claims Conference granting funds for such schools?

Schonfeld argued at the meeting for immediate action and *The Jewish Chronicle* reporter wrote: 'The second part gradually gained in impetus, concluding with a general shouting match in which Dr. Schonfeld's voice was not drowned.' The body was set up and a number of very Orthodox Jewish schools which were not state aided were represented on it. Schonfeld always took a particular interest in these, because it was very difficult, financially, to keep them going. As they were offering a good Jewish religious education, whether they were part of the JSSM or not, they could count on his support. The fight went on.

NOTES

1. *The Jewish Chronicle*, 24 December 1954.
2. *The Jewish Chronicle*, 17 December 1954.
3. *The Jewish Chronicle*, 11 February 1955.
4. *The Jewish Chronicle*, 23 September 1955.
5. *The Jewish Chronicle*, 5 May 1955.
6. Ben Yitchok, *Jewish Tribune*, 7 October 1999.

# 8  Surviving a Tumour

Although the London County Council had ensured that Jacob Crystal was reinstated as Head Master at Avigdor, it was still not happy with the infrastructure of the school. In 1956 the inspectors agreed what progress needed to be made and gave the school till 1958 to make the necessary improvements. They did not happen. Eventually, in exasperation, the LCC decided to withdraw state aid from the school, which was the kiss of death for its future. The community were horrified and, naturally, expected Schonfeld to feel the same way. After all Avigdor had been the creation of his father, it was the first JSSM school and it had been a flagship in its day. Schonfeld saw it differently, according to one of his closest friends at the time. He pronounced himself well satisfied, because the withdrawal of state aid gave him the perfect excuse to get rid of Crystal at last. He decided he could close the school and transfer the children to other JSSM academies, such as the newly state-aided Hasmonean, which had the added advantage that it was in a better location for the communities from which Avigdor drew its intake.

The withdrawal of state aid from the Avigdor was, however, considered a disgrace for the community, particularly by those who had never supported it and opposed its religious philosophy. They were only too happy to crow. Even *The Jewish Chronicle*, which was usually even-handed, published a leader which stated that the withdrawal was the 'inevitable consequence of the reckless policies pursued by the Board of Governors'. It did not spell out what the reckless policies were, but it clearly suggested that Schonfeld should be replaced.

Crystal resigned in September 1959 with a year's salary, and the school building changed to one for girls from the beginning of the Autumn term. The state aid still had a year to run and Schonfeld did not appeal the LCC's decision. There was some talk in parliament on the subject in May 1960. The government pointed out that the school had never become the grammar school for 300 which was originally envisaged. There was no evidence that changing it to a girls' school would solve the problem and, therefore, requests for an enquiry would be refused.

Eventually Schonfeld used the premises in Lordship Road for the Avigdor Primary School.

Schonfeld had always been unlikely to win against Crystal, the Council authorities and the able legal team which backed them both up. He was now, on occasions, irrational in his approach. To add to his problems, he was still getting severe headaches and he was now going deaf in his left ear. His reaction times had slowed down and he was becoming quite a dangerous driver. Something was definitely wrong with his health, but for years he kept the symptoms to himself. It was in 1961 that Solly lost one of his oldest friends: Harry Goodman died at the end of the year at the early age of 63. They had been very close for a long time and Solly would miss Goodman's support and advice very much.

The Swinging Sixties dawned with son, Victor, now 20, Jonathan 16 and Jeremy nine. Of the children, Victor rejected any religious approach, Jonathan accepted the Charedi philosophy and Jeremy was comfortable in any camp. To some extent Solly remained isolated at home as far as the lifestyle of the Charedim was concerned. Judith, brought up in the United Synagogue, had not changed her own views, though she did not try to change Solly's either. The whole Hertz family were equally middle-of-the-road. Samuel and Leon Hertz were rare visitors, though Josephine and Judith were close. Josephine phoned or came round at least once a day. Ruth was in New York and contact with her was severely limited. Apart from Josephine there was little sympathy for Solly's position. From his point of view, there was little to admire about the lives the Hertz offspring had made for themselves. Getting on with all the in-laws is seldom a simple matter, though.

There continued to be considerable arguments within the Hertz family about the distribution and handling of the income from the former Chief Rabbi's literary output, and Solly was forced to take sides with Judith against some of the other siblings, which did not help family relationships. There was a major row in 1964 between the children about the royalties, and this particularly upset Judith who disliked materialism at the best of times. The problem was that Hertz's will left the English language royalties to the girls and those from the rest of the world to the boys. However, as the Holocaust had destroyed the demand on the Continent, the division was inequitable and this proved a cause of contention over the years. Samuel Hertz continued to deal with the publishers, initially without asking a fee for his time and effort, but it was a fraught situation. Samuel was a canny dealer in shares and had a good portfolio, but inflation always eats into a fixed income. The old Chief Rabbi had far-sightedly ensured in his will that an independent solicitor was one of the trustees and the nominee had a difficult task dealing with the different interested parties.

One good thing which had emerged in the earlier discussions was the agreement with the publishers, Soncino, in 1960 to produce a new and glossier edition of the Hertz Chumash, which was aimed at the American market and sold very well indeed. Royalties did come, primarily, from the Hertz Chumash and they were split between Judith, her two sisters and two brothers. Over the years, the book became the standard work for most of the American Orthodox congregations.

In 1960, looking for a new challenge, Schonfeld had considered the possibility of writing a new Chumash, based on the Hertz edition. Remembering the years Hertz had devoted to the editing of the work and the amount of clerical help he received, this was an exceedingly ambitious plan on Schonfeld's part. Samuel strongly opposed the idea, as he felt it unnecessary to create competition from another volume when the Hertz Chumash was doing so well. It was agreed that Solly would abandon the idea.

There remained, however, serious disagreements between Schonfeld and Samuel Hertz. They nearly went to court in 1963 and Solly eventually agreed a fee for Samuel of £850 a year, linked to the Swiss franc. By 1967 the fee was worth £1,100 as the Swiss franc strengthened against the pound. Further rows went on from 1967 to 1969, the bones of contention now being who was to publish what, as well as who got what. In America the alternative choices were Soncino, who did a good job but only paid 7½ per cent royalties and Bloch, who would pay 15 per cent if they could break Soncino's monopoly of distribution rights. Judith's sisters joined in the wrangling and many bitter letters passed between the contending parties.[1]

Schonfeld had produced another book in 1963 called *Why Judaism?* The most notable book at the time on the subject had been written by the distinguished American author, Herman Wouk, but the *Jewish Exponent* in Philadelphia felt that *Why Judaism?* was 'better, for there is more genuine learning, a surer feeling for words, and a more mature sympathy ... He does a good job.' Which was praise indeed, for Wouk was a world famous writer.

On the other hand *The Jewish Chronicle* had not been impressed with his 1958 *Message to Jewry*, which its reviewer complained was an: 'over generalised and pedestrian recapitulation of old themes, which in this unhelpful generality may mean very much or very little'. What can be said with certainty is that whatever Schonfeld wrote, his philosophy never strayed far from the straight and narrow and he hammered the traditional message home. The publishing arm of the JSSM had now produced ten books up to 1963. Three were Solly's, three were JSSM text books and there were some minor works by Hertz. The Hertz prayer book, as distinct from the very popular Singer prayer book, still sold well and, as late as 1972, the public bought more than 800 copies.

The school rolls at JSSM were now beginning to show a marked improvement. The seven schools within the organization were looking after 2,000 children in all and the idea of an education in a Jewish school was becoming slightly more acceptable to the community at large. The boys' site in Holders Hill Road was already so fully utilized that the Council initially refused permission for a synagogue to be built in its grounds. But Schonfeld still was not satisfied. He had homed in on the need for still more pupils when he addressed the Glasgow Yeshiva on their prize-giving day in 1961. He told the audience that, as there would not be another influx from the Continent, the British Charedi community would just have to grow its own crop of leaders and scholars. The infrastructure necessary to do this was slowly coming. For instance, Schonfeld had opened the Chaye Olam North West London Talmudical College in 1960 for an advanced level of study. It started life with only fifteen students, aged between 16 and 20. All the luminaries turned up suitably dressed in homburg hats, but Solly could be seen in his customary top hat, which he always believed was more appropriate if he was performing a ceremony. Rabbi Dunner would wear a top hat throughout his very long ministry.

When the boys' school finally became state-aided officially, the financial difficulties decreased, but with state aid came the increased involvement of Barnet Council. Instead of Avigdor's LCC nominees, the Board of Governors now included Barnet representation, though their governors would often not attend meetings or played little part in the deliberations. Schonfeld brooked no argument with his wishes anyway. There were also governors appointed by the trustees of the schools, who represented Adath communities. If, however, any of them chose to oppose Schonfeld, they soon found themselves replaced. If the heads of the trustee synagogues now saw less of Schonfeld as their religious leader, they still gave him carte blanche to run the schools as he saw fit.

Meanwhile, the project for Jewish community centres in Israel had had to be abandoned. There was no enthusiasm to replace the donor who had gone to prison. The relationship between the Charedim and the Israeli authorities was continuing to deteriorate anyway. Motorists driving through some parts of Jerusalem on the Sabbath risked having their cars stoned by those who considered such behaviour sacrilegious in the holy city. On the other hand, the protests against mixed bathing in Jerusalem a few years before had resulted in the heavy-handed treatment of peaceful protesters by the authorities. Schonfeld had been particularly concerned at the manner of the arrests in 1958 which were, in some cases, followed by nine-month prison sentences.

The Charedim, trying to maintain the laws of the Torah, were in conflict with the right of a democratic government to make laws approved by a majority of the electorate. Ella, in Israel now, had her own agenda. In 1964 she worked hard to raise £20,000 to set up a Youth Centre in Jerusalem in memory of her husband. Her aim was to try to keep young Jews off the street by giving them something constructive to do. She was 75 years old at the time, but still firing on all cylinders.

For Schonfeld, in Britain, the Holy Land problem was the attitude the JSSM should adopt towards the Israeli government when discussing it in school. How should the teachers deal with questions on Israeli government decisions which went against Jewish law? Where many schools would not dream of taking sides in a political discussion, Schonfeld had no compunction about stating the Charedi case. Where the effects of Israeli government decisions were contrary to the biblical law – raising pigs for human consumption, for instance – the decisions were much resented in Charedi circles. Some teachers did not even want the pupils to sing the Israeli national anthem. Schonfeld was going to continue to follow the *din* (Jewish law) and would not support the Israelis uncritically.

The Jewish community in Britain at the time was strongly pro-Israel as that country fought to survive. Schonfeld's criticisms of Israeli actions were widely rejected, but his feel for popular public relations opportunities still functioned well when the occasions presented themselves. In 1961 *The Times*, no less, reported the clearing of a hospital ward in Brixton prison so that the son of a prisoner on remand could have his circumcision in the presence of his father. Schonfeld conducted the service and commented that it was undoubtedly the first time in Britain that the ceremony had taken place in jail.[2] The father had, in fact, been imprisoned on an extradition warrant and Schonfeld had another day in court to plead that the parent should be freed on bail for the High Holy Days. This time the judge turned the request down. It was not, of course, just opportunism on Schonfeld's part. He believed completely in the causes he supported but he made the most of them. On another occasion he was asked by the press to comment on the execution of Adolf Eichmann, who had played a major part in implementing the Final Solution. Schonfeld supported the verdict handed down in Jerusalem. It was a contentious point in religious terms because capital punishment had been effectively outlawed in Jewish law for many centuries. One Sanhedrin was reported in the Talmud to have sat for seventy years, and during that time had sentenced one person to death. It was still known as the Bloody Sanhedrin.

Schonfeld's health was now deteriorating further. He officiated at a wedding in 1960 where the bride distinctly remembers that his address was so eccentric that some of the guests thought he was drunk. It was not every day or even every week, but there were a slowly increasing number of occasions where things just were not right. He might put it out of his mind by blaming overwork or dismissing the attacks as a temporary problem but, sooner or later, he had to face the fact that the symptoms would not go away. At last he decided to see his doctor who recommended him to Valentine Logue, a highly skilled Australian neurosurgeon at London's Middlesex hospital. After the necessary tests had been concluded, the news was very bad. Schonfeld had a growth at the back of his head which definitely had to be removed. Senath considered it likely that the tumour could have been growing in size for ten years or more, which would have accounted for his occasionally odd behaviour, but the effects of the illness were now far worse than that. The tumour was now at a stage when only major surgery would give Solly a chance of many more years of life. It was so large that Solly was not at all sure that he would survive the operation. This was obviously a major concern, but Schonfeld looked to the future, not in terms of his own mortality, but in working to ensure the continuing progress of his schools.

The closing of the Avigdor had been carried out relatively smoothly. The best teachers had transferred to Hasmonean. Richard Grünberger had gone to the Boys' School to take over the Jewish Studies programme and Morle Grunfeld did the same job at the Girls' School. It was the overall control, though, that concerned Schonfeld and he was not at all convinced that Walter Stanton would be sufficiently qualified from a religious point of view to maintain the JSSM's ethos. He decided to sound out others, although at times to suit his own timetable, as usual. One Sunday at lunchtime he rang one of the senior Hasmonean masters. David Jacobson's presence was demanded instantly. The fact that he was eating his lunch was of no interest. 'Now', said Solly. He had rung one head teacher at 1 o'clock in the morning. 'It's 1 o'clock', groaned the head. Solly told him to consider himself lucky that it wasn't 2.30! Jacobson duly headed off to Highgate to discuss who might take over, and they did agree on who was the best qualified.

Happily, the operation was a success and Schonfeld pulled through. In 1965 when Solly was finally released from hospital, and after months of recuperation and rehabilitation, he had changed. Physically, he was deaf in one ear, he had lost the movement of one side of his face and the left side of his mouth had a pronounced droop. In operations of this nature the surgeon has to work very close to the facial nerve and in those days could not always avoid damaging it. The overwhelming appeal of Solly's physical presence was seriously diminished. He was told by his doctor that he could not drive any more but, according to one of his close friends, he continued to do so on a very occasional basis. Usually, however, he would use the Tube, arranging meetings at various stations. He walked with a stick now to help his balance and often took the opportunity to study or work on the train. He had given up smoking as soon as he knew how ill he was and the good news was that the tumour was not malignant. He could no longer drink alcohol and *kiddush* on Friday nights (which involves a sip of wine) was delegated to Jeremy.

In future Schonfeld would have difficulty in speaking clearly from the pulpit and his ability to command an audience was undermined. He had been a powerful orator before the operation but he was never to be so again. In future he would often not be coherent in his arguments either. The operation affected his reasoning. The face, the voice, some of the energy and the charisma were damaged, but what remained intact was his determination. Struck a terrible physical blow, he never had any intention of giving in to the handicaps he suffered. He would never relax his efforts and he continued in his endeavours unbowed. For a man who had always believed he had the Almighty on his side, the possibility must exist that he would have wondered why that support had apparently faltered, but 'Schonfeld kept his religion deep within him'.[3]

Solly knew now that he would never attain a higher post than he had already achieved. For a man who still retained considerable ambition – he was only in his early 50s, when so many reach their peak in their careers – it was the wrong moment to realize that from now on his progress would probably be downhill. He was still happy with his decision to bring in Rabbi Padwa to deal with the legal problems of the UOHC. As he dismissively remarked on one occasion, 'I'm happy to have Padwa. I didn't want to pasken on chickens [judge their fitness for consumption] for the rest of my life.' If this totally underestimated the gravity of many legal questions which came before the UOHC court, it did emphasize that, as in most organizations, there is a lot of tedious minutiae involved. Schonfeld was never, if he could avoid it, a details man.

As the years went by he would start to have good and bad days. The deterioration in both his physical and mental strength would run him down slowly in the last twenty years of his life. He would become very argumentative. One good friend said – and many others voiced the same sentiments – that 'he would argue with everybody about everything'. The damage to Schonfeld's health was largely kept within the family. There was almost a conspiracy of silence to play down the adverse effects. Everybody in the community wanted to accept that he had made a full recovery with few after-effects and the true facts were safe within a tight circle. Even Jeremy had been told that he could not discuss it with his closest friend at Hasmonean. The doctor was, of course, bound by his Hippocratic Oath not to discuss the condition of his patient and was even more happy to cooperate as he was another of the refugees whom Solly had saved before the war.

Within a few months of the operation Schonfeld was finally able to preside over the dedication of a new synagogue building, attached to Hasmonean Boys' school. This project had taken some years to come to fruition. The necessary finance had to be found and planning permission had also taken a long time to obtain. Schonfeld, however, had always wanted somewhere better than the school hall for services and he brought together a lot of the local supporters of the Adath to try to create a community. He had always known that the crucial time to cement a boy's adherence to the religion was from the age of 13 onwards. Up to bar mitzvah their involvement was considerable as they learned their part in the service for the great day. In the years after that there was not the same outside influence. Whether they attended synagogue outside of school would increasingly be their own decision. The alternative attractions of the wider world would impinge on their thinking to a greater extent. He had seen what had happened to Kibo and David. Providing a rallying point for Judaism within the school was an important counterbalance.

The synagogue was built with a high degree of optimism. They called their community the North Hendon Adath and although the founder members were only about eighty in number, the synagogue could seat 300 men and 150 women. It was not an architectural marvel; the religious commitment, however, could stand comparison with any major school chapel congregation.

On Sunday 19 September 1965 the new synagogue was consecrated. Schonfeld confined himself to saying the prayer for the Royal Family, consecrating the synagogue and giving a benediction. The major addresses were given by others and it was certainly wise for Schonfeld not to extend himself in those early days after the operation.

The morning services in the new synagogue gave the boys comradeship during their prayers. Many found the daily routine a nuisance, like another lesson, but they remained involved. The 45-minute *shacharith* service was conducted by sixth formers in rotation and the sight of hundreds of boys wearing *tephillin* must have been a great joy for Schonfeld and the other ultra-Orthodox teachers. Or again, once a year, there is a festival called Chanukah and candles are lit to commemorate a victory over the Greeks in post-biblical days by a group called the Hasmoneans. The whole school would be found in the synagogue singing a particularly stirring song of the festival and the memory of that day would remain with a lot of the boys for many years after. It was from those successful Jewish leaders over the Greeks – the Hasmoneans – that the school took its name.

Schonfeld would regularly attend the morning assembly at both the boys' and the girls' school. In his heyday his handsome presence had been the object of admiration at the girls' school. As the years went by now, he would repeat the same jokes he had told many times before. Where the children had laughed at them the first time, they gradually started to laugh at him. For the teachers it was a sad sight.

By December 1965, however, he was in the thick of controversy again and working at nearly his old pace. It was obvious that he wanted to prove that, even after the operation, he was not to be written off. A suggestion was made to form a Conference of European Rabbis and Associated Religious Organisations. The Chief Rabbi was to be the President. Schonfeld was asked to comment as the UOHC had refused to join and with the title of Presiding Rabbi, he was still seen as their spokesman. Schonfeld stated flatly that he did not believe in the usefulness of a middle-of-the-road body. It was hardly a ringing endorsement of the Chief Rabbi's status, but Schonfeld did attend the meeting in Munich and addressed the assembly, along with Rabbi Munk.

In that same December he also attacked mixed schools, although the government was all in favour of co-education in its comprehensives. He told the girls at their Annual Speech Day, where the guest of honour was the distinguished Professor Dame Kathleen Lonsdale, that mixed schools played no part in Judaism. He suggested 'it made the girls boyish and the boys girlish'. During the war, of course, the school at Shefford had been co-educational, but Schonfeld would have excused that as an emergency situation which was corrected as soon as it was possible to do so. In the twenty-first century, reports would suggest that single-sex girls' schools do, in fact, produce better exam results, but co-education remained a major plank in the manifesto of the Labour party.

In the same month Schonfeld also attacked the Liberal wing of the Jewish community, saying that their marriage unions – often with one partner who was not halachically Jewish – should be labelled desecration rather than solemnization. If that section of the community was in favour of compromise, Schonfeld was not.

He would continue to have victories. The bad days would only gradually come to exceed the good ones. When Margaret Thatcher became Minister of Education in the 1970s there were a number of discussions between Schonfeld and one of a handful of Conservative Jewish MPs, Sir Henry d'Avigdor Goldsmith. Goldsmith reported back afterwards: 'We always came off second best!'[4]

If the young Schonfeld was no more, the middle-aged rabbi's reputation and standing still made him a living legend. There were so many in the community and around the world who owed him their lives. Very naturally, for them he could do no wrong. It was certainly not his fault that he had had to survive such a terrible illness and it was felt that his selfless devotion to so many good causes over the years was likely to have been a major contributing factor. It was like seeing a badly injured war veteran; every allowance would be made for him for the rest of his life. Admittedly, there were some – those he had outsmarted, outshone and overruled in the past – who bore grudges. Where they had any authority, they would welcome the fact that the lion was wounded and take their petty revenge. They were, however, in a very small minority. What happened more often than not was that, with the passing of time, negative memories faded.

As far as his personal finances were concerned, Schonfeld had always lived from hand-to-mouth. He knew he had any number of rich friends who could never repay their debt to him; he would ask for their help for his projects and the cheque books would come out readily enough. Schonfeld felt it was demeaning, however, to accept charity for himself and he struggled on as best he could. On several occasions the Adath lay leaders tried to get him to accept a salary increase. He always turned them down on the grounds that, if he was to get an increase, then all the other synagogue officials should have one as well and the Adath, in his view, simply could not afford the additional expense.

There was a steady income of £30 a week from the Letchworth Shechita Board. He would receive £10 a week from the Kedassia pension fund when he retired and in 1963 Rabbi Dunner confirmed that Judith would receive £7.50 a week throughout her lifetime. It was a paltry sum but at least Judith had the income from the royalties on her father's books. In 1970 they were worth £750 a year. When Judith eventually died, her sons returned to Rabbi Dunner at the Adath all the money which had been given to her as a widow by the organization. Receipt was acknowledged.

Schonfeld also had the royalties from his own books, of course, but these were minimal. When he was asked to officiate at a wedding, funeral or a bar mitzvah, the parents would be likely to send him a cheque as well; those he could accept without losing face. It was still little enough with a house to keep up in Highgate, three growing sons and the cottage in the country. From now on Matching Tye would acquire dust and mildew, the wallpaper discolouring and the windows covered with cobwebs until it was eventually sold in 1980.

By 1966 things had not improved. There was now £390 a year from the Kedassia Restaurant, another £390 from the Schechita Board and another £390 for the office of Presiding Rabbi. It did not measure up to the £30 a week he had previously received from the Board, but then there were other sources of kosher meat available and it was a competitive market. At least Victor and Jonathan were close to independence.

The retirement of Israel Brodie brought to the helm of the United Synagogue a former pupil of Schonfeld's, Immanuel Jakobovits. He was another disciple of Samson Raphael Hirsch and he wrote: 'I have never ceased to be influenced by his attitudes, nor ever wanted to abandon them.'[5] It was not just the shared common philosophy, however, that bound him together with Schonfeld. Jakobovits also said: 'In November 1936, travelling alone, I set off for London, having been accepted as a boarder at the Jewish Secondary School in Stamford Hill, of which Dr. Schonfeld was principal in name, and presiding genius in fact.'[6] Jakobovits always felt he owed a great deal to Schonfeld and admired what he had achieved.

As far as Jewish education was concerned, the new Chief Rabbi had come to the same conclusion as the man who had saved him before the war. That only a network of Orthodox Jewish schools could underpin the community's future. In this, of course, he was no different from any other Chief Rabbi, but Jakobovits had two advantages over his predecessors. First, he had an example to follow and that guiding light was Schonfeld. It was the stricken rabbi, from the ranks of the Charedim, who had proved that it was possible to marry a strong Jewish educational curriculum with an equally intense programme of secular studies. Jakobovits had watched the progress of Schonfeld's schools over the years and he had seen the commitment of the Hasmonean pupils. Jakobovits' second advantage when it came to the development of new schools was an organization created by his secretary, Moshe Davis, called the Jewish Educational Development Trust (JEDT). It was led by a dynamic retailer called Stanley Kalms (later Lord Kalms and, for some years, Treasurer of the Conservative party). Davis and Kalms recruited a group of very rich, very powerful Jewish businessmen, all of whom were prepared to commit themselves to the cause. As they were all happiest running their own companies, it was agreed that each entrepreneur would take responsibility for creating one school in a designated area. A typical example was Alan Sugar (later Sir Alan and the star of the TV programme 'The Apprentice'). Sugar was the founder of Amstrad, so he was comfortable with the rather lesser problem of sorting out the educational needs of the large Jewish community in Ilford on the eastern outskirts of London. He was fired with enthusiasm and a new school was financed and built with commendable speed and efficiency.

Jakobovits would have liked to have worked more closely with Schonfeld, but the elderly rabbi was not as keen. There was sometimes the suspicion in his mind that Jakobovits, originally a member of the Adath, had joined the opposition. In any event, Schonfeld, having always maintained the JSSM's independence, was not about to change his policy. It was also pertinent that while, on a personal level, he was perfectly prepared to trust Jakobovits, the memory of his battles with the United Synagogue's Honorary Officers over the post-war school funds stayed in his mind.

To any unbiased observer, it would also have seemed unlikely that the autocratic rabbi could work well with the entrepreneurs, and on Schonfeld's good days he knew that his ability to take on the world, if necessary, was no longer there. His old friend and guru, Rabbi Michoel Ber Weissmandl had died in 1957. Miraculously, Weissmandl had lived to see National Socialism ended; Hitler's boast of a 1,000 year Third Reich had lasted just twelve. After the war was over, Schonfeld had kept in touch, still getting Weissmandl's advice as he had all those years before in Tyrnau and Nitra. Many years after the rabbi's death Solly would start to ring America to talk problems over with Weissmandl's son, who also became an eminent rabbi. Although, to the outside world, Schonfeld was a law unto himself, behind the scenes he would listen to those whose opinions he valued. As far as the world was concerned, however, he kept this very much to himself. As time went by Schonfeld might need the help of the JEDT, but he kept them at arms length. Jakobovits was not invited to speak at the schools or to participate in their activities. Schonfeld would get very annoyed if anybody suggested inviting him to do so. On the other hand, if Schonfeld was asked about his relations with Jakobovits he was quick to point out that some of the Chief Rabbi's children were educated at Hasmonean.

For his part, no matter how often Jakobovits might be asked to restrain Schonfeld from some of his more eccentric, even outlandish, actions, the Chief Rabbi would never support Schonfeld's opponents in public. He felt he owed Schonfeld his life, he was in favour of the most rigorous Jewish education possible, he approved of the growing emphasis on the boys going from school to Yeshiva before university and, as the JSSM wasn't broke, he wasn't going to try to mend it. What he did recognize was that the effects of the operation had reduced Schonfeld's capacity to run the JSSM, but if his attempts to help were misconstrued, he was not prepared to do anything to make Schonfeld's life difficult. He was only willing to watch on the sidelines and try to act as a backstop if there was an emergency. With his personal background, Jakobovits always recognized that Schonfeld was the pathfinder for what he wanted to achieve in greater measure.

If Schonfeld was a poor man, he remained rich in the regard in which he was held by so many of his friends. In 1964 Victor Hochhauser had written to the former Home Secretary, Chuter Ede, to ask him to recommend Schonfeld for a Life Peerage. Ede had called Schonfeld 'father of the Distressed Persons scheme' and regarded him very highly. R.A. Butler had also been approached some years before with the same idea. The concept was a proposal whose time had not yet come. Only one rabbi, other than Brodie, had been given even a knighthood. That was Hermann Gollancz, who had done sterling work in the East End of London much earlier in the century. Schonfeld was a far more controversial figure than Gollancz and one of the politicians who was important if the idea of the peerage was to be approved, was Lord Hailsham, who had acted for the defence in the Crystal court case. Hailsham was not a Schonfeld supporter.

Schonfeld's phalanx of benefactors very generously helped to finance the good causes in which he was interested. Even so, there could be serious difficulties. One of them promised him £10,000 for a new classroom, as long as it was not used for religious purposes. Schonfeld took the money but did use it in that manner. So the donor refused to pay and Schonfeld took him to court. The judge heard the evidence and then told the two litigants that, although he was not Jewish himself, he did have a Jewish wife. In the judge's opinion this case, if unresolved, would reflect poorly on the Jewish community and he, therefore, advised the protagonists to go away and settle it out of court. Which they did – and Schonfeld continued to get help from his friend thereafter. It was a pity that all the court cases in which Schonfeld was involved did not end in the same way.

At Hasmonean Boys' School, 1965 saw the arrival of Rabbi Meir Roberg who would play an important part in the development of the school in the years to come. Roberg was exactly the kind of Jewish teacher who was in very short supply. He had been educated at Manchester Grammar School and read Classics at London University where he got a First. He was very keen on cricket and spent as much of his time watching Lancashire at Old Trafford as he could. Yet he had gone to Gateshead Yeshiva and had also studied in Israel. His teacher training had been at Birkbeck and for five years he was the head of the Jewish Studies Department at the ultra-Orthodox Yavneh Grammar School. This had got into financial difficulties and been taken over by the JSSM. Getting Roberg too was a real bonus. Within a few years an attempt was made to poach him for the vacant post of Deputy Head at JFS, but it was not difficult for Schonfeld to persuade him to stay at the Hasmonean. The more Orthodox the teacher, the more appealing the level of priority given to Jewish studies at Hasmonean. One of the most significant attributes of the Jewish teachers at Hasmonean was always their dedication to their jobs. Typical was Rabbi Isaac Abraham, whose grandfather had fled Baghdad for China, who was, consequently, a native of Shanghai and had survived. He was short in stature, but his sheer personality and dynamism made him very popular with the pupils. For Abraham, the maintenance of good Jewish teaching was nothing less than a sacred duty, and so it was for his colleagues as well. The pay might have been poor but the satisfaction of a job well done was immense.

Jewish Studies were to become more intense. Some new parents paid for teachers to give their children additional lessons before and after school. This spurred on the regular Jewish Studies teachers to develop a Yeshiva stream to prepare boys to go on to yeshivas after they had finished their schooldays. Hasmonean was the only school that could effectively prepare the boys, and this ensured that they stayed with the JSSM and were not lost to other academic centres.

Stanton and Schonfeld complemented each other very well for many years. Where Stanton was very organized in his approach to problems, Schonfeld was equally spontaneous. So Schonfeld pushed Stanton to get on with new initiatives and Stanton prevented Schonfeld from going overboard with wild flights of fancy. Stanton also guarded the secular curriculum. He had moved from membership of the United Synagogue to the Hendon Adath synagogue and he became a staunch supporter. This was partially because he had been very impressed by a visit the school had received from Rabbi Leib Gurvitz, the Rosh Yeshivah at Gateshead. Gurvitz had been equally impressed with the school and, in terms of British Orthodoxy, Gurvitz's approval of the work of a Jewish headmaster was the equivalent of at least a CBE, if not a knighthood. Nevertheless, Stanton was fearful that the increase in the emphasis on Jewish Studies might easily make inroads into the teaching of secular subjects. He maintained the balance.

The Jewish Studies programme included two periods a day and a lecture every morning from 8.40–9.20. There was another voluntary session after school from 4.30–6.00 and another on Sunday. Classical Hebrew was taught as a language. It was typical of the support that Schonfeld could call on, that the printing of a special volume on parts of the Gemorah was paid for by one of the benefactors. Technically, the book covered common aspects of the Gemorah, rather than whole sections, which was the Hungarian way of teaching it in their Yeshivahs, and probably the way Schonfeld had learned from his father, Victor.

One text book that was not used was the Hertz Chumash, even though this was by far the most popular version of the first five books of the Bible at the time and the royalties, of course, benefited the Schonfeld family. Nevertheless, it was not liked by the Charedim. Hertz had chosen to illustrate the text not only with commentaries from rabbinic authorities but from Christian theologians as well. This approach was rejected by the Charedim. Hertz had edited a popular work for the Jewish community, but the boys at school studied more deeply and needed a work which, in particular, explained the thinking of a still very influential rabbi, the eleventh-century Rashi, far more fully. So an alternative chumash was used instead.

The standard of teaching of secular subjects was enhanced by the recruitment of two very able brothers, Nachum Ordman who taught physics and Jack Ordman, maths. Their exam results over the years would be exceptional. It was not unusual for Jack Ordman's sixth form class to all get 'A' grades at A Level. This was very unusual at the time. A number of teachers devoted much of their working lives to the school. Gerald Gerber taught Maths and Jewish Studies at Hasmonean from 1961 to 2001. Of course, not every teacher could be brilliant. Whilst the best of Hasmonean education was first class, the boys who did not shine in a subject found that the teachers of lower sets could be less effective, a problem common in almost any school, though.

What was rarer in academic circles was stopping school inspectors from doing their job. Yet in the winter of 1969 the Headmistress of Hasmonean Prep would not admit the inspectors who visited the school, on the grounds that they had come without warning. The inspectors called the police because they were within their rights, but Schonfeld supported the head teacher. He said he had recently complained about the Department of Education before a parliamentary committee. Under these circumstances he considered that any inspector's report was liable to be biased. He conducted his own case when he was prosecuted for obstructing the inspectors, lost it hands down, and was fined £10. When the new decade dawned, this could well have gone down as one of the minor court cases in which he would be involved.

In the United States Moses had dabbled successfully in metals, textiles, property and commercial fishing. He was a pillar of the Orthodox community in Mamaroneck in New York and he later taught journalism at New York's Pace University. All-in-all Moses was a polymath, employed as well as a drama critic and highly regarded as a painter and sportsman before cementing his professional reputation as the doyen of UN correspondents.

Ella, now in her late 70s, continued to focus the attention of the family on her health and well-being. A string of letters poured out from her flat to the children, a considerable number of which involved complaints of one kind or another; the main concern was, of course, that they did not contact her often enough. When Senath's marriage to Ernest collapsed, Ella tried for years to act as a marriage broker for her daughter, but without success. She would never take any financial help from her and, in later life, Senath was herself sometimes in need. In 1967 she asked Moses for help and, as always, Moses provided it.

Ella continued to live in Israel, where Senath would settle as well in 1973, as a consultant for the famous Hadassah Hospital in Jerusalem. Ella had by now grown into a rotund, silver-haired figure. She continued to be pro-active; in 1962 she had wanted to swap a plot of land she owned in Jerusalem to create a home for Jewish beggars. Moses pointed out that investing the money she could get for the plot would produce a third of the money he regularly gave her, but this was not an argument she wanted to hear. She also accepted help from David and Kibo after she moved to Israel permanently but she would never take anything from Senath. Daniel also made her a 'director' of a property company which paid her generous fees.

Unfortunately, in 1967, when he was only 54, Daniel died of a heart attack during the Festival of Sukkot. It was a very bad year for the Schonfelds, as Ella had a growth diagnosed that same autumn and she needed a major operation to have it removed. The operation was successful but she slowly declined over the next few years and finally died in 1971, back in London, when she was 82 years old.

The effect of his own operation made Schonfeld's efforts to raise money less vigorous than before. He recognized that new blood was needed to reinvigorate the JSSM but a suitable candidate to take over from him was extremely difficult to find. The combination of rabbinic learning and an ability to develop a business was in short supply. Schonfeld endeavoured to recruit a prominent rabbi in the United States and even sounded out a couple of very senior rabbis in London, but to no avail. He remained the only ecclesiastical leader prepared to devote his life to the JSSM and, of course, without charging for his efforts. Schonfeld never drew a salary from the JSSM. Seldom could it be said more truly that a man's permanent occupation was a labour of love.

In 1969, on the 40th anniversary of the start of the JSSM, the intention was to clear the indebtedness of the five schools. There was now a total of £75,000 in long-term borrowings. As he said at the time, 'the deficiencies had grown apace and the income has been nothing like it used to be'. It was not for want of examining every possible avenue. One of his relatives remembers introducing her husband to him. 'How much do you earn?' asked Schonfeld hopefully.

The anniversary dinner was held at the Central Hall in Westminster and the Earl of Longford was the guest of honour. *The Jewish Chronicle* reported that half of the JSSM's now 2,500 pupils paid no fees and that there was an annual deficit of £20,000.[7] Schonfeld launched an appeal for £100,000 for more classrooms, a new block at Hasmonean Prep and other improvements to the infrastructure of the schools. In the meantime the JSSM continued to live from hand to mouth. Jack Lunzer, Hugo's son, would take money to the office on a Friday, for the frequent occasions when Solly would turn up with a post-dated cheque or a pressing bill. Prompt aid would often need to be forthcoming if the teachers were to be paid that week.

NOTES

1. Schonfeld archives, University of Southampton.
2. Ibid.
3. Rabbi Meir Roberg in conversation with the author.
4. Ibid.
5. Meir Persoff, *Immanuel Jakobovits, A Prophet in Israel* (London and Portland, OR: Valentine Mitchell, 2002).
6. Ibid.
7. *The Jewish Chronicle*, 11 November 1969.

# 9  Good Growth and Bad Growth

The early 1970s were marked by an explosion in inflationary pressures. Prices in Britain rose by up to 20 per cent a year and this unforeseen crisis placed an immense strain on Schonfeld, like so many others. Not only was he physically unable to seek out financial support with the same vigour he had in the past, but also many of his supporters now had their own cash flow difficulties and found it more difficult to write him the cheques on which he depended. Schonfeld's own finances suffered as well. There were more arguments about the royalties. The independent solicitor that Hertz had insisted on being one of his trustees decided to take all the children to court, in order to clarify a number of points on distribution rights and publishers. The solicitor's views prevailed. There was a lot of money involved. In the first half of 1975 the Soncino Press sent in a payment for royalties of £2,855. The sales of the Hertz Chumash had realised £62,000[1] but the royalties still had to be split among Hertz's children and the money paid far fewer bills because of inflation.

The formerly trimly turned-out Schonfeld was now becoming a shabbier figure. The Deputy Headmaster, Meir Roberg, remembers visiting him one winter in his North London office. The old rabbi was sitting in a freezing room wrapped in a holed blanket. He asked Roberg if he'd like him to turn on a small electric fire. The blanket he used for the same purpose at Highgate had belonged to his father-in-law, the Chief Rabbi. He had a small electric foot warmer underneath it as his feet got cold. He liked to be surrounded by familiar pieces of bric-a-brac, like an art-deco standard lamp he'd found put out as rubbish somewhere. In fact, Schonfeld liked his office the way it had always been, but it did give out a stern message that money should be spent on good causes and not on frivolities. Judith, of course, still had the house in Highgate and there was also the cottage in the country. In addition the children were now financially independent, but it must still have been difficult for Solly and Judith to remain independent and make both ends meet.

What could have made things much worse was the constant litigation in which Schonfeld seemed determined to be involved. If he had never lost his love of the law courts, the 1970s were to afford him many opportunities to enjoy the cut and thrust of legal action. In almost every instance the result was disastrous, as he lost case after case, but nothing could stop him from occupying the limelight which such occasions allowed.

One of the earliest actions concerned the Hasmonean Preparatory School in the late summer of 1972. The Edgware Adath synagogue and the school owned the building between them. The rabbi died and Schonfeld wanted his flat for additional classrooms for the school. So he had the door padlocked, prevented the daughter of the dead rabbi from removing her father's possessions, stopped the new rabbi from occupying the flat and then employed security people with an Alsatian dog to ensure the flat was not entered. The Alsatian was reported to have attacked the new rabbi when he arrived to take possession.

The synagogue's Honorary Officers went to court and the judge was very critical of Schonfeld's conduct. He said it was 'difficult to sympathise with his attitude or to condone his conduct'. He awarded costs against Schonfeld personally and these included the time of the Attorney General's office, which represented the interests of the Charities Commission. Schonfeld was specifically barred from using the Trust Funds of the JSSM to pay for the expense. When asked to comment, Schonfeld said airily: 'I am not interested in money', but Schonfeld's supporters club would have had to come to the rescue again. People would have cringed at his unjustified arrogance, but Schonfeld would have said he had acted in strict accordance with the object of his life's work, even if he had gone about it in the wrong way, which he would never admit. He had wanted more room to educate more Jewish children and everybody knew he would go to extreme lengths to try to ensure that he was able to do so. The problem was that his judgement was increasingly letting him down. He was growing more eccentric in his actions with the inevitable consequences. The damaging effects of the brain operation ten years ago were slowly increasing.

The financial position of the Girls' School deteriorated rapidly as soon as Schonfeld decided that it should have a new location in Page Street in Mill Hill. The sale of the old Parson Street site brought in a lot of money but not enough to settle all the debts and to pay for the kind of fine new school buildings that Schonfeld wanted for the girls. It was hoped to defray the costs by having a petrol company take a lease on part of the site for a garage, but this imaginative proposal came to nothing.

Originally, at the beginning of the 1970s, Schonfeld had conducted lengthy discussions with Barnet Council on the possibility of the Girls'

School becoming state-aided and the Council had come down in favour of this if the school governors would play their part. The Conservatives were back in power after Ted Heath had won the 1970 election, and they had been the party which favoured grammar schools; massive comprehensive schools were strictly an idea of Harold Wilson's Labour government. So Schonfeld felt that a suitable deal could be struck with the Conservative Barnet council. Barnet's building plans for their schools in 1972–73 were approved by the government and included the Girls' School's move to Page Street. The work was expected to start in 1974–75 and even though the country's worsening economic position soon made it necessary for Barnet to cut back, the Page Street move was retained. So the council wrote to Schonfeld in July 1974 for a letter of formal agreement which was needed by late September at the latest. To the council's surprise and chagrin, Schonfeld did not reply and eventually Barnet had no option but to defer the project.

The problem, the ramifications of which on Schonfeld the council could not have appreciated, was that the election of 1974 had changed the political scenery. Labour were back in power, comprehensives were the flavour of the month again and the government had ruled that no state aid would be given unless there were at least 900 pupils in the school. This was not seen as a problem by Barnet. Putting Hasmonean girls together with Hasmonean boys on the same Page Street site would be an excellent solution, from their point of view. It would achieve the synergy of having teachers for both, instead of needing two of each. The classes at Shefford during the war had been co-ed and nobody had objected to that. The Holders Hill Boys' site could be sold and it would help finance the project, since it was in a good residential district. The inadequate building could be replaced by a brand new one. What could be simpler?

For Schonfeld, however, the prospect was nightmarish. The world had changed since Shefford. Those were the days when nobody was allowed into the Royal Enclosure at Ascot if they had been divorced. Those were pre-pill days when premarital sex was frowned upon by the majority of people in the country. It was before the Swinging Sixties and the lifestyle of the pop world. For Schonfeld the nation's sexual mores had collapsed. In itself, this was not a problem; it was not even a new problem. Religious Jews had kept to their values in the times of the sexual promiscuous Greek and Roman empires. They had managed during the flagrancy of the Carolingian Charles II and of the Regency England of George IV. They could do so again. The UOHC was not going to compromise on matters touching Jewish law or work with those who *were* prepared to compromise. Only a while back, in 1971, the Board of Deputies of British Jews voted to give rabbinic status to the Reform and Liberal movements. Immediately, the UOHC had walked out on the organization and they have never returned. The large Charedi section of the community are now only represented on the Board by the Federation of Synagogues, which is still to the right of the United Synagogue but is now to the left of the UOHC.

As far as the Charedim were concerned, the sensible course of action to adopt in this modern sexual gale was to batten down the hatches; to protect the Charedi youngsters from being swamped by the prevailing standards. This was not, however, going to be easy if the boys and girls were thrown together in the sixth form at a combined Hasmonean. The council could see no objection to the boys and girls being in separate classes in their early years. When the numbers slimmed down in the sixth form, however, it made no sense to them to have two classes of ten, one for boys and one for girls doing, for example, A Level biology. It would make financial sense to have one class of twenty. This was particularly the case when there was an economic crisis, 20 per cent inflation a year and a desperate need to enforce any cuts possible in government expenditure. After all, this was the decade when the International Monetary Fund had to be called in to agree what could be done about the ailing British economy.

Schonfeld decided that he would have to stall. The fact was that to accept state aid was to risk a potentially disastrous pregnancy among the girls. Just one would be enough to seriously undermine the image of the JSSM. Where a non-religious school might shrug its shoulders and simply deny any responsibility, this would not be accepted among the ultra-Orthodox, if the JSSM created the conditions by which such a situation could occur more easily. In some ultra-Orthodox circles a young couple meeting to consider marriage are invariably accompanied by a chaperone, much as in Victorian England. The very slightly less Orthodox will still meet in public, in the lounges of hotels or in restaurants. The idea that a Charedi bride might not be a virgin would be considered totally unacceptable. Never mind the Permissive Society and the gossip pages of the tabloids. This was the Charedim in the 1970s and they kept themselves entirely separate from fashionable attitudes. If it was forbidden in the Bible, that was far more important than the transitory behaviour and opinions of pop stars and sex goddesses.

There was, however, no categorical proof that mixing the two schools would create such a problem. It might be common sense that it could happen, but to poor parents wanting a better education for their daughters, the prospect of state aid for the girls was their dream. Schonfeld was doing his best by taking 10 per cent of the girls free.

Another 40 per cent were paying half fees and only 50 per cent the full charge. Administratively, it was also a problem to get the fee payers to actually pay up; times were hard and if they could delay settling a bill, many would need to do so. There were also some parents who simply took advantage of Schonfeld's soft heart and the school's administrative inefficiency and did not pay when they could have done so.

For whatever reason, the financial picture became increasingly gloomy. Even so, Schonfeld continued to stall. The council wrote to him continually for a decision on Page Street. At the Governors' meeting in December 1976, it was recorded that state-aid was hoped for within twelve months. A year later, however, in January 1978, the Governors agreed to defer the subject yet again until a later date. The Minutes recorded that: 'the assisted status was so fraught with angry opposition that pressing forward with it now would be likely to cause severe damage'. Where the angry opposition was coming from was not officially specified.

Schonfeld was not a free agent in acting as he did. He had to take into account that to maintain the popularity of the Hasmonean schools, he needed to continue to merit the support of the Charedi community. There was also the point that, although it was not clear who exactly the schools' trustees were, they were all Charedim. Even if he had tried to join the two schools together, they would have rejected the idea out of hand. Normally they left him severely alone to get on with developing the JSSM, but the prospect of co-education would have stirred them into action. He could not, therefore, agree to making Hasmonean a co-ed comprehensive, even if he had wanted to – which he did not – and he equally could not tell the council that. To make matters even more delicate, it so happened that two of the senior councillors, Rosa and Joe Freedman, were often in the Mayoral chair and were members of the Reform Synagogue and totally opposed to the views of the Charedim. Schonfeld infuriated them both on several counts.

To add to the problems of simply balancing the school books, there was the need to pay for the continuing construction on the new Page Street site. Schonfeld sold his office in Stamford Hill to deal with some of the bills. This was acceptable, but the school buildings were sacrosanct and there could be no question of selling any of those unless there was a suitable alternative school building available. No school would ever be closed. Schonfeld moved his office to a flat above the *shtiebl* in 5 The Bishops Avenue in Hampstead Garden Suburb, which did have the advantage that it was much closer to his home in Highgate. The *shtiebl* had become his regular place of worship since he left the Adath in 1960, although he carried on walking long distances to give sermons further afield, in Golders Green and Hendon in particular.

The physical conditions of the infrastructure at both schools were impossible, though for different reasons. For example, at the boys' school there were not enough chairs for the pupils to sit on. This was because the school was packed to overflowing. The economic problems of the country were leading more and more families to consider a free Jewish school education for the first time. The breach in the wall of contempt for such institutions, based on an unfavourable comparison with public schools, had been widened by the crisis. Schonfeld could see that now was the time to strike by taking the extra children he was offered.

Before 1969 Hasmonean Boys' had been considered a two-form entry school – sixty-six children a year could be accepted in two classes of thirty-three pupils. In 1969, though, the governors had been able to justify a move to a three-form entry, as applications for places continued to increase. Barnet approved the growth although it knew the building was much too small to accommodate the extra number of pupils. The minimum approved area for a school with 600 pupils was 2,700 sq. metres. The Holders Hill Road site was just over 2,000 sq. metres, inadequate by no less than 30 per cent. If that was not crowded enough, by 1975 there would be 616 boys at the school and by 1978 there would be 646. This, after Schonfeld had given the council a promise never to exceed 540.

One reason for the deceit though was humanitarian. During the decade the situation in Iran became increasingly dangerous for the Jewish community, as the Shah's position deteriorated in the face of the opposition of religious fundamentalists. The Jews in Iran started to leave and a large number were quietly accepted as immigrants, temporary or otherwise, by the British government. The Iranian Jews were a wealthy community and they were not inclined to wait and see if another Hitler was going to take power at home.

Many Iranian Jews arrived in Britain and a lot of them were on their way to America. While they worked on finalizing their visas, they had to educate their sons. Schonfeld took them at Hasmonean. How, though, could he explain to Barnet the importance of looking after Iranian Jewish children? Barnet, of course, knew exactly what was going on, and kindly looked the other way for as long as it could. One of the teachers remembers being asked by Schonfeld to look after the Iranian kids. They all attended morning prayers where *tephillin* (phylacteries) are placed on the head and arm. The Iranian children only had one set of *tephillin* between them. So each one put them on in turn and then passed them to his neighbour. The teacher also remembers, though, that the children knew all the prayers by heart.

The infrastructure at the Boys' School was seriously inadequate in many other ways. For example, the school building had no secondary fire escape. Providing one was the responsibility of the Governors. The council brought this potentially calamitous situation to their attention in the summer of 1977 and on five subsequent occasions in the next eighteen months; nothing happened. There were four governors appointed by Barnet Council but either they were not kept informed by their own Education Department, which seems very unlikely, or the subject was simply left off the agenda at Governors' meetings. The Trustee governors remained docile. Their attitude was probably influenced by their memory of the occasional governor in the past who had disagreed with Schonfeld and had subsequently failed to be reappointed; *pour encourager les autres* had worked. It was equally nonproductive to state a case and only see it approved if Schonfeld liked the idea.

What the council was entitled to rely on was that the situation was temporary. If the school was moving to Page Street, then why spend a lot of money on a building which would shortly be defunct? Schonfeld knew it would not be, however, but still could not even find the money to improve the playground. By now Meir Roberg, as Deputy Head Master, was taking some of the load off the shoulders of the increasingly rheumatically handicapped Stanton. Both knew very well that the roof leaked, the heating was never adequate, the playground was potentially dangerous, and the playing fields were usually waterlogged throughout the winter. In cold weather many children sat in class, wrapped up in anoraks.

Schonfeld's priority was not the building, the playground, the fire escape or even the cleaning. What mattered to him was the education he could provide. The science block, for example, had the largest budget for new equipment and was well endowed. In October 1972 a new Great Hall had been inaugurated and a cabinet minister had been the guest of honour, talking of British foreign policy under the Schonfeld presiding eye. Eight hundred pupils had attended from the Boys' and Girls' Schools and nobody had mentioned the absence of a fire escape.

The proportion of time given to Jewish Studies had now been increased by Schonfeld to two lessons a day, much to Stanton's concern. The headmaster felt sure that the move would alienate many parents, as half the school roll was from the ranks of the United Synagogue. He worried unnecessarily, however, as the parents were happy with the school's exam results, particularly with Stanton and Roberg, and they did not wish to make any changes.

In day-to-day matters, Schonfeld was always on the phone to Stanton, who would be inclined to hold the phone away from his ear as the Chairman of the Board of Governors went on and on. Roberg found Schonfeld much less difficult on educational subjects. 'He would admit he was wrong. He was not unreasonable. He could be persuaded. Dawkins [Dr Jack Dawkins, the Barnet head of Education] admired Dr. Schonfeld for his pluck and tenacity, but found him impossible to work with.'2

Rabbi Ephraim Kestenbaum's fund-raising efforts for the girls' school proved insufficiently successful, though this was partially due to some of the money raised being used by Schonfeld to pay other kinds of bills. The creditors were piling up and Rabbi Kestenbaum still had the responsibility delegated by Schonfeld for keeping the show on the road. At one point the Page Street site was sold by Schonfeld and then had to be bought back. Schonfeld's wealthier friends guaranteed enormous sums until the problems could be sorted out. Even so, suppliers now started to sue for their money. In 1976 the builders went to court and got a judgement against the JSSM. They took a charge on the school premises and Schonfeld appealed to the Jewish Educational Development Trust to come to the rescue. The Trust had been doing sterling work in creating new Jewish schools but were not averse to helping an old established one. The Chief Rabbi continued to feel in Schonfeld's debt. At an emergency breakfast meeting an old Schonfeld supporter immediately offered a £100,000 guarantee against the bank overdraft. The JEDT had helped before and this time granted £25,000 unconditionally. By the end of November they had helped the JSSM to clear the entire debt. Schonfeld was still much admired and the JEDT officers reported little difficulty in raising the money that was needed. In return for the JEDT's help, Schonfeld made a number of undertakings, including a promise to repay the JEDT when it was possible to do so. In all the JSSM had needed £92,500 but, as a result of the selling of the Girls' School's old premises, this promise was honoured. The school deeds were returned, but it might not be so comparatively painless if such problems occurred again.

Kestenbaum had poured a fortune of his own money into the Girls' School over the years, to expand Parsons Street and make both ends meet. Faced with a seriously deteriorating financial position, Schonfeld discussed the possibility of downsizing the girls' school in order to sell off part of the site to pay off more JSSM debts. Kestenbaum, who had devoted so much time, effort and money in building up the Girls' School was, naturally, very much against the idea and said so. After many years of harmoniously working together in a joint effort, their different approaches undermined their relationship. Schonfeld had now reached a point where he could not take opposition from anybody and the two fell out. When the teachers were not paid their June salaries, thirty-five of them issued a writ against the JSSM, though this was withdrawn when the cheques finally arrived. Kestenbaum had had enough, though, and resigned.

At the Girls' School, the foundation stone had been laid in April 1975 but the initial space available was considerably less than had been utilized at Parson Street, in spite of the new Litman Hall and the Rosa Gabe and Solomon Cramer rooms. There were now cases where girls were being taught German at the front of a classroom and French at the back.

In the summer of 1977, Kestenbaum reemerged as a Barnet nominee on the Board of Governors of the Boys' School. Schonfeld took steps to ensure that he was very seldom told when the meetings would take place. At the one meeting he did attend in October 1977, he disagreed again with Schonfeld, who rose from his chair and hit him with his stick. He further threatened Kestenbaum that if he attended a meeting again, his son, who was a pupil at the school, would suffer. Kestenbaum was patched up and displayed the injury at his local police station. When he had calmed down after a totally unwarrantable attack, he decided not to make a charge, but he certainly could have done. It was a poor reward for Kestenbaum who had put in so much hard work over so many years.

It was also in 1977 that the Girls' School finally moved into the Page Street site. The building still had not been paid for and the builders were taking legal action. It turned out that the Assembly Hall was unsafe and could not be used. There would appear to have been faults on both sides. Last minute loans from friends avoided the possibility of the school actually being closed. Schonfeld now took the opportunity to print note paper which stated quite clearly that Hasmonean was state-aided and divided into two departments, boys and girls. The boys were, of course, state-aided and both schools were part of the JSSM. But the girls' school was not state-aided and Barnet objected to the note paper as misleading, which it certainly was. They asked Schonfeld to stop using it but he continued to do so.

Fund raising continued as new bills continued to pile up. In late 1976 Schonfeld had gone north to discuss the problems with the Hubert Trust, one of the main Charedi charitable organizations. They had agreed to lend him £50,000 and that had relieved pressure from the builders for payment for the Girls' School premises. It was a typically generous gesture on the part of the Trust, though even greater sums had come from others over the years as gifts. In December 1977

Schonfeld appealed to the Clore Foundation for support and the famous entrepreneur sent £15,000 to the JEDT for the Girls' School. It was later contended by Schonfeld that the JEDT had not passed that money to the JSSM, but it was stupid to fight with the only organization which was guaranteed to be able to come to the rescue again if it chose to do so.

Schonfeld did not make matters any easier by deluding himself that his talents also included those of a developer. He gave instructions to create buildings at the Girls' School for which there was no planning permission. He employed direct labour who did a bad job and he allowed insufficient depth for the foundations of buildings. He ignored the need to get permits as he had ignored so many council rules and regulations in the past. Only this time he was not dealing with the education department and armed with a sound case that his educational teaching standards were working well. Now he was up against planning and building inspectors who would be held responsible if they allowed unsafe structures; only a few years before a block of flats had collapsed in South London, involving fatalities, and that was every planning department's nightmare.

Within the Adath, Schonfeld still tried to be helpful. It was becoming increasingly difficult to find homes at a reasonable price in Stamford Hill and a number of young married families moved as much as half an hour's walk away from the area. Though they were prepared to walk to the synagogue on the Sabbath themselves, they soon found that this would be impossible when they had small children to bring too. What was needed, they decided in 1975, was a new synagogue. While this breakaway was unpopular with the home shul, Schonfeld understood the problem and set out to find them premises. When he did so, the price was £6,000. Schonfeld said that if they raised £2,000 among themselves, he would get £2,000 from the Burial Society and raise the other £2,000 for them himself. It was a most generous offer – but the families turned it down. They simply did not want to be beholden to the old man. They were afraid that they would lose their independence, the same argument that Schonfeld had used so often to maintain his own.

It was in 1975 that Otto Schiff died at the great age of 96. In his later years Schiff was not a well-known figure in the Jewish community and, with his passing, his major contribution to the rescue of Jews from the Continent before the war was almost forgotten. By contrast, in 1978, the death of Eli Munk in Israel was widely regretted. Munk had retired from his synagogue in Golders Green in 1969 and gone to live in Jerusalem. Now, at the age of 77, his life had come to an end. 'Munk's' synagogue would revere his name far into the future.

Schonfeld was still in the driving seat, directing the JSSM ship through the financial gales towards the harbour of massive and successful Jewish education. When, eventually, moves would be planned to replace him and destroy his power, one member of the committee undertaking the work sent in his resignation to its Chair and wrote that he could not 'In good conscience take part in any action that will, at this stage of his life, forcibly remove from office the one man responsible for, among other things, the creation of the major Orthodox school system in London.' The official trustees among the UOHC communities were also reluctant to act. Rabbis Padwa and Dunner were among approximately ten rabbis who met weekly to discuss UOHC community problems. Schonfeld seldom attended and now, when asked to do so to discuss complaints made against him, declined to do so. Nobody felt able to take issue with this.

Throughout the 1970s Schonfeld retained his one powerful secret weapon. Without entrance exams, in impossible working conditions, his pupils managed, year after year, to perform scholastic miracles; their results improved year-on-year, a substantial proportion of them finished up in the professions, they produced large numbers of students for Yeshivas and universities, they finished up as fine rabbis and they made a nonsense of the idea that ivy-covered walls were essential for educational success.

Even when the school roll was 525 at the beginning of the decade, the sixth form had ninety-five pupils. Of these sixteen left to go to university and thirty to *yeshivot*, many to go on to university afterwards. Many more started immediately to study to become lawyers, accountants and doctors. Three boys got into King's College, Cambridge and four old boys got first-class degrees. For a comprehensive with no entrance examination, it remained a staggering performance when viewed through the eyes of the Barnet Education Department.

Not that entry into the school was always conducted by the rule book. There is a letter on record from as far back as 1971, when the Barnet Education Department decided they had to voice their concerns about Hasmonean to the Town Clerk. They were worried, they said, that boys might be accepted as pupils from outside the borough, which was only allowed if there were no suitable applicants from within the area. Furthermore, they might be coming from private preparatory schools, rather than from the state schools, which should take precedence. As the letter said, Schonfeld 'frequently attempted to admit pupils to the school in a manner which is contrary to the normal admissions procedures of the Local Education Authority'.[3] And the department were entirely correct.

The top echelon in Barnet saw the results, though, and Barnet were not about to rock the boat. They had three grammar schools in the Borough; Henrietta Barnett Girls School, Queen Elizabeth School for Boys and Hasmonean. Of the three only the Hasmonean had no entrance exam. Yet it had no difficulty producing similar exam results to the other two, and that was after allocating a substantial chunk of the school day to the Jewish Studies curriculum. As far as Hasmonean Boys' was concerned, Barnet would often argue about withdrawing state aid because of the refusal of Schonfeld to toe the line; then they always agreed to give him more time and that they would consider the matter again at a future meeting.

The results spoke volumes for the dedication of the teachers, but there was a degree of chaos on the periphery of the common room. The head of Barnet education would report: 'The methods used by the Hasmonean Boys School to inform me about staffing appointments and related matters were haphazard and in my view totally unsatisfactory ... not infrequently the first information received regarding the appointment of a teacher is when that teacher reports for duty.'[4] In addition to this, some teachers paid by the council also taught at other JSSM schools which were not state-aided. This situation was totally unacceptable to the authority but continued nevertheless and, if anything, worsened. The official would also complain: 'In April 1977 I reluctantly agreed to the payment retrospectively of full salary to X, an unqualified person who had, without my knowledge, taken up teaching duties at the school in January 1977.' The teacher lasted another year. Bureaucratically, it was all inexcusable.

Of course the teachers could have reported the illegalities to their union to organize complaints to go to the council, but none ever did. The education of the children took precedence over their heavier workload. Indeed they had ample justification for their own complaints. For reasons which were never explained, their salary cheques ceased to come direct from the Council. When they had done so, they always arrived on time. Now it was requested that the money be sent to the school and, on a number of occasions, the teachers were paid late. The financial situation was getting that desperate. Walter Stanton, as the Headmaster, poured oil on troubled waters to the best of his ability. He reckoned that half his time was taken up unscrambling Schonfeld's disputes with the educational and local authority officers.

There was justification for Barnet being confused. They were accustomed to working with their schools in the borough through either the Head Teacher or the Chairman of the Governors. At Hasmonean they found requests and information arriving from Stanton and Schonfeld, but also from the Clerk to the Governors, the Deputy Head Master, heads of departments and the School Officer. Letters arrived on their desks without Stanton's knowledge and sometimes against his wishes. On occasions letters on the same subject would come from both Schonfeld and Stanton, with contradictory arguments. One explanation is that Jews are accustomed to having to deal with their own problems and many dislike handing over the authority to do so to others. So the scenario at Hasmonean would have been considered by many in the community to be not unusual.

The core problem was, of course, that there was no counterbalance to a declining Schonfeld. If that role should have been played by the Headmaster, he had given up long ago. If he was unhappy at what went on at Governors' meetings, Stanton would get up and leave because he knew he could not win if Schonfeld had made up his mind. The Board of Governors always had a majority of Schonfeld supporters anyway. It changed rapidly in membership during the 1970s, so that Schonfeld's experience was greater than that of the Trustee governors. Of the eight foundation governors sitting on the Board in October 1976 only two remained in office two years later. Furthermore, the eight seats had been filled by fourteen nominees during that period. A lot of worthy Adath congregants did not enjoy being cyphers.

In addition, Stanton was in constant pain now from his arthritis. His hands were swollen and gnarled, though he still managed to lay *tephillin* every morning, with the help of the senior boys who would bind the leather straps on his arm and head for him. In the school offices Schonfeld would be on to him and the other school officials on a very regular basis. There were disagreements, and shouting matches were not uncommon. Eventually some officials simply put the phone on their desks and carried on with their work while Schonfeld bellowed down the line at them.

If the results at the Boys' School were admirable, those at Hasmonean Girls were even more remarkable, given the academic leadership available. The qualifications of one teacher turned out to be one A Level in needlework. After the Head Teacher had left in 1976, a replacement was taken on by Schonfeld but soon departed. Another was appointed who resigned when she became pregnant. It was alleged that she was then paid 'a substantial monthly sum but did not attend the school', which would have made the financial position worse. After that Schonfeld decided the school should be run by four deputy headmistresses. Schonfeld never lost his sense of humour entirely. As he said at the time: 'Four heads are better than one'. There was still no board of governors at the

Girls' School or even a board of management. Schonfeld now appointed and dismissed, interfered and sometimes contradicted himself. Kestenbaum had done his best to restrain him from his wilder ideas but Kestenbaum was no longer involved. On one occasion in 1978 Schonfeld excluded two girls, but one of their fathers was a barrister who immediately went to court. It was yet another disaster. Schonfeld had accused the father of not being Orthodox but lost the case and had to withdraw the allegation and take the girl back.

The main barrier to academic success for the Girls' School was that the lack of facilities led to the disintegration of the sixth form. Parents who wanted higher education for their children were not satisfied with the inadequate leadership and the poor infrastructure. Most good schools will accept additional students who are qualified to start in their sixth forms, so the girls could be moved easily. JFS, for example, was a popular alternative.

If it was easy enough to pick holes in the way the Boys' and Girls' Schools were run, the vast majority of the day-to-day schooling proceeded effectively under Stanton and his deputy, Rabbi Roberg. The ethos of the schools was particularly commendable. There was very little bullying, the children gained spiritual and ethical support from the teaching and practice of Judaism, and enthusiastically gave time to raising money for charity and visiting old people's homes. They were not angels, there were exceptions, but overall they were a hard working group of students, encouraged by their parents and taught by a dedicated staff.

The non-Jewish teachers normally looked upon the Orthodox aspects of the school with amused tolerance. One teacher was asked at a parents' evening how a boy was getting on with his English studies. 'Not bad at all', said the master, 'for a school where English is a foreign language!'

One major problem which split the school into two camps was its approach to the State of Israel. The more the government of Israel moved away from the Orthodox norms, the more antagonism it created with the Charedim in Britain, and the JSSM was the creation of the Charedim. As long ago as 1949 the European Executive of the Agudas Yisroel had declared that to celebrate Israel Independence Day was contrary to the Shulchan Aruch, the standard codification of Jewish law. At the time Schonfeld had attacked the ruling but now, nearly thirty years later, some of the teachers were so ambivalent about the State that they even tried to prevent the boys from singing the Israeli national anthem. In the Spring of 1976 the school's Israel Society invited the Chief Rabbi to address them on Israel's Independence Day and he accepted. Schonfeld had still never invited Jakobovits to talk at the school. He continued to fear what he considered would be the undermining influence of the United Synagogue, if they were able to gain a foothold in the running of the JSSM. In addition, to Schonfeld, the standards of observance acceptable to the United Synagogue remained inadequate. Stanton was away on holiday in Israel and Schonfeld decided that the only way to prevent the Chief Rabbi's address was to close the school on the day in question and on this he insisted. Calculated or not, it was an insult to both the Chief Rabbi and the Zionists in the school. Boys wrote to *The Jewish Chronicle* to protest and, when Stanton returned, he declared himself against the ruling. 'I disagree with the decision. I am a religious Zionist', he told *The JC*.[5]

The governors held the reins of power, though, and the school did close. Barnet were told that the closing of the school was *due* to Israel Independence Day, not that it was to prevent it being celebrated. When the Education Department discovered the truth, they decided not to risk being cast as bulls in delicate religious china shops. Stanton fought back. He organised a special assembly the day before the anniversary when Israel remembered its war dead, and on Independence Day the Israel Society held its meeting at a nearby hall. It was packed and Jakobovits spoke. In addition, a number of the senior boys went to the Israeli Embassy to pay their respects.

Schonfeld's decision was attacked in a *Jewish Chronicle* leader but his action would have been supported in Charedi circles. It was a striking illustration by the Charedim of the rejection of the creation of a secular state in Israel. This, after all, had always been known as the Holy Land and its rulers were not living up to its historical credo. Many of their actions gave immense offence to a wide range of international Orthodox opinion, not just among the Charedim.

The contrast between the financial and administrative problems and the ethos and results of the schools, summed up perfectly the dilemma which faced the school parents and many others. Within the Charedi community there was enormous regard for Schonfeld. He had saved so many of the lives of the senior figures, or of their relations. They might laugh at him behind his back for his patrician accent and his increasingly incoherent speeches. They might resent his autocratic approach, his inadequate paperwork and his normal refusal to admit that even the faintest possibility existed that he might be wrong. Nevertheless, they would rally to his defence if he was under attack and many would be infuriated if his methods were being questioned in any way.

At the schools, the same was true. The boys might now snigger at his facial deformity and his repetition of the tired old jokes. Nothing, however, could take away from him the fact that the JSSM was, above all else, his creation. One could search far and wide for years and never come up with anybody else who would sacrifice his health, his finances, his whole later life to the one objective which the vast majority in his community considered the most important task they had to achieve; to keep Orthodox Judaism alive in Britain through the education of the children. And he had carried out that objective for forty-five years without ever being paid for it.

Admittedly, Schonfeld wanted untrammelled power. For example, he continued to resist the suggestion that the schools should have Parent-Teachers Associations. He admitted you might raise £10,000 through a PTA but he said you would also get 10,000 headaches. It was only partly because he did not want to give up an ounce of his power. It was also partly because he felt that what was not known would not hurt anybody.

One new parent, however, came from a sturdy stock of refugee survivors and found a way through the impasse. The lady was hands-on and what she saw of conditions at the Boys' School filled her with dismay. She recognized that the place was a dump. Windows broken, toilets filthy, inadequate cleaning standards throughout the building, insufficient equipment and general administrative chaos. Now if 600 boys are put into an inadequate building they are unlikely to keep it in pristine condition. What is more, the headmaster should always be, first and foremost, concentrating on the educational standards. Yet here was a sick man, with severe rheumatoid arthritis, constantly badgered by Schonfeld and without the support of a Parent-Teacher Association. Stanton could only bear so much. It was fortunate that in 1974 this one parent – who still wants to remain anonymous – grasped the nettle at the Boys' School. She persuaded Stanton to allow a group of mothers to come into the school and start to clean it up. One mother who surveyed the conditions and had a sense of humour, said 'A bomb. First, a bomb!' Over the next few years, slowly but surely, conditions started to improve. It was done very quietly. The daily linen was washed at home and neither the parents nor the press ever heard of it. As a general rule, most parents had little idea of what was going on behind the scenes. The corollary, however, was that, as the women worked, they became aware of more serious problems; members of the staff started to whisper of money going astray. The financial controls were inadequate and the opportunities for petty theft were numerous. To make matters more complicated, there were seven different bank accounts. The mothers remained unthreatening and Schonfeld came to grudgingly cooperate with them. If there was ever confrontation, the women held their own. Complimenting one of them on one occasion, Schonfeld said, 'You have the brain of a man'. The feminine elements of political correctness did not come easily to him. Whatever the disagreements, though, the two sides had one common objective; to educate the children as well as possible.

There were also complaints about the use of the money in the Benefit Funds for both the Boys' and the Girls' Schools. These were under Schonfeld's sole control. Surrounded by overdue bills, he must have found it tempting to pay off all sorts of creditors and help with cases of hardship, not necessarily associated with the schools. As word spread, a movement eventually started to get a proper investigation carried out. The school administrators delayed providing answers. They fell back on asking for a letter with the full details of the outstanding points. They got a string of them at the end of March 1977. Three weeks later they had sent no reply but, at that point, there was a burglary at the school. The only things that were taken were the accounts books.

At the annual general meeting of the Golders Green Beth Hamedresh (Munks) in 1977, a committee was approved to look into Jewish education in their locality. It was an excuse; what they really wanted to look at was the JSSM and, as one of its trustee communities, they were well entitled to do so. The committee was chaired by Aron Vecht, a distinguished scientist, and it included experienced professionals and businessmen. The committee started to delve into the problems of the JSSM. They soon learned more about unpaid bills, legal actions, money unaccounted for and a wide variety of additional financial problems. The money situation eventually deteriorated to the point where, in early 1979, Meir Roberg was reduced to writing to the parents at the Boys' School to ask for a donation of £10. It was to pay for a new boiler at the school as the old one had proved totally inadequate during the winter frost.

In 1978 Moses wrote to Solly and told him 'I do believe you enjoy a fight', and it remained true. In October of that year Schonfeld wrote a sound defence of the position of the Right Wing in *The Jewish Chronicle*, citing his authority to do so: 'as titular head of the Union-Adath Yisroel'. Etymologists, though, would have recognized the weakness implicit in the word 'titular'. As far as the new fight looming on the horizon was concerned, however, it was going to be a pretty one-sided encounter. The problems became even more critical when the committee learnt that Schonfeld was in serious danger of being prosecuted by the Inland Revenue; a lot of money due to them from the school had gone astray. Something had to be done and done quickly. It was the Attorney General who decided that it would be necessary to go to the High Court to get a receiver appointed for the JSSM. The legal position was that the JSSM was a charity and a charity has beneficiaries. The beneficiaries were the pupils and their interests were safeguarded, *in extremis*, by the Attorney General. In the late 1970s this was Sir Michael Havers, and it was his task to see that the interests of the children were being properly protected. Affidavits were produced and a date was set for July 1979.

It was a very difficult situation for the committee to handle. Non-Jewish authorities were going to sit in judgement on an intensely Jewish concern. They were doing so with the agreement of the Trustees and they were, together, going to attack the reputation of an icon. The risk the committee members took was of suffering the one penalty which could be imposed by their community; ostracism. Even today, twenty-five years later, some will only speak off the record about the events of those days. They recall individuals in authority who were Schonfeld supporters and who were outraged at what they saw as bringing the community into disrepute. They often did not speak to them, thereafter, for years.

In 1978, however, the financial situation grew ever more precarious. In February the JSSM received a writ for unpaid building work. In April the company got a judgement for £5,000 with a further £1,000 to be paid in May. They asked Barnet if they could take the furniture at the school. The Council told them that it belonged to Barnet. Further court action followed. In March 1979 another writ came for equipment provided for the new lab. This one was dismissed on technical grounds and the JSSM stalled by not providing evidence on time and getting an extension. The Quantity Surveyors wanted £17,000 for aborted work they had carried out at the Girls' School and the engineers wanted £22,000. The situation could not be allowed to continue in this way.

One of the final straws was that the salary cheques for the teachers at the Girls' School bounced, yet again, in December 1978. A date for the court hearing was agreed. In a good cause, the committee would do the right thing, but for Schonfeld it was the beginning of the end.

NOTES

1. Schonfeld papers, University of Southampton.
2. Rabbi Roberg in conversation with the author.
3. Dick Bird in conversation with the author.
4. Ibid.
5. *The Jewish Chronicle*, 30 April 1976.

# 10 The Final Years

The summer term of 1979 was the last in which Schonfeld would rule over his beloved JSSM. On 20 July, under the Trustees Act 1925, Mr Justice Walton approved the appointment of a receiver to sort out what had become an impossibly tangled financial mess. As the judge said in the court that day, there was an 'absolutely deplorable' possibility of the schools being seized and sold to pay off the creditors.

Nobody knew how much was owing. Nobody knew for certain which of the trustees were responsible for the running of the JSSM or who governed the charity. For the best part of fifty years it had been Schonfeld's personal project. Whatever the rules may have said, whatever governors, local authority nominees or those invisible trustees may have preferred, at the end of the day the final decision had always rested with Schonfeld. It was partly because nobody was willing to take over and have to deal with a complex organization. It was also because Schonfeld had done a tremendous job in building the JSSM and everybody acknowledged that fact. Now, when challenged, many of the Trustees made Schonfeld's hegemony abundantly clear as they hurried to absolve themselves of any responsibility for the chaos.

If it ever came to the crunch, Schonfeld had always dealt with rebellious trustees and the governors by falling back on one incontrovertible fact; he was accepted as the sole religious authority in the running of the schools. If push came to shove, every disputed decision could be forced through by him on the grounds that it was a religious matter. That was the solid foundation of his power and it had never failed him before.

Now he could cope no longer. The judge asserted that 'affairs are being dealt with in a most improper manner'. The Charities Commission only had the 1975 accounts, though draft accounts up to April 1977 had been recently lodged with it. After a two-day hearing the judge approved the appointment of a receiver for the movement, hoping that he would 'perform the usual miracles that receivers are sometimes capable of'. It was to be a tall order.

The Committee who were parties to the court case were thankful for what they saw as two mercies. Firstly, that while the dirty linen was being washed in public in evidence, the press did not notice what was going on. The headlines would have been excruciatingly embarrassing to the Charedim but publicity was avoided until after the receiver was appointed. And, secondly, that Schonfeld was in court throughout the hearing but did not say a word. The Committee thought the situation was bad enough without one of his outbursts. By now it was difficult to know if Schonfeld would provide a rational argument or a diatribe.

The judge set out the terms of reference in delicate terms; he told Schonfeld that whilst the rabbi was responsible to the court on high, he, the judge, was responsible to the courts on earth. He asked for respect for both responsibilities.

It was totally out of character for Schonfeld to stay quiet. The objective of Sir Michael Havers was to have a receiver appointed and Schonfeld knew it. He would fight the appointment in the future, tooth and nail. Why he did not make his case during the original court hearing is difficult to understand. Equally, it is hard to work out how pressure might have been brought to bear on him to achieve his agreement to stay silent. In any event, that was what happened and everybody was delighted it had worked out that way. It was destined to be a very short honeymoon period before the old Schonfeld approach reasserted itself.

Having achieved their aim, the choice of receiver for those who had brought the action was a delicate one. Everybody wanted the JSSM to continue, educationally, as it had done over the years. Its results were outstanding and although Barnet's Education Department had a string of technical complaints, Hasmonean Boys' School remained a star in their firmament.

Barnet had over 100 schools in the Borough, including a number of sink schools. The Education Department was not short of work for its limited staff. If the occasional teacher was appointed at the Hasmonean without their approval, if the agenda for governors' meetings sometime arrived later for their appointees than regulations provided, even if Schonfeld packed Hasmonean Boys' School with far more pupils than the maximum agreed with him, it was still producing results of which any borough could be proud. That summer no fewer than ten of the sixth form had achieved four 'A' grades in A Level examinations. Even better, these results came from boys who had not been selected because of their superior abilities at the age of 11. They had been chosen because they came from Orthodox Jewish families. To have a state school doing better than many public schools was a real feather in Barnet's cap.

It was suggested by many critics of the JSSM that if it was in a financial mess, it was the responsibility of the UOHC to bail it out, it was a school for Charedi children. The fact was, however, that in 1979 almost half the boys were from United Synagogue homes, not from those of the Charedim. Some of the Charedim might have preferred it otherwise. They might have found the observance of the *mitzvot* by some of the United Synagogue children less stringent than they would have wished. They might have feared such behaviour could be contagious. In the future when schools that were prepared to adopt a stricter regime came into existence, they might be their choice for their children. Nevertheless, it had always been Schonfeld's belief that he would not increase the number of youngsters setting Charedi standard in later life if he only recruited pupils from Charedi families. For fifty years that had been the JSSM's position.

Everybody wanted the problems resolved without undermining Schonfeld's reputation. He was greatly admired by much of the community for his tireless work over so many years, having grown the JSSM from the thirty pupils he inherited, to the 2,000 the movement was responsible for in 1979. Even the lawyers representing those opposed to Schonfeld did their best to explain away the shortcomings in his performance in recent years. The barrister for the Attorney General said: 'one knows that many men of God keep their eye so much on the next world that their conduct in this world is not easy to follow'. If face-saving melted into patronising comment on occasions, the counsel certainly did not go for the jugular.

In a generous tribute, *The Jewish Chronicle* spoke for the majority of the community when it said that the appointment of a receiver:

> cannot and must not be allowed to destroy the remarkable record of Rabbi Dr. Solomon Schonfeld in the educational field. He was the architect and lynchpin of a network of schools which were for long supreme in this community in their academic standards, both secular and religious, and the envy of others who sought to emulate their example.[1]

JFS supporters, no doubt, swallowed hard. It had been though, by any yardstick, a remarkable achievement. So now there had to be a receiver appointed who understood all this. Who could recognize the importance of maintaining the *mitzvot* at the school – or keeping to the religious minutiae – depending on your point of view. Lord Fisher was the President of the Jewish Board of Deputies at the time. It was he, together with the Chief Rabbi, who came up with the name of Bernard

Garbacz as the man who should be appointed by the Attorney General on behalf of the Charities Commissioners, Barnet and the original committee. Garbacz was a chartered accountant with an impeccable record of helping good causes. He was well known in United Synagogue circles as a totally reliable and efficient professional. Better than that, though: Bernard Garbacz was very Orthodox. He might not have been ultra-Orthodox but he came from a rabbinic family and he had not fallen any measurable distance from the bough. From a long association with the school as a parent, Garbacz also knew, or suspected, where many of the financial bodies were buried.

Garbacz knew that he was in for a rough ride. It was also going to take up a great deal of his time, but he had no intention of charging a penny for his work. In the end his bills would have been £50,000 (the equivalent of £150,000 today). That would have added to the £212,000 he told the creditors in January 1980 was the total indebtedness of the JSSM. Garbacz did not own the practice, Landau, Morley, where he was the senior partner. There were other partners and they included non-Jews as well as Jews, but all agreed with him not to charge. It was ironic that later on there would be allegations that he was stretching out the work in order to increase his fees, when the truth was he was not charging any. As, traditionally, it is not the done thing in polite circles in Britain to parade one's generosity, Garbacz did not consider the rumour-mongers worthy of any response.

The early decisions Garbacz had to make were body blows for Schonfeld. The engine room of the JSSM had announced that he would, as usual, be addressing the pupils at the schools at the beginning of the Autumn term. Garbacz, however, wanted the schools to carry on without disruption, as if nothing had happened while the boys and girls were on their summer holidays. He could not risk the danger of Schonfeld speaking against the appointment of a receiver before the assembled pupils and staff. He might have recalled the school splitting into two camps over the Israel Independence Day lecture. So he got a court order to ban Schonfeld from the schools he had nurtured. For Schonfeld to be denied access to the schools over which he had sweated blood for all of his adult life must have been heartbreaking. There would now be a gap in his life, a chasm which could never be filled. To make matters worse, the Albert Hall had been booked for a massive celebration to mark the Golden Jubilee of the JSSM in March 1980. With the parlous state of the finances, and the creditors at the gates, Garbacz had no alternative but to cancel the function. This, too, must have hurt Schonfeld very badly. There would be no official recognition of all that had been achieved over those fifty years.

The old man had not been in court when the receiver was finally appointed. He welcomed him officially afterwards, though: 'Mr Garbacz is a nice kosher man. Why shouldn't I work with him? I am entirely happy with the choice of Mr. Garbacz. He has no bee in his bonnet about the Orthodox.'[2] It also helped the early relationship between the two that Garbacz had a child at the school. Aubrey Rosen, the JSSM's official treasurer, backed up Schonfeld, saying that Garbacz was a friend rather than a foe.

Schonfeld's initial praise for the receiver contrasted with his blend of persecution complex, paranoia and conspiracy theory when it came to the creditors. In attempting to explain the JSSM debts, Schonfeld was intemperate again when defending the movement: The claims were 'only inflictions that people have conjured up that we can't always face up to. They are not obligations, they're inventions, concocted impediments, from people who want to tear off another bit of our flesh.'[3] If he had been rational, he would have known very well that the claims were well documented and anything but spurious. On a radio programme he attacked Barnet Council and particularly Rosa Freedman: 'They are the devils because they have an anti-Orthodox woman at the head of the Committee.'[4] This was very unfair. Rosa Freedman might not have held Schonfeld's religious views, but she was a highly respectable woman and her husband was a good solicitor who had also served as mayor. She defended the council with dignity, saying, quite correctly, that they had done all they could to encourage all the schools in the borough and, certainly, Barnet had been patient in the extreme with the JSSM. She said the teachers and Council 'have done an excellent job under extremely difficult circumstances', which was true. Schonfeld and the Freedmans had met on several occasions and the latter told anyone who would listen how difficult he was. Rosa Freedman had met with him as late as September 1978 when the discussion had centred on state aid for the Girls' School. Schonfeld pressed her on the question of whether this would result in the school classes having to be mixed. Mrs Freedman was more concerned to write the following month to emphasize that the government would not pay for bringing the Boys' School up to scratch.

Schonfeld's language was not in any way calculated to help his cause. When he went on that the troubles were due to the fact that: 'nobody really wanted to help me', and complained of 'personal animosity against me and anti-Orthodox elements' he only made matters worse. He vigorously defended his opposition to the solution of amalgamating the boys' and girls' schools. He said he would 'not allow 14 year old girls to be deflowered by 16 year old boys'.[5] In fairness, if that was over-dramatic, it was not unknown in the country at large.

The JSSM debtors were also numerous. Garbacz soon discovered a considerable number of parents at the Girls' School who owed fees, many of whom had done so for several terms. Schonfeld would never have expelled a child because the fees were outstanding. As the accounting system was chaotic, the list of debtors had, unfortunately, been allowed to rise unchecked. The damage caused by the loss of Kestenbaum had come home to roost. When dealing with the fact that so many of the parents of the girls were not paying the correct fees, Schonfeld repeated the defence he had applied for the previous fifty years. He said that he might not have charged them, but he had given a good Jewish education to a lot of girls who could not otherwise afford it. In cases of financial hardship, this was undoubtedly true.

As was to be expected, the JSSM debts were detailed in official documents, sworn affidavits, court proceedings and legal correspondence. On Schonfeld's side there were no financial records. When Garbacz started to try to make sense of the JSSM accounts, he found no accounts books at all. If there had ever been any, they had disappeared. Many had gone in the burglary at the school in 1977. One accounts book had even disappeared from the offices of a former auditor. The choice of explanations was administrative inefficiency, a cover-up of malpractices, or burglars who stole accounts books to order. Effectively, Garbacz had to start from scratch to find out who was owed what. A receivership which he expected to last a year at most, stretched out to nearly three.

As the receiver, he, naturally, approached the Hon. Treasurers of the JSSM for help in sorting out the mess, but they had every reason to insist that they had been officers of the charity in name only. There was ample evidence from other officials that all the financial decisions had always been made by Schonfeld.

The views of the Jewish community were often introspective. Dayan Myer Lew, one of the most senior rabbis in the United Synagogue, said in the pulpit that it was 'very deplorable that the intervention of the Attorney General [on behalf of the Inland Revenue] had been invoked'. Dayan Lew was a distinguished rabbi but he had no apparent understanding of the Attorney General's responsibilities. Havers could well have responded that he was only trying to get the £34,390 which was owing to the Inland Revenue in tax. Barnet had paid the salaries of the Hasmonean secular-studies teachers. From the money they provided, tax and National Insurance had to be deducted; the latter came to £34,390 and it was well overdue. What had happened to the cheque Barnet had sent the school to pay the Inland Revenue, nobody knew or would ever admit finding out. As it must have been deducted from a Barnet Council bank account, it would have been easy to trace the account in which it had been lodged. Frankly, it could have gone to pay any one of dozens of outstanding bills. £34,000 was a lot of money, though; about £120,000 today. There obviously was the possibility that the money had been embezzled by one official or another. Whoever was responsible, it happened on Schonfeld's watch, so he was inevitably the one held accountable. Schonfeld could have gone to prison if the £34,000 had been used for other purposes than paying the tax and it clearly had. Nevertheless, what happened to the money was never made public.

Lew was, effectively, suggesting that the community should have stumped up the cash, so that the problems would never become public. It was true that the community had a common interest in burying this potential scandal, but the major question was, of course, who would come up with the money? The £200,000 that Garbacz spoke of would be £600,000 today.

Garbacz appealed to the community to volunteer. The main stumbling block was that potential donors were afraid that, if they did write a cheque, the money would not be properly handled by Schonfeld. He had been successfully raising money to improve the schools since 1933 but his financial credibility was now seriously in doubt. Nobody believed then, and nobody believes now, that a single penny of the missing money had ever been taken for Schonfeld's personal use, but the fact could not be gainsaid that at least £34,390 had not ended up with the taxman.

Schonfeld's public endorsement of Garbacz's appointment did not stand the test of much time. With Walter Stanton due to retire, there was a need to appoint a new headmaster. In fact, when the receiver was appointed, Dr Mett, an educational adviser, had also been recruited to help in that capacity, but he did not stay in the post for long. As the courts had given Garbacz total authority over the affairs of the JSSM, he had to deal with this problem as well. Schonfeld objected strongly to the receiver undermining him, in a matter that he still considered to be his responsibility. In a letter to Garbacz, Schonfeld wrote: 'So I discover that you have wolves' teeth hidden in your sheepskin mouth. I shall, therefore, only issue my ruling and send a copy of this letter to *The Jewish Chronicle*.'[6] Schonfeld's words were those of a very sick man.

If, logically, Schonfeld knew that he had been deprived of his power to run the JSSM as he felt best, he never acknowledged the fact. A deluge of letters flowed from his office, attempting to wrest the moral and legal high ground from the receiver. In his letter to Garbacz on a replacement for Stanton, he laid down his law: 'Please take note that any body, other than the governing body, defined in Paragraph 2 of both the Instrument and Articles of Government for Hasmonean, who purports to appoint a head teacher over any one of the Hasmonean schools, will be guilty of false pretences, and any individual so "appointed" is not appointed.'

There are echoes of Shakespeare's King Lear: 'I will have such revenges on you both ... I will do such things – what they are yet I know not – but they shall be the terrors of the earth.' He had rescued the rabbis by persuading the Home Office to grant the visas, he had saved the Kindertransport children from the Nazis, he was convinced he had the Almighty on his side and he had, therefore, always believed that no task was too great. His lifelong creed was that he would never give in. For those who owed him their lives, who had supported his efforts to develop the JSSM against all the odds, for those who grudgingly admired him, and even for his enemies, it was a tragedy of Homeric proportions to see the disintegration of a great man. The debilitating effects of his illness were daily becoming more difficult to throw off and everybody recognized that he really could not be held responsible for his actions. Judith, a silent bystander, must have suffered acutely from his decline. Nevertheless, the law had to take its course.

Schonfeld certainly went down fighting. Garbacz did his best to cushion the fall. He had indeed sent his sons to Hasmonean and respected Schonfeld's achievements. He never failed to treat Schonfeld with the utmost courtesy. At the same time he had to do his job and Schonfeld was not helping. He was very ill, but he rallied for a last hurrah; over his dead body was anybody going to take the total control of the JSSM away from him. For most of the next year he fought Garbacz tooth and nail in the courts. From October 1979 until August 1980 he instituted six court cases to try to overturn the actions of the receiver. In the winter of the previous year Schonfeld had fired his solicitors and this certainly did not help. Now, in October, Schonfeld challenged Garbacz's right to appoint a head teacher for the Girls' School. Schonfeld did not turn up in court and he lost. 'It is quite clear', said the Vice Chancellor, Mr Justice Megarry, 'that the authority of the receiver must include the ability to appoint teachers, including head teachers'. In February Megarry granted an injunction to prevent Schonfeld from interfering in Garbacz's work. Again, Schonfeld did not attend.

Garbacz had needed the support of the court because, as he wrote to Schonfeld: 'you have been soliciting sums of money from various individuals ... indicating to the donors concerned that the moneys you were collecting were on behalf of the Jewish Secondary School Movement'. If money was raised, it was for Garbacz to use it to pay the creditors, not Schonfeld.

Schonfeld reacted angrily that he was 'prepared to take up your sordid information as it so vividly reflects my own challenge against your organisation [the Jewish Educational Development Trust] of which you are an advertised trustee'. There were no grounds at all for confusing Garbacz's two roles and indeed Garbacz had written to the JEDT the month before when they had said that the organization was: 'not prepared, at present, to offer its help to the JSSM, as was done previously'. Garbacz asked publicly: 'How can they spend £2 million on a primary school in Kingsbury and not see the merit of investing £165,000 – even on a short term loan basis – to restore the financial credibility of the JSSM.'

Garbacz knew the answer; it was because of the independence of the JSSM from the JEDT schools, which Schonfeld had not been prepared to surrender in any way. The total independence of the JSSM educational efforts had made him many enemies. In fairness, the JEDT had bailed him out handsomely once before. That had not solved the problem for long, though, and a group of high-powered businessmen were not about to send good money after bad.

Schonfeld retained a great deal of affection, even in these difficult days. On Chanukah in December 1979 the JSSM held its annual service at the Synagogue on the second day of the festival. Schonfeld took the service and the boys and girls, together with past members of the schools, made up a congregation of 1,100 to show their regard for him. Schonfeld addressed them, as usual, as 'Young ladies and young gentlemen' but he realized this would be one of the last occasions he would see them. As he told them from the pulpit: 'I am an old man. I won't last very much longer.' It was an occasion with very sad undertones, but the attendance was a wonderful illustration of the affection in which Schonfeld was still held.

In March 1980 the battle continued. Early in the month Megarry told Schonfeld to send the court a list of the contributions he had received. This time Schonfeld appeared before Mr Justice Goulding and conducted his own case. He said he was only trying to help repay the debts by raising money: 'Does the receiver want to remain receiver forever?' He also opposed the appointment of Rabbi Moshe Young to be Head of the Girls' School. 'No man can be headmaster of the girls' school. It is not our way.' The judge found against Schonfeld and mildly complained that he found the rabbi's language 'immoderate' and his behaviour 'ill advised'. He said that 'Like many men of advancing years, he saw only his own viewpoint'. Schonfeld was ordered to pay costs.

Even the courts, though, were as gentle as possible with Schonfeld. Like Garbacz, they were not about to kick a man when he was down. Schonfeld, however, continued to fail to recognize the true position. When he still had the chance to influence the future, he did not take it. In April, Mr Justice Whitford had told Garbacz to have a scheme for the future administration of the JSSM settled in chambers before bringing it to the court for approval. He said in passing that it was: 'a matter of great regret' that Schonfeld had not come to court again. Schonfeld could have played a part in the development of a plan for the future, but he let the opportunity slip. Perhaps nobody knew how ill he was, least of all himself.

In July a year had passed since Garbacz's appointment and Schonfeld was back in court again. This time he was appealing against the March decision to stop him interfering with Garbacz's work. Lord Justices Templeman and Brightman took one look at the list of other complaints that Schonfeld wanted to discuss and held that they were not a quorum. He ought to have three Lords of Appeal, not the two of them. The counsel for the Attorney General pointed out that further litigation would be the 'greatest disincentive' for contributions to be obtained to pay the debts, but the Appeal Judges did not agree. Schonfeld would have his full rights and Schonfeld responded 'God bless you, my Lord'. Money – that nobody had – was being spent like water on legal fees, but the tragedy would drag on into a further act.

At last, in August, Templeman and Brightman were joined by Lord Justice Buckley and heard Schonfeld plead extravagantly that 'to impose a receiver on a human being is a reversion to slavery'. He dismissed the JEDT as the 'Jewish Educational Demolition Trust' and said that they had blocked funds from the Clore Foundation which had been provided to help settle the Girls' School's debts. He returned to the subject of Rabbi Young's appointment at the Girls' School. 'It's not the Puritan way – we don't want them running around in their knickers when a headmaster is in the hall.' Such inappropriate language was unlikely to carry much weight with Lords of Appeal. Templeman summed up. He acknowledged Schonfeld's great record of service to the Jewish community, but said that he 'had no understanding of English law when it came to the appointment of trustees'. The truth was, though, that Schonfeld had now deteriorated to a stage where logic and common sense had deserted him.

Once again costs were granted against Schonfeld and the judges mercifully refused him permission to appeal a hopeless case to the House of Lords. Schonfeld had fought and lost every action in the last year and now he had come to the end of the legal road. Garbacz would have breathed a sigh of relief whilst bitterly regretting the humiliation that Schonfeld had brought upon himself, the waste of time and the immense waste of money.

Another unresolved question is where did the money come from to pay all the legal bills? Schonfeld might have done his own legal work and friendly solicitors might not have charged for their time. Nevertheless, he was up against QCs and the expenses can mount up if you have to pay the other side's costs. The expenses must have been very high and Schonfeld, everybody agreed, never had any money, personally. Where he might have used the funds of the JSSM for legal cases in years gone by, he was no longer able to do so. The finances of the JSSM were now firmly in the hands of Garbacz. So somewhere in the background there must have been supporters, still willing even at this point to back him with hard cash. They asked for no credit for their generosity, but the school structure Schonfeld had built up over many years would never have got off the ground without the support of quiet and devoted helpers behind the scenes. Men like Freddy Greenwood, Victor Hochhauser, Jack Lunzer, Bernard Kahn, Louis Mintz, Benny and Adolf Schmidt-Bodner, Sam Stebba and Sir Sigmund Sternberg – to name just a few of his long-term backers (and with apologies for those omitted) – who had made very substantial contributions to the success of the JSSM over the years. Schonfeld still retained their affection and gratitude. These debts so many people owed him for the lives of themselves and their families, made any argument about the merits of his handling of the JSSM finances of little import. Certainly, nobody has ever suggested that the legal costs were not paid, so the money had to come from somewhere.

As soon as Garbacz had been appointed, he started to try to raise the funds he needed to settle the JSSM debts. In October 1979 he wrote an open letter to the community:

> I need £165,000 to pay off creditors, the majority of whom are not members of the Jewish faith, and if they are not paid in full and quickly, it will be to the everlasting shame of the Anglo-Jewish community. Consequently, there is no way that I will ask the court to sanction any scheme of reconstruction for the JSSM unless all creditors are paid in full.

As far as Garbacz was concerned there would be no arrangement by which the creditors would be asked to settle for so much in the pound. If they were due the money, Garbacz expected the community to come up with it all. Initially, the appeal effectively fell on deaf ears. Three months later only £9,000 had been raised. Garbacz wrote to both the

Chief Rabbi and the President of the Board of Deputies to express his 'total disillusionment' at the community's reaction to the problems of the JSSM.

Eventually, Garbacz was reduced to threatening to close the Girls' School unless the parents gave him substantial help. In 1980 there was £16,000 owing in unpaid fees. Only 140 of the 310 girls in the school were paying the full fees while the other 170 were either paying reduced fees or nothing at all 'on the basis that either they cannot afford to do so, or will not pay'. Garbacz also threatened to post a list of thoseparents in arrears on the school notice board. As a result, at an emergency meeting in November 1980, donations and pledges totalling £26,000 were forthcoming. The position was still deteriorating, however. Garbacz pointed out to the parents that the running costs of the Girls' School were £90,000 a year but fees produced only £55,000.

The support that the receiver had every right to expect from the three Adath communities who were trustees of the school was simply not forthcoming initially. Garbacz pointed out that families affiliated to one of the Adath communities were allowed to pay reduced fees, and these amounted to a subsidy of £21,000 a year. It was a gift that the JSSM could no longer afford.

The reaction to the threat of closure was as expected. *The Jewish Chronicle* was highly critical: 'If the Hasmonean Grammar School for Girls closes at the end of this term ... it will be a damning indictment of the Orthodox community, more particularly that part of it identified with the Union of Orthodox Hebrew Congregations and the Adath.' As so many of the children came from United Synagogue homes, this was too narrow a criticism; if correct, the leadership at the United Synagogue should have been equally subject to the same damning indictment.

Eventually, there was an agreed solution that all the debts would be initially settled through a temporary loan of £200,000 from the Israeli Bank Le'umi. In a year or so Garbacz was able to pay off the loan after prolonged negotiations with the JSSM trustee communities. There were also many generous benefactors who agreed to come out of the woodwork when it became obvious that Schonfeld would have no say in the way their gifts were utilized.

One of the Conservative ministers in the Department of Education, Sir Rhodes Boyson, also weighed in and saw to it that the Girls' School got state aid in 1984, thus stopping the main cause of the JSSM's continuing financial haemorrhaging. It surely had to help as well that Margaret Thatcher, the Prime Minister, was MP for nearby Finchley and that there are more Jews in Barnet than anywhere else in the country. If that seems overly pragmatic, what the JSSM had lacked for years was a healthy dose of pragmatism.

In 1982 Garbacz was able to tell the court that his job was done and that he could be released from his responsibilities. He was not sorry. Apart from the stress of public debate, which was often unfairly and irresponsibly antagonistic towards his approach, he found that four or five visits a week to the schools were necessary to ensure that the right policies were in place and being followed. Sorting out the mess had been three years of hard work but Garbacz was satisfied; the schools would continue now under more prudent financial controls.

When considering the whole unhappy episode, one point tends to be overlooked: that the JSSM's assets far exceeded its liabilities. The value of the school premises as real estate ran into the millions, and that value was the result of efforts over the years which were led by Schonfeld. The Boys' School was valued in 1979 at £1.5 million, Page Street was worth £2 million and other school property a further £2.5 million. If, before state aid, the Girls' School had been moved to a smaller site, or even closed, the value of the Page Street acreage would have eliminated the JSSM's debts ten times over. The Movement was not, however, a commercial enterprise. It remained – and still remains – more of a sacred trust, dedicated to preserving and expanding a special form of education.

It is a matter of conjecture whether any other British ethnic and religious community would have considered the financial problems of its faith schools to be a personal responsibility. Sufficient numbers of the Jewish community did. Psychologists might well have a field day writing theses on why they felt that way. The answer has to be that they were in a tiny minority: while most of the Jewish community did not feel it was their responsibility to stave off the threat of Garbacz's everlasting shame, in the end, there were sufficient religious men and women who did. If any of the creditors were Jewish and uncommitted, they should have been grateful that not everybody held their views.

When Garbacz handed over responsibility for Hasmonean to the new governing body, the Boys' School still had 570 pupils on a site which was too small for that number, but the roll was, at last, far more in keeping with the agreement reached with the Council nearly fifteen years before. There were now thirty-two full-time and twelve part-time staff under the leadership of Meir Roberg as Head Master. Jewish studies occupied 25 per cent of the curriculum and, on the secular side, the school took pride in its new zoology laboratory and the advanced science laboratory. In a report issued at the time there was the pious hope that 'the school will move to a new site within the next few years',[7] but at the time of writing that has not happened. As the level of public morality has continued to decline, in terms of underage abortions nationally, it is not surprising that the Charedim have been in no hurry to merge their schools.

When Garbacz left the scene, the Girls' School had 316 pupils, with seventeen full-time and twenty-seven part-time staff. This was less than for the boys, but the girls only took Jewish studies for eight hours a week, so fewer teachers were needed for that part of the curriculum. The school was soon able to point to a 75 per cent pass record for O Levels and 90 per cent for A Levels, as the perceived need to leave before reaching the sixth form receded. Both schools were performing well and have continued to do so. They are officially regarded as one six-form-entry school which just happens to be housed in two different locations.

Kibo died in 1981, aged only 63, but Zuzanna would live for another twenty years. In the autumn of 1981 Solly had to go back to the Middlesex Hospital where he had had the original operation, to have his condition checked. He was not happy there and he did not put up with the situation for long. On Yom Kippur, with the remnants of his old iron determination, he discharged himself, tottering into the street in his pyjamas and dressing gown and hailing a taxi to take him home. It was obvious that his mind was now seriously disturbed and he had become very difficult for Judith to handle.

In February 1982 he reached his 70th birthday. A big celebration was planned at Hendon Synagogue but Schonfeld did not feel well enough to attend it. Judith Grunfeld urged him to go and another of his old friends, Lady Hazel Sternberg, a relation by marriage, added her voice and picked him up in her car to take him to the party. It was a tremendous gathering, designed to recognize all he had achieved, and as one journalist wrote: 'If everyone who owes something to Schonfeld were to turn up, they could fill the Albert Hall.' The synagogue was full of ghosts. Samson Raphael Hirsch who had inspired Avigdor, Avigdor himself, Ella, 'the Queen Mother', Israel Kestenbaum and David Gestetner who had supported him initially, Harry Goodman, Michoel Ber Weissmandl and Joseph Hertz, his father-in-law. Many of his long-time allies were in the hall, particularly Judith Grunfeld.

The event was too much for him. He was uncertain where he was, left early and from that night on his condition deteriorated markedly. He started to shake and his speech became unclear. He began to repeat himself and though he spoke with deliberation, too often now what he said made no sense. His walking became more unsteady, even with his stick, until he eventually had to take to a wheelchair. Initially it was possible for Judith to look after him but soon it became necessary for him to have round-the-clock nursing. Handrails were installed in the house and the wider family settled down to deal with a steadily worsening situation. At Christmas one of the nurses took him in her car to see the lights. He could no longer speak but his pleasure was clear.

Technically, Schonfeld had obstructive hydrocephalus with an extensive peri-ventricular oedema. In layman's terms, he had water on the brain. This is a natural condition, but it is usually dispersed through a channel which, in Schonfeld's case, had become partially blocked. It is possible to put a tube into the brain and drain the fluid off in that way, but Schonfeld's condition had deteriorated to a point where it was decided that this would not do any good. His illness was almost certainly linked to the tumour he had suffered twenty years previously.

The cost of looking after Schonfeld was horrendous for the family. In 1982 the nursing bill was £20,628 (the equivalent of £50,000 today). Family and friends paid for just over half of it. In 1983 it cost another £20,000 and the shortfall was another £10,000. Judith Grunfeld sent out appeal letters to the thousands who owed their lives to Schonfeld's efforts before and after the war. Most of her appeals fell on deaf ears, for there are none so deaf as those who will not hear. If Solly had known, he would have shrugged. He had performed the *mitzvot*, he had saved the lives, he had been inspired and supported by the Almighty; that would have been enough.

In December 1983 he had a brain-stem stroke and his doctors gave him two weeks to live at the most. He slipped quietly into what appeared to be a coma for the next eight weeks, with members of his close family and some of his old friends sitting by his bedside all the time. Kibo's recently bereaved widow, Zuzanna, came from seven till ten most mornings, sharing shifts with Judith and her sons. As David Rosenfield, a passenger on the Kindertransport recalled later: 'I sat with him for hours when he was ill'. The Chevra Kadishah of the Adath sat with him at night, reciting psalms or studying Torah.

For many there was so little which could be done to repay the debt they would always owe him. Towards the end both his nurse in the hospital and his son, Jeremy, were still sure he could hear what was being said, though he could not respond. In his last days the marks of the anxiety and tension left his face. He lay waiting to die in peace. He passed away at 8.00 in the evening on 4 Adar, 6 February 1984, which happened to be his Hebrew birthday. It is a rabbinic tradition that to die on one's birthday is a sign of particular virtue. That would have meant a lot to Solly.

The official cause of death was bronchopneumonia, which the

medical profession refers to as the Old Man's Friend. The pneumonia puts an end to all the suffering and certainly it comes as a blessed release to many patients.

It was estimated that as many as 1,000 people went to the funeral at the Adath cemetery in Cheshunt. The Adath waived their usual fees and the consecration of the tombstone in March 1985 was also massively attended. Judith Grunfeld might have wondered where all the support had come from, which was so noticeably missing when she'd made her appeal to defray the cost of the nursing.

When the Chief Rabbi, Immanuel Jakobovits, was told of Schonfeld's death, a mutual friend lamented that it was the end of a chapter. Jakobovits corrected him. He said, 'You are wrong. That's the end of a book.'[8]

NOTES

1. *The Jewish Chronicle*, 20 July 1979.
2. *The Jewish Chronicle*, 27 July 1979.
3. Ibid.
4. BBC Radio London, 'You don't have to be Jewish', September 1979.
5. *The Jewish Chronicle*, 17 August 1979.
6. *The Jewish Chronicle*, 5 October 1979.
7. Derek Taylor (ed.), *Jewish Education 1981/1982* (London: Jewish Educational Development Trust, 1982).
8. Joe Lobenstein in conversation with the author.

# 11 Epilogue

On the fourth floor of the Hartley Library at Southampton University is the Special Collections Division, within which there are the collected papers of Solomon Schonfeld, kept in no less than 800 boxes. Amongst the documents that can be studied are the Minute Books of the Chief Rabbi's Religious Emergency Council, the certificates of Schonfeld's semicha, a vast array of letters from his mother in Israel and all his working files. These include such details as the history of his father's last illness, the letter agreeing to settle Ms Grolman's breach of promise accusation, and Solomon Schonfeld's last blue British passport. The archive is as comprehensive as any researcher could possibly wish.

Indeed, it is remarkable that so much has survived. How many letters do people keep for fifty years? How many organizations have a full history of their work over half a century? Why did Schonfeld never throw anything away? Why did he hoard it all, as if the faded papers and the worn notebooks were as precious as diamonds? Particularly as, in life, he always insisted on looking to the coming years rather than the past.

Perhaps he saw the records as his legacy. What he really valued in his lifetime were the results of the work he had done, and it could be that he left all the details behind for posterity. It is very common to want to leave a record, even if he did say that only the future was important. The archives are a kind of genizah too; the rule is that documents in Hebrew are not to be thrown away. So they are kept in a spare room or even a tomb, because the language is holy. Perhaps, to Schonfeld, because he believed he was doing the work of the Almighty, he might feel the details should also be kept intact. He kept it all: both material which was favourable to him, and also some which a man, anxious only to maintain his reputation after his death, might have thrown in the fire.

Schonfeld never wrote his memoirs and when it was suggested that he should, he replied: 'Certainly not. If I were to blow my own trumpet the Almighty wouldn't do what I wanted any more.' When he died, however, his praises were trumpeted from all quarters. He had been a self-starter all his life and what he had planted would continue to bear fruit in the years to come.

There was no need to put his antiques, jewellery, gold sovereigns and share certificates in a safe deposit, because he had none of these. He was only rich beyond the dreams of avarice in terms of the lives he had saved and the quality of the education he had provided for so many thousands of young people. He was immensely successful in his efforts to keep the flame of his Orthodox beliefs shining brightly on his Charedi bridge. When he gave up the helm, the numbers of the Charedim continued to rise substantially every year, but it is the founders of any movement who have the most difficult task. If he ever wondered whether it had all been worthwhile, the great piles of documents could have reassured him that it had, even if he would always have fretted that he might have achieved more.

Throughout the ranks of the Charedim and beyond, Schonfeld was a great man, but in what did his greatness lie? Not in the events of his last years. Henry V, the victor of Agincourt, is recognized as one of our greatest warrior kings, but then Henry was lucky. He died at the age of 35, just seven years after the great battle. It was the long-forgotten Henry VI who had to deal with the economic havoc caused by his father's extravagant war. Schonfeld lived out his full life span and died far from the limelight, without the peerage Victor Hochhauser had tried to get for him, and without the financial support he so richly deserved from so many of those whose lives he had saved. His schools, over which he had slaved for nearly fifty years, had been taken from him by the courts, and given to younger, fitter, equally professional and, therefore, more competent men to run. He lost his last court battle in August 1980 and was dead three and a half years later, in February 1984.

The Union of Orthodox Hebrew Congregations has also changed. No longer is the organization wedded to Samson Raphael Hirsch's *Torah im derech eretz* philosophy. The more isolationist philosophy of the Chassidim is in the ascendant within the Charedi ranks. All the evidence is that Schonfeld never fought the Chassidim because they were heading in the direction he favoured. He far preferred this to the continual lowering of standards in Jewish observance which characterized a larger proportion of the Jewish community in Britain in his early years. He certainly valued the cultures of other civilizations, but whilst the *Torah im derech eretz* approach encouraged such a marriage, the dominant partner would always be the Torah, the Talmud and the Shulchan Aruch. Schonfeld never had any problem with that.

There seems little doubt, however, that, while Schonfeld would never fight the Chassidic approach, he never belonged to that way of thinking himself. He was recognized within the UOHC in his later years as not quite being 'one of us'. Where, for example, Rabbi Dunner's obituary in *The Times* would point to the fact that he very seldom strayed outside the confines of the community, the same could never be said for Schonfeld. He not only tried to keep open his contacts with those that were Orthodox but less observant – the United Synagogue members – but he also wanted to keep up his contacts with the non-Jewish authorities.

With increased affluence the move to the right changed the Adath and the UOHC. Many of the community's foremost families in the 1930s left the Stoke Newington district for more prosperous neighbourhoods. A considerable number are to be found today in Hampstead and they seem to have in common a feeling of betrayal; that in moving to the right from *Torah im derech eretz*, something precious has been lost. Equally, of course, after the war the Chassidim mourned the loss of the towering structure of Talmudic learning which had taken so long to build up in countries like Poland, Czechoslovakia and Hungary, and which perished in the concentration camps. Their aim was to rebuild it anew. There was an immense determination to replace those who had died, but the outside world was rejected, partially because it had proved totally unable to prevent the calamity.

Schonfeld, too, had seen the horrors at first hand. He had, for example, lost his friends in Slobodka, where he went to study for his semicha. There were 25,000 Jews in that town in 1933. In 1959 there were 5,000 who had settled after the war. About fifteen of the Schonfeld and Sternberg uncles, aunts and cousins were killed as well. Schonfeld grieved, but he was fortunate. He had the behaviour of the British people to prove to him every day that some nations did observe moral and ethical codes. He knew there was no need to withdraw into a shell in Britain, but he could not be expected to persuade those who had suffered so grievously that this was always going to be the case.

'It could happen here' was a popular refrain in many Jewish families, because the Final Solution had come out of the blue in their Continental homelands. The refugees would be wary of trusting any country in future, even one with the unblemished record of the British over three centuries. Like the Jews in the Wilderness, the generation of slaves – to fear in this case – would have to die out before the confidence of the community could be restored. And in the meantime, most would pass on their fears to their children.

The Chassidim knew Schonfeld's views, they respected his efforts on their behalf, but he was an obstacle to the line they wanted to take. Schonfeld became more peripheral to his community in his later years, as his intellectual powers declined after the operation to remove the tumour. On the other hand, in his last years at the helm of the JSSM, many of his colleagues suffered from what is now called Founder's Syndrome – the inability of an organization to be rid of a leader who has become a liability.

Schonfeld's claim to greatness will stand the test of time, perhaps more for his educational achievements than for anything else. Single-handedly he managed to change the perception of Jewish schooling for the Jewish community in Britain. When he started his work for the JSS in the 1930s, for the vast majority of British Jews, Jewish schools were *infra dig*. The mainstream would look down on those who were reduced to giving their children such a second class education. The only exceptions where a Jewish environment was acceptable were at two public schools where it was possible for minute numbers of rich children to combine a modicum of Jewish studies with the full panoply of secular education. The Jews' Free School was also acceptable for those who could not afford a public school for their children, but it was not considered to be of a sufficiently high academic standard. This increasingly was not true but, at the time, the JFS's reputation was rooted in its past.

By 1984 when Schonfeld died, the whole image of Jewish schools had been massively improved. Instead of being discussed behind closed curtains and amidst sniggers, they were on their way to becoming the choice for one third of the Jewish children in Britain. New schools had been built by the massive efforts of the JEDT, but the man who had made Jewish schools respectable to an increasingly middle-class community was Schonfeld. If he had not shown what could be achieved by the success of the Hasmonean Schools, Jakobovits would have found it far more difficult to get the support he needed from the powerful industrialists who supported him, or to fill the schools when they were built.

The difficulties of his last years – the financial chaos, the receivership, the lost court cases, the debilitating illnesses – give the impression that his life ended sadly and in personal failure. That was not the case at all. On the grand scale, it was precisely in those years that he won his lifelong battle – to change the perception of Jewish education for large swathes of the Jewish community. As his powers waned and failed, the applications for school places soared.

As one obituarist summed it up, 'Jewish education was considered eccentric in the 1930s. Anyone without his stamina, determination and self-assurance would have given up.'[1] Only Schonfeld had the necessary 'stamina, determination and self-assurance'. Of course he was a maverick. According to one of his strongest supporters: 'He stood no nonsense – or what he regarded as nonsense. He had an innate disdain for committees and displayed little love for democracy.'[2]

In addition, Schonfeld put advanced Jewish studies, as part of a lifestyle, back on its rightful pedestal for thousands of people. When the sixth formers left Hasmonean at the end of his tenure, a large number of them would go on to university, but a sizeable proportion of them would go first to yeshiva. Yeshiva and university were put on adjoining educational pedestals. That was down to Schonfeld too and, in later life, the lessons they had learned at school were not forgotten.

Not all the credit, of course, belongs solely to Schonfeld. He could not have achieved his objectives without the generous financial help of a wide range of supporters; the Lunzers, the Kestenbaums, Kahn, Greenwood, the Sternbergs and many, many others. He had over the years the dedicated support of any number of teachers who put the importance they gave to religious education above their standards of living; Judith Grunfeld, Walter Stanton and Meir Roberg were just three leaders of that large and dedicated team.

What all his supporters would agree on though was that, without Schonfeld, it would not have been possible to win the battle for the minds of the community. On his 70th birthday Chaim Bermant was given the job of summing up Schonfeld for *The Jewish Chronicle*. He repeated the words of the Rabbi's critics: 'He's impossible ... aggressive, intolerant, arrogant, a fanatic, a bigot, a trouble maker, irresponsible'. Bermant pointed out in addition, however, that his old friend was 'One of God's Cossacks'. Schonfeld would have had no argument with this. As he told the congregation from the Dollis Hill synagogue pulpit once: 'Everything is too peaceful. Let us get together and have troublemakers for Judaism. Let us have contested elections. Let us run down a few people.' The status quo he encountered originally was leading to mass assimilation. To shift its progress into a new direction was never going to be possible without a substantial input of verbal dynamite.

There was, of course, another side to Schonfeld. In an article in 1986, after Schonfeld's death, Bermant quoted one of the children rescued after the war:

> He was like a God in his uniform. He looked absolutely wonderful ... he had this twinkle in his eye ... he was so human, such a warm person. He could have been a film star. I adored him.

Admittedly, Schonfeld was a better man to have on your side than against you. Was he, fundamentally, undemocratic though? His own view on the subject was printed in his *Universal Bible* in 1955. 'Democracy has its limited uses, but the ultimate government of the people for the people should be by the wise and the good, however few they might be.' Bermant added to this reference: 'And his working definition of a wise, or indeed, a good man, would be somebody who agreed with him.' On balance, Schonfeld was not a practicing democrat.

Bermant felt he had the answer to one of the crucial questions about Schonfeld's life. He wrote: 'he has never had a full outlet for his abilities, ambition and almost explosive energies. He was ... like a war horse harnessed to a Brougham and the experience was good neither for himself nor, indeed for the Brougham.' This comment was amusing journalism but way off the mark. If the Brougham was the Kindertransport or the JSSM, a war horse was needed to lead the charge of a very light brigade of believers and Schonfeld filled the role admirably.

One of the threads that runs through Schonfeld's life was that he did not have Hamlet's problem. Schonfeld never had any intention of meekly suffering 'the slings and arrows of outrageous fortune'. As far as he was concerned the job was 'to take arms against a sea of troubles and, by opposing, end them'. His methods of opposing them might vary, but the determination to go that route never wavered. Schonfeld is remembered for being extremely confrontational. In his youth, he confronted by means of skilful negotiation, charm, intelligence and persistence. In later years, though, he would, on many occasions, in marked contrast, confront for the sake of confrontation and do it clumsily.

It could not have been through bad luck, anti-Semitism or vicious opponents that he went to court so many times in his later years. He seemed to get withdrawal symptoms if he was not regularly addressing a judge. The setting held so many attractions for him. It was not just that in court he occupied the limelight, which he had lost in his normal life as his powers and authority waned. It was also that, every time he was in court, he was mixing with the good and the great again. No matter how often he lost, no matter the criticism levelled at his head by judges and lawyers, during those days in court he was important again in the wider world. He would be reported in the newspapers, his views would be read and he would get relief for the frustration every opinionated individual suffers from their inability to change the world to their point of view.

Confrontation boosted Schonfeld's self-esteem. Increasingly sidelined, respected but ignored, he needed to prove to himself that he still counted – and confrontation was one way of doing this. It would have been a classic response to the position in which he found himself, when his power base collapsed with the end of the CRREC and the death of Hertz.

What does seem a sad loss is that, as a consequence, there were few brand new conquests after 1960, when he was only 48. The best executive years of Schonfeld's life may have produced a marvellous result in the schools but they did not constitute a fresh challenge. The thought always remained with him that, perhaps, he could have done even more, given the opportunity. On the other hand, his health diminished and it is to that weakness that the comparative lack of new initiatives in his later life should fairly be attributed. After the operation in 1965, his decision making was often impaired and even the most successful CEOs, given their few years in the sun in their 50s, need good health to make the most of them.

What Schonfeld put into the balance to outweigh his shortcomings was leadership, determination, belief, positive thinking, a vast love of children, immense kindness and a capacity for work which was still of a high quality for many years after his terrible illness struck him down. Schonfeld was a great salesman. He begged for money all his adult life and he had the disadvantage that he did not raise it for one of the more popular Jewish charities like supporting Israel or for the handicapped within the Jewish community. He begged for an initially unfashionable, widely denigrated and unglamorous cause: Jewish schools. Fortunately, he had a remarkable, instinctive understanding of the principles of marketing. He appreciated the need for the endorsement of his product by those in the public eye; the national leaders who were prepared to associate their names with the schools. He also knew the value of maximizing the image of a product by making it sound larger than it was.

It was Schonfeld who created the Needy Clergy War Fund, the Jewish Soldiers Services, the Jewish Internees Welfare Organisation, the National Council for Rescue from Nazi Terror, the post-war Religious Reconstruction Fund, the Committee for Proclaiming Jewish Ethics, the European Union of Orthodox Jewish Congregations and the Community Centres for Israel organization. They all sounded impressive, even if, on occasions, there was not much substance behind the letterhead on the note paper. Schonfeld might have been contemptuously dismissed as a *schnorrer* by his critics, but that was carping. Like the Biblical prophets he successfully sold his visions and beliefs to a lot of the people.

Behind all the grandiose titles there was always to be found the same driving force, the one man who knew what needed doing and pretended a mass of other people did too. Schonfeld also succeeded because he had the priceless belief that he was doing the work of the Almighty. Everything was possible for him simply because of that. It was what he had in common with all his supporters; they all had the same confidence. It is always possible that, on occasions, he may have mistaken the Almighty's message, but his faith was the powerhouse which drove him on.

For those who have no similar conviction, it is, perhaps, difficult even to contemplate that such motivation is genuinely possible. In a scientific, materialist, hedonistic age of world powers and power blocs, it is very easy to believe that no one man can make a difference and that without the strength of committees, associations, parties and armies there will be no progress. Schonfeld believed that one man, given enough determination, could make a difference. He proved it triumphantly before, during and after the war.

In retrospect, it was not the number of lives that Schonfeld saved that was so remarkable. It was the fact that he saved *any*. That *he* saved any. Not this committee or that organization. Although Schonfeld's power base was the CRREC, that was always a facade for Schonfeld himself. He was the powerhouse and his was the innovative mind behind the work.

The formation of the CRREC started the Schonfeld legend, which would last the remainder of his life and which still survives. Schonfeld saved several thousand lives, but in a decade during which nearly 30 million died in the Second World War, a few thousand is not a very large number. The bureaucratic machinery of Anglo-Jewry saved many times that number and got precious little credit for it, when the bones of the history of the pre-war efforts came to be picked over. Why Schonfeld and not Otto Schiff, Norman Bentwich or Neville Laski? There were a number of reasons.

First, Schonfeld was a one-man band. He had a large number of devoted helpers but there was only one leader. The CRREC was not a committee organization. Schonfeld was never a very good chair of a committee. The Council was a commando group headed by one charismatic Scarlet Pimpernel. In his younger days, when Schonfeld did his best work, it was usually when he could make final decisions without much outside involvement.

Second, Schonfeld became best known for the children he saved – many referred to them as Schonfeld's children – and there is far more publicity mileage in a trainload of children than in a much larger number of adults. Of course, he saved many adults as well, but the children were the main story.

Third, Schonfeld epitomized the possibility of the underdog winning against immeasurably superior opponents. He was Peter Pan, rescuing the potential victims from the implacable enemy. He was Robin Hood too, taking entry visas from the rich and powerful establishment leaders and giving them to the often neglected Orthodox minorities. He was Superman, solving impossible bureaucratic problems with innovative thinking, which nobody else matched. He was built like a hero, he behaved like a hero, and the forces massed against him crumbled a little in the face of his determination.

Schonfeld was not, however, taken in by his own image and reputation. When asked in later life how many people he had saved, he replied 'How many *didn't* I save?' His record shows he would never have been complacent enough to think there was nothing more he could have done. Missed opportunities would have upset him for years after. It is also true that in those terrible years between 1933 and 1945 it was vitally important to believe that victory was possible, no matter how unlikely it looked. By all the rules of warfare Britain should have been beaten. That she won was not just down to Hitler's blunder over Dunkirk (Von Runstedt, the German General, was stopped by Hitler from getting to the port first). It was not just because of the superiority of the Spitfire and the determination of the British people. It was because the British believed Churchill when he said they could win. And many saw in legends, like Schonfeld, the power of the individual to snatch victory from the jaws of defeat.

There is also the point that it's much more difficult to feel loyalty, affection and respect for an organization, than it is for a charismatic individual. You could see, listen to, shake hands with and applaud Schonfeld. It was far less easy to do the same with any bureaucratic body, in spite of the great work the Jewish agencies carried out and the enormous efforts they made. The press always tries to get a human element into a good news story. With Schonfeld that was easy.

Schonfeld's other remarkable achievement was the increase in the size of the Charedi community in Britain. There are two ways of developing a community; first, people can have lots of children. Charedi families have always been large but the aftermath of the Holocaust gave them an extra impetus. Their determined and incredible long-term aim was to replace the six million Jews who had died in the Holocaust. Only by doing so could they show the world that Hitler's Final Solution had achieved nothing. They set out to have large families.

The other way was to evangelize, something that has not been on the Jewish agenda for centuries. In fact, it has produced enormous problems in an Orthodox Jewish context for at least 1,000 years, simply because it's very difficult indeed to convert to Judaism. Not only do Orthodox Jews not encourage converts, but also there are not that many people willing to convert in the first place, particularly considering the way the Jews have been treated over the centuries. So the only way to increase the size of the community is by getting Jews from less Orthodox backgrounds to join the Charedi communities.

When he started on his task, Schonfeld inherited a public relations image for the Charedim which had a number of negatives. Of these, poor, foreign, common and extreme were top of the list. To a considerable extent, it was the Hasmonean pupils who slowly but surely changed the brand recognition within the community. The schools produced hundreds of doctors, accountants and lawyers. A high proportion of them prospered in business. In days of yore this would have led to a lot of them leaving the religion in order to progress further, by gaining acceptance into society and by conforming to the religious beliefs of the majority population. This is what had happened to any number in the past, who had been educated at Christian public and grammar schools. It still does and in large measure. But most of the Hasmonean former pupils were cast in a different mould and were helped to stay within the ranks of Orthodox Jewry because they lived in a more multi-racial society. The pressure to conform to the majority view was much lower. The majority of them were happy in their Orthodoxy and they had had dedicated teachers to educate them in the Charedi way of life. They showed others, by example, the advantages of greater observance, in terms of Jewish family life, high moral and ethical standards and strong, integrated communities. Alongside Schonfeld and with his encouragement, Joseph Dunner transformed the possibility of higher education for women in the community; the practice of going to Sem.

Over a long period of time, the continuous movement in the community as a whole, away from observance of the mitzvoth, was brought to a halt. It had been going on for more than a century, but in many families the hitherto exceptional alternative of adopting a greater degree of observance became more frequent. Although the percentage of young British Jews who married out of the faith increased and affected about half the community, this substantially reflected a breakdown in religious belief which, for example, equally affected many Christian denominations. Of those who remained involved in Judaism, there was an increasing shift in the other direction. It was consequently the centre ground that suffered the greatest losses. This Jewish radicalization posed no threat to the general public, as other varieties of fundamentalism might. As Woody Allen once said, you don't feel it necessary to cross the road if you're approaching a Jewish accountant!

So Schonfeld's greatest permanent legacy was that one third of British Jewish children would attend Jewish schools by the turn of the century. All of a sudden, carrying out the mitzvoth would start to be more acceptable and even fashionable. A large, committed core emerged. It was not just the ultra-Orthodox who followed the age old rulings. Those on their periphery, an increasing number of the members of the United Synagogue, also started to practice more. Even if they did not join the Charedim, they were very often sufficiently influenced to bring a greater appreciation of Torah learning and practice into their own lives.

There is a good illustration of this in a ritual called Tashlich. During the festival of the New Year, Jews hope that they will be forgiven for the sins they committed during the course of the previous year. Traditionally, they figuratively cast their sins away by throwing pieces of bread into a stream. Chief Rabbi Solomon Herschell used to bring the City of London to a halt in the early part of the nineteenth century when, during one afternoon, he led a vast array of Orthodox Jews through the streets of the City to the banks of the Thames to perform the ceremony. Fifty years later Chief Rabbi Nathan Marcus Adler said that the practice was old fashioned and it went out of favour. By 1945 it was a forgotten *mitzva*, hidden in the back of the prayer book. In 2008, however, in Hampstead Garden Suburb in London, hundreds of members of the families of the local United Synagogue Jewish community were to be found by the banks of a neighbouring stream reading the prayers and throwing in the bread.

So the Charedi ranks would now, once again, include plenty of barristers, merchant bankers, stockbrokers, eminent surgeons, the cream of the crop. That was down to Schonfeld, perhaps at several removes, but he had made it that much more likely, by sending out into the world thousands of young, well-educated and, most importantly, committed Orthodox Jews.

His educational legacy, however, is not just the JSSM in the Jewish community. The pre-eminent position of the Hasmonean Boys' School in the borough of Barnet may have dropped a mite. On the other hand, JFS in Brent has become the best school in the borough. The point is, however, that it is now accepted within the community that Jewish schools can provide an excellent all-round education and, therefore, that faith schools are relevant. The standards are recorded in the statistics of exam results and the degrees earned by the former pupils. The relevance is to be measured in the contribution the pupils make to the society in which they live, in the happiness of their home lives, in the negligible number of delinquents and criminals, and in their list of priorities. If the warmth and solidity of Jewish family life is admired by the general population, it is revered by the Jews all over the world.

It always needs to be recognized that the main reason for Schonfeld's success was the quality of the pupils who were available to him. He always knew that. His contribution was to harness their potential, but they were a remarkably talented source of educational material, and they had the spur of their parents pushing them on to academic success.

On this point, as in all others, the Talmud was always perfectly clear; the law stated that the correct role models for the people were the wise, not the rich.

Schonfeld's critics often accused him of being inconsistent and of becoming more extreme in his views as the years went by. For example, his early qualified support for Zionism is contrasted with his unilateral decision to close Hasmonean in 1976 on Israel Independence Day, in spite of the opposition of Walter Stanton and almost all of the pupils. The suggestion that Schonfeld should have stuck to his original position of support for Israel obviously works both ways: the Zionists had not stuck to their 1930s position. The intimated religious position of the Zionists in the 1930s was that if Israel came into existence, it would be an Orthodox Jewish country. The fact that many of the Zionists were near-atheists was not a trait which was much publicized. When Haham Gaster supported the Zionists when Theodor Herzl, the Zionist leader, first came to Britain, Gaster knew that Herzl was not Orthodox in his views, but he hoped that, as the movement developed, this secular attitude would change. So did Schonfeld, and both would have been disappointed. In the 1930s the Zionists tried to discriminate on exit visas in favour of their followers rather than the Orthodox. This memory would have rankled with Schonfeld in his relations with the State of Israel.

If Schonfeld had to choose between supporting a secular Jewish state and supporting a Charedi approach to Judaism, he would have been betraying the latter if he had supported the former. It was no contest; if the Israelis were going to be secular, then they risked forfeiting the support of the Charedi – and Schonfeld would always be found marching in the Charedi ranks. It is important to notice, however, that the initial change was not in the Charedi, but rather it was in the Israelis so often coming down on the non-observant side when they created the laws of their state. Did Herzl ever proclaim that the farms of the future National Home for the Jews would be able to raise pigs without condemnation?

In 1948 when the State of Israel was proclaimed, the question was widely discussed of what use the Jewish diaspora would be in the years to come. The argument was that they had served their purpose in maintaining the existence of the religion until the Jews were able to recover the Holy Land. With the State of Israel, finally, a reality, it was suggested all that they needed to do was emigrate to the country, their job done. One answer today is that pockets of the Charedim outside Israel – as well as a substantial number within the country – are ensuring that Orthodox Judaism will survive. Again, there are a lot of Jews – possibly a majority – who believe that Orthodox Judaism should be modernized which, effectively, means placing less emphasis on the performance of the *mitzvot*. Their only problem is that too many of their children cease to practice Judaism at all. With their grandchildren, the evidence is that there will be fewer still. With the Charedi communities, it is a very different picture.

There can be no doubt that many of Schonfeld's positive qualities in his prime were eaten away and turned into negatives as his strength waned and the effects of the tumour took its toll. The man who could talk government departments into breaking their own rules for refugees, became the man who would refuse to accept the dictates of the Barnet Education Committee when they were just doing their job. The leader who could inspire his staff to far greater efforts than they thought possible, finished his tenure as principal of the JSSM with many of his senior staff trying to keep well away from him. The inspiring leader declined into a figure of fun for many, and a mere shadow of his former self. If he had wanted an unblemished record, he would have had to die from the tumour when it was operated on in 1965. But even in his decline, the schools he loved turned in better and better performances every year. After his death they would do better still.

In 1995 Hasmonean Primary School finally got state aid, after raising £550,000 to bring its infrastructure up to the necessary standard. It was still dedicated to Schonfeld's *Torah im derech eretz* approach and still drawing most of its support from United Synagogue children. 'We are not trying to produce Yeshivah bochers', said one Chairman of the Governors (it should be *bocherim*). For all that, by 1999, as many as 95 per cent of the Hasmonean boys leaving the school did go on to Yeshivah and 87 per cent of the girls went to Sem.

Public figures are usually judged by the effect they have on the national stage. This is, however, to ignore their responsibility to the families they come from and decide to produce. By that yardstick, Schonfeld was a good and very loving father, a devoted husband for forty-four years and a lifelong friend and supporter to his parents, siblings and children. Though his duties took him away from the family on innumerable occasions, his sons remember him as still having plenty of time for them. He made every effort to be home in time for their bedtime when they were young. That they did not all accept his religious views happens in a vast number of families; children do not always follow in their parents' footsteps.

That Schonfeld made mistakes cannot be denied but as one old friend said: 'he survived an illness which would have felled a lion. It is easy to avoid errors if one does nothing; it is impossible to avoid them if one attempts everything, and his achievements, even when set against his errors, are monumental.'[3]

It is too often taken for granted that Schonfeld never took a salary for his work for the JSSM. When there was only one school in 1933 and thirty pupils, the excuse that the organization could not afford to pay its principal might have been justified, if only by necessity. When, however, there were a network of schools and 2,000 pupils, the Chief Executive – which was Schonfeld's role – should have been paid a good salary. Certainly, anybody else who took on the job – unless they had independent means – would have demanded it before accepting the post. The efforts to find a suitable replacement in the late 1960s could well have foundered on the fact that there was no provision for a first class benefits package for the successful candidate. Of course, it could be questioned whether Schonfeld was in earnest in seeking a successor, but he would know that there had to be one eventually and we have the evidence that he discussed a successor before he had the operation in 1965.

Judith only outlived Solly by three years. The fund raised for Solly's nursing had not been exhausted and the children felt that it should be given to his widow, who had considerable need for it. Instead it was transferred into a charitable fund and Judith received a small income from the interest it earned.

Wolfe Walter Stanton died in 1989 and Meir Roberg, who had become head of the Girls' School as well in 1984, took early retirement in 1993. He is still a much sought-after adviser on Jewish education in many parts of the world. David Schonfeld died in 1995, Moses in 1998, Senath in 2001 and Jacob Schonfeld is, happily, still with us, having celebrated his 80th birthday. Judith Grunfeld also suffered an incapacitating stroke in later life and died in 1998 at the age of 95. Of all the characters in the book, she was the only one about whom you never hear a bad word. Dayan Padwa died in 2000 and Rabbi Joseph Dunner in 2007. Padwa had been the principal rabbinic authority of the UOHC for forty-five years and Dunner had served the Adath for sixty years.

In 1997 Schonfeld's old *shtiebl* in The Bishops Avenue was sold by the Adath amidst much contention. There was a great deal of affection for its rabbi, Chaim Wilschanski, and less concern for the uses to which the money realized from the sale could be put. The house had contained Schonfeld's office as well in later years but there were now other Charedi synagogues within walking distance.

Schonfeld is remembered whenever the survivors of Schonfeld's children or the old Hasmonean pupils have a reunion. In 2003 a permanent memorial to the children on the Kindertransport was unveiled at Liverpool Street railway station in London where they had first arrived. It first took the form of a huge glass suitcase in which were some of the few possessions the children could bring with them when they left their parents, usually for ever.

The prep school is now, officially, the Solomon Schonfeld Hasmonean Primary School. He is remembered in the creation of Schonfeld Square in Stamford Hill, a housing estate developed by the Agudas Yisroel Housing Association. The name was proposed by Judith Grunfeld and would have pleased Harry Goodman as well. Ruth Lunzer, Schonfeld's devoted secretary, was the guest of honour of some of the girls who had been rescued from Poland after the war when they had a reunion in 1997. They had not forgotten how carefully she had nurtured them on a daily basis when they had first arrived. Ruth Lunzer died in 2008.

In 2005 the Avigdor Primary School was no longer viable. The school roll had fallen from over 200 to just 100 pupils. The problem was that it had always been a co-educational school and mixing boys and girls, even at such an early age, was now frowned upon in the Charedi circles dominant in Stamford Hill. The protection of the children against the onslaught of the standards of an ever more permissive society now included segregation of the sexes at primary school level. It was ironic that when the school closed at the end of the summer term that year, the results obtained in the national Standard Attainment Tests (SATS) were the highest of any school in Hackney. But then in 2005 Hasmonean Boys' School in Barnet was the seventh best performing state school in the country.

As the generation of Second World War refugees dies away, Schonfeld's efforts on their behalf will become a footnote in the history of those terrible times. There is every reason to hope, however, that his legacy of the importance and relevance of faith schools will help to create future generations of good citizens.

The last word should go to the one who worked alongside him for so many years and knew the public man best: Dr Judith Grunfeld. Here she is speaking at the 70th birthday celebration in 1982:

> God has many messengers. And while we give thanks to Him, we must feel deep gratitude to those who were worthy of being His human agents. [Solomon Schonfeld] organized, collected, planned, equipped, petitioned and used his influence and his God-given sparkling personality to save the lives of his unknown Jewish brethren in deadly peril ... with the spark of his ingenuity and the force of his personality, he could march through closed doors; talk to deaf ears; melt stubborn hearts; bend the iron rules and cut the red tape ... his voice could penetrate through the most Anglo-Saxon stillness and stir it with the flash of his eye, his sparkling

youth and his zest for life. His whole being was directed towards one aim; to bring just one more person over, to rescue just one more life ... to place one more name among the chosen ones, to choose one more for life on the slippery, treacherous road to safety, to carry one more child into the haven of freedom and future – one more, more, and still more.

Where could you find a better purpose in life?

NOTES

1. Chaim Bermant, *The Jewish Chronicle*, 19 February 1984.
2. Joe Lobenstein in conversation with the author.
3. Chaim Bermant, *The Jewish Chronicle*, 19 February 1984.

# Bibliography

Adath Yisroel Silver Jubilee Book, 1936.
Alderman, Geoffrey, *The Federation of Synagogues 1887–1987* (London: Federation of Synagogues, 1987).
Black, Gerry, *JFS: The History of the Jews' Free School, London, Since 1732* (London: Tymsder Publishing, 1998).
Bolchover, Richard, *British Jewry and the Holocaust* (Oxford: The Littman Library, 1993).
Copeland, A., (ed.), *Dayan Grunfeld Memorial Anthology* (London: Dayan Grunfeld Memorial Library, 1980).
Dansky, Miriam, *Rebbetzin Grunfeld: The Life of Judith Grunfeld, Courageous Pioneer of the Bais Yaakov Movement and Jewish Rebirth* (Brooklyn, NY: ArtScroll/Mesorah Publications, 1994).
Freud-Kandel, Miri, *Orthodox Judaism in Britain since 1913: An Ideology Forsaken* (London and Portland, OR: Vallentine Mitchell, 2006).
Golders Green Beth Hamedrash, *The Blessing of Eliyahu* (London: Golders Green Beth Hamedrash, 1982).
Gould, Julius and Shaul Esh (eds), *Jewish Life in Modern Britain* (London: Routledge & Kegan Paul, 1964).
Grunfeld, Dayan Dr Isidor, *A Memorial Anthology to Dayan Dr. Grunfeld* (London: Dayan Grunfeld Memorial Library, 1980).
Homa, Bernard, *Footsteps in the Sands of Time* (London: 1990).
Kahn, Cynthia, *Wild Water Lilies* (Beack Publications, 2005).
Koschland, Bernard, 'Tylers Green Hostel', *Jewish Historical Society of England* (June 2006).
Kranzler, David, *Thy Brother's Blood: The Orthodox Jewish Response During the Holocaust* (Brooklyn, NY: ArtScroll/Mesorah Publications, 1987).
Kranzler, David, *Holocaust Hero* (Jersey City, NJ: Ktav Publishing House, 2004).
Kranzler, David and Gertrude Hirschler, *Solomon Schonfeld: His Page in History* (New York, Judaica Press, 1982).
Morris, Benny, *Righteous Victims: A History of the Zionist-Arab Conflict, 1881–2001* (New York: Random House, 2001).

Rabinowicz, Harry, *A World Apart – The Story of the Chasidim in Britain* (London and Portland, OR: Vallentine Mitchell, 1997).

Schonfeld, Solomon (ed.), *In Memoriam, Rabbi Dr V. Schonfeld*, compiled by Naphtali Lipschütz (London: 1930).

Schonfeld, Solomon, *Jewish Religious Education* (London: JSS Books, 1943).

Schonfeld, Solomon, *Message to Jewry* (London: JSS Books, 1958).

Schonfeld, Solomon, Standard Siddur Prayer Book (London: JSS Books, 1973).

Schonfeld, Solomon, *Jewish Religious Education, II* (London: JSS Books, 1977).

Schonfeld, Victor, *Life's Purpose* (London: Jewish Post Publications, 1958).

Shatzkes, Pamela, *Holocaust and Rescue. Impotent or Indifferent? Anglo-Jewry 1938–1945* (New York: Palgrave Macmillan, 2002).

Taylor, Derek, *The Chief Rabbis 1664–2006* (London and Portland, OR: Vallentine Mitchell, 2006).

Taylor, Derek (ed.), *Jewish Education 1981/1982* (London: Jewish Educational Development Trust, 1982).

Tomlin, Chanan, *Protest and Prayer. Rabbi Dr Solomon Schonfeld and Orthodox Jewish Responses in Britain to the Nazi Persecution of Europe's Jews 1942–1945* (Oxford: Peter Lang, 2006).

Yisrael, Yismach, *Historical Essays to honour Rabbi Dr. Israel Porush, OBE., on his 80th birthday* (Sydney: Australian Jewish Historical Society, 1988).

# Index

21st Army Group, 86, 87
Abraham, 3, 89
Abraham, Rabbi Isaac, 140
Abramsky, Yechezkel, 29, 44
Adath, 14, 17, 19, 20, 23, 25–7, 30, 42, 43, 53, 55, 70, 74, 80, 94, 97, 98, 104, 110, 111, 115, 117, 120–4, 130, 134, 136, 138, 153, 160, 174, 177, 178, 181, 192
Adath Yisroel congregation, 7, 8, 10, 19, 21, 22, 25, 60, 71, 81, 83, 97, 98, 119, 148
Adler family, 70
Adler, Chief Rabbi Hermann, 105
Adler, Chief Rabbi Nathan Marcus, 189
Aguda, 13, 21
Agudas Yisroel, 13, 51, 157, 193
Air Ministry, 75
Albert Hall, 116, 166
Alexandra Palace, 75
Allen, Woody, 188
Ambassador Hotel, New York, 64
Ambulance, Mobile Synagogue, 86
America, 3, 6, 13, 37, 42, 47, 64, 73, 74, 77, 78, 85, 92, 94, 95, 98, 104, 105, 111, 119, 120, 122, 129, 138, 142, 149
American Federation of Labour, 106
Amstrad, 138
Anti-Semitism, 22, 37, 40, 46, 50, 51, 55, 74, 91, 184
Arabs, 12, 49, 78, 84
Ark, 66
Ascot, 146
Ashdod, 121
Ashkenazi, Rabbi Zevi, 25
Ashkenazim, 7, 25, 119
Astor House, 94
Astoria Cinema, 90
Attlee, Clement, 34, 85, 110, 117
Attorney General, 145, 161, 165, 168, 172
Auschwitz, 73
Australia, 132
Austria, 5, 11, 13, 40, 41, 48, 50, 51, 56, 57, 59, 62, 68, 70, 71, 88, 118
Austro-Hungarian Empire, 5
Avigdor Primary School, 128, 193
Avigdor School, 95, 103, 104, 109, 113, 115, 127, 130, 132

Baeck, Rabbi Leo, 59
Baghdad, 140
Bahamas, 78
Balcon, Michael, 35
Baldwin, Stanley, 46
Balfour Declaration, 12, 49
Bangladesh, 8
Bank Le'umi, 174
Barbican Mission to the Jews, 56
Bar mitzvahs, 44, 45
Barnato, Barney, 106
Barnet Council, 130, 145, 146, 148–55, 158, 161, 164, 166–9, 175, 189, 191, 193
Baumgarten, R., 87
Baywater Jewish Schools, 27, 65
BBC, 24, 31, 117
Beau Bessian camp, 78
Behr, Samuel, 103
Beis Ya'akov Seminary, 123
Belarus, 5
Belgium, 38, 54, 92
Belsen, 86, 87
Ben Gurion, David, 38
Bentwich, Norman, 59, 80, 186
Bergen-Belsen, 87
Berlin, 27
Bermant, Chaim, 63, 183, 184
Bermuda, 85
Beth Din, 19, 26, 29, 41–4, 118, 124
Betinsky, Ruth, 64
Bible teaching, 110
Biggleswade, 67
Birkbeck College, 140
Bishops Avenue *shtiebl*, 148, 192
Bliss, Arthur, 116
Blitz, 73, 74, 81, 105
Blood libel, 91
Bloody Sanhedrin, 132
B'nai Brith, 116
Board of Deputies of British Jews, 37, 38, 52, 77, 85, 88, 147, 165, 174
Board of Orthodox Jewish Education, 119
Boer War, 75
*Book of Jewish Thoughts*, 82
Bosnia, 50
Boult, Adrian, 116
Boyson, Rhodes, 174

Braude, J., 107
Brent, 189
Brightman, Lord Justice, 192
British Council, 79
British Expeditionary Force (BEF), 73
British Union of Fascists, 49
Brixton prison, 131
Broder, Moses, 103
Brodetsky, Selig, 77, 85
Brodie, Chief Rabbi Israel, 88, 102–4, 106–8, 126, 137, 139
Buckley, Lord Justice, 172
Bulgaria, 39, 78, 139
Butler, R.A., 34, 98, 139

Cambridge University, 23, 31, 81, 109, 154
Cambridge University Jewish Society, 117
Canada, 73
Carmel College, 104, 114
Caro, Rabbi Joseph, 7
*Casablanca*, 64
Catholics, 41, 71, 93
Central British Fund (CBF), 93
Central Hall, Westminster, 119, 143
Chamberlain, Neville, 55
Channon, Henry (Chips), 84
Chanukah, 124, 135, 171
Charities Commission, 145, 163, 166
Charles II, 146
Chassidim, 5, 10, 11, 53, 116–18, 124, 125, 180, 181
Chaye Olim North West London Talmudical College, 130
Chelsea, 96
Chevra Ben Zakkai, 11, 20, 83, 98
Chevra Kadishah, 42
Chief Rabbi, 6, 7, 135
Chief Rabbi Religious Emergency Fund, 51
Chief Rabbi Religious Emergency Council, 51, 52, 55–8, 61–4, 74–6, 78, 79, 82, 83, 87, 88, 92, 94, 100, 179, 184, 186
China, 140
Christians, 1, 14, 30, 35, 56, 93, 97, 141, 188
Church of England, 15, 46, 55
Churchill, Winston, 187
Circumcision, 3, 10, 39, 131
Claridges Hotel, 31, 43
Clifton College, Bristol, 104
Clore Foundation, 153, 172
Clonwyn Castle, 93
Cohen, Abraham, 103
Cohen, Joyce, 92
Cohen, M.J., 103
Cohen, Sir Robert Waley, 8, 9, 31, 32, 34, 47, 50, 52, 59, 74, 80, 81, 86, 99, 101
Committee for Proclaiming Jewish Ethics, 119, 185
Committee of British Relief Societies Abroad (COBRA), 94

Communism, 2, 16, 24, 29, 116
Community Centres for Israel, 121, 130, 185
Conference of European Rabbis, 135
Conquy family, 25
Conservative party, 146
Council for German Jewry (CGJ), 57
Council of Jewish Day Schools, 125, 126
Court of Appeal, 113
Cousinhood, 115
Cramer, Solomon, 152
Crystal, Jacob, 109, 110, 112–15, 127, 128, 139
Cutner, Solomon, 83
Czar, 16, 50
Czechoslovakia, 5, 22, 50, 55, 56, 59, 75, 181
Czechoslovakia Refugees Fund, 63

Dachau, 66, 123
*Daily Prayer Book*, 83
Davis, Moshe, 137
Dawkins, Jack, 151
Dawson, Lord of Penn, 18
de Valera, Eamonn, 53
Debrica, 92
Denmark, 73
Denning, Lord, 113
Department of Education, 141, 174
Depression, 27, 31, 37
*Dictionary of National Biography*, 24
Displaced Persons Camp, 91, 92
Dollis Hill Synagogue, 183
Dunkirk, 73, 187
Dunner, Aba, 121
Dunner, Rabbi Josef, 121, 123–5, 130, 136, 154, 180, 188, 192

East End, 8, 139
East Prussia, 123
Eda Charedit Beth Din, 118
Ede, Chuter, 139
Edgware, 81
Edgware Adath, 145
Edinburgh, 71
Education Act, 1944, 98, 105
Eger, Rabbi Akiba, 11
Egypt, 3
Ehrenpreisz, Rabbi Marcus, 39
Eichmann, Adolf, 131
Eire, 53, 93
El Alamein, 77
Enfield cemetery, 14, 19
Enlightenment, 9
Epstein, Dayan Isidore, 112
Establishment, 40
Eton, 32
European Union of Orthodox Jewish Organizations, 119, 185
Eysinck, Hans, 24

## Index

Far Rockaway, 64
Fascism, 24, 49, 75, 116, 138
Federation of Synagogues, 7, 8, 10, 101, 115, 147
Feldman, Dayan, 32
Feldman, Edith, 64
Ferber, Rabbi Hirsch, 19
Fink family, 16, 30
First World War, 12, 13, 26, 38, 49, 75
Fisher, Lord, 165
Fisher, Sam, 110
Fleischman, Saul, 64
Foreign Office, 12, 59, 84
France, 54, 68, 71, 85, 92
Frankel, William, 109, 110
Frankfurt, 5, 11, 34
Frederick the Great, 3
Freedman, Joe, 148
Freedman, Rosa, 148, 167

Gabe, Rosa, 152
Gaelic, 7
Galbanum, 36
Garbacz, Bernard, 165–76
Gaster, Haham Moses, 19, 32, 34, 41, 44, 50, 52, 190
Gateshead Yeshivah, 66, 95, 102, 140
Gemorah, 141
George III, 85
George IV, 146
George V, 94
Ger, Rabbi of, 53
Gerber, Gerald, 141
German Jewish Aid Committee (GJAC), 38
Germany, 5, 6, 10, 22, 27, 35, 37–40, 43, 45, 46, 48–51, 53, 55–62, 66–8, 70, 73, 77, 91, 92, 96, 112, 116, 121
Gertler, Mark, 106
Gestapo, 87
Gestetner, David, 16, 18, 62, 176
Ghetto, 9, 20, 40
Gibraltar, 25
Glasgow, 64
Glasgow Yeshiva, 130
Goddard, Lord Justice, 113
Golders Green, 22, 27, 95, 115, 12, 149, 153
Golders Green Beth Hamedresh (Munk's), 42, 56, 122, 154, 160
Goldrei, Charles, 43
Goldsmith, Henry d'Avigdor, 136
Gollancz, Hermann, 139
Gompers, Samuel, 106
Goodman, Harry, 21, 23, 27, 28, 52, 56, 73, 110, 126, 128, 176, 193
Gorell, Lord, 86
Goulding, Mr Justice, 171
Greeks, 2, 14, 68, 135, 146
Greenwood, Freddy, 173, 183
Grocers Company, 20
Grolman, Ms, 41, 42, 69, 179

Grosvenor House Hotel, 44
Grünberger, Richard, 132
Grunfeld, Dayan Isidor, 35, 44, 109, 110, 119
Grunfeld, Dr Judith, 28, 34, 35, 60, 65, 68, 79, 89, 110, 111, 117, 176–8, 183, 192, 193
Grunfeld, Maurice, 109, 132
Guardianship Act 1944, 86
Gurwitz, Rabbi Leib, 140

Hackney, 193
Hadassah Hospital, 142
Hagadas, 82
Haifa, 70, 78, 119
Hailsham, Lord, 114, 139
Halpern, Bertha, 40, 41, 70
Halpern, Dennis, 103
Halpern, Rabbi Eichanon, 118
Halpern, Philip, 103
Hamburg, 22
Hampstead, 81. 181
Hampstead Garden Suburb, 61, 189
Harlow, 79
Harrow School, 106
Harvard University, 96, 104
Hasmonean Boarding School, 103
Hasmonean Boys' School, 95, 103, 112, 120, 127, 130, 132, 134, 135, 137–41, 146–50, 152, 154–8, 160, 164, 167, 168, 170, 175, 176, 183, 188–91, 192
Hasmonean Girls' School, 110–22, 132, 135, 137, 141, 145–8, 150–3, 156, 157, 160, 161, 167, 168, 170–2, 174–6, 188, 191, 192
Hasmonean Preparatory School, 141, 143, 145
Hasmonean Primary School, 65, 98, 104, 191
Hasmonean Yeshiva Stream, 140
Hasmoneans, 135
Hatikvah, 110, 137, 157
Havers, Michael, 161, 164, 168
Hays Office, 31,
Heath, Ted, 146
Heathrow, 113
Hebrew, 83, 110–12, 125
Hebrew University, 176
Henrietta Barnett School, 155
Henry V, 180
Henry VI, 180
Herbert Oppenheimer Nathan & Vandyk, 21
Hertz Chumash, 129, 141, 144
Hertz, Daniel, 51
Hertz family, 128, 144
Hertz Forest, Israel, 119
Hertz, Chief Rabbi Joseph, 19, 22, 26, 27, 29, 32, 34, 42–4, 46, 47, 50–3, 57, 58, 64, 69–72, 80, 81, 86, 97–102, 115, 128, 130, 141, 144, 176, 184
Hertz, Josephine, 128

Hertz, Judith, 22, 22, 58, 68–71, 79, 80, 97, 98, 128, 129, 136, 144, 176, 177, 192
Hertz, Leon, 128
Hertz, Rose, 22
Hertz, Sadie, 70
Hertz, Samuel, 128, 129
Herzl, Theodor, 12, 190
Highbury County School, 16, 20
Highbury Secondary School, 27,
Hilfsverein, 51
High Court, 161
High Wycombe, 56
Highbury County School, 16, 20
Highbury Secondary School, 27
Highgate, 71, 72, 80, 98, 132, 137, 144, 148
Hiroshima, 89
Hirsch, Rabbi Samson Raphael, 4, 7, 10, 11, 14, 20, 117, 137, 176
Hirschell, Chief Rabbi Solomon, 7, 189
Hirschians, 4, 5, 9, 11, 18
Hitler, 22, 37, 48–50, 55, 71, 73, 77, 138, 149, 187
Hochhauser, Victor, 83, 116, 119, 139, 173, 180
Hogg, Quintin, 114
Holland, 53, 66
Holocaust, 55, 73, 77, 84, 88, 92, 105, 128, 131, 181, 187
Homa, Bernard, 17, 27, 30
Homa, Ramsay, 30
Home Office, 38, 43, 53–8, 60–4, 85, 86, 93, 101, 123, 139, 170
House of Commons, 49, 84, 85, 90, 127
House of Lords, 114, 172
Herbert Trust, 152
Hungary, 4–6, 25, 27, 48, 70, 78, 83, 96, 116–18, 141, 181

Ilford, 138
India 8
*Individuality in Pain and Suffering*, 96
Inland Revenue, 160, 168
Intelligence Training Centre, 95
International Monetary Fund, 147
Iran, 149
Isaac, 3
Isle of Ely, 84
Isle of Man, 75, 76
Israel Independence Day, 157, 158, 166, 190
Israel Labour Party, 125
Israel, State of, 12, 13, 18, 38, 89, 94, 110, 118–21, 125, 130, 131, 140, 142, 153, 157, 158, 179, 185, 190
Israeli Embassy, 158

Jacob, 3, 86
Jacobson, David, 132
Jakobovits, Chief Rabbi Immanuel, 137–9, 151, 158, 165, 174, 178, 182
Janner, Barnett, 32

Jerusalem, 13, 16, 118, 130, 131, 142, 154
Jesus College, Cambridge, 31
Jewish Agency, 13, 84
*Jewish Chronicle, The*, 16, 34, 40, 44, 63, 64, 86, 88, 98, 101, 102, 106, 109, 110, 116, 126, 127, 129, 143, 158, 160, 165, 169, 174, 183
Jewish Day School Trust for Greater London, 107
Jewish Educational Development Trust (JEDT), 137, 138, 151, 153, 171, 172, 182
*Jewish Exponent*, 129
Jewish Refugee Committee (JRC), 48, 51, 59, 101
Jewish Internees Welfare Organization, 185
*Jewish Religious Education*, 82
Jewish Religious Education Board (JREB), 99
Jewish Secondary School Movement (JSSM), 15, 24, 26–8, 30, 32–5, 41, 43, 44, 61, 63–5, 82, 89, 93, 95, 96, 98, 100, 104, 106, 107, 109–17, 119, 122, 126, 127, 129–32, 137–40, 142, 143, 145, 147, 148, 151–5, 157–75, 182, 184, 189, 191, 192
Jewish Servicemen's Kosher Food Service, 119
Jewish Soldiers Services, 185
Jews' College, 94, 112
Jews' Free School (JFS), 15, 35, 65, 98, 100, 102–4, 106, 107, 140, 157, 165, 182, 189
Joint Emergency Committee for Jewish Education, 80
Jones, Sir George, 32, 89
Joseph, 86

Kaganovitch, 17
Kahn, Bernard, 66, 67, 92, 173, 183
Kahn, Joyce, 67
Kalms, Stanley, 137
Karaites, 3
Karachi, 95
Kashrut, 22, 42, 67, 76, 80, 82, 86, 87, 115
Keats, 69
Kedassia, 42, 43, 97
Kedassia pension fund, 136
Kedassia restaurant, 137
Keren Hayesod, 13
Keren Hatorah, 79
Kestenbaum, Rabbi Ephraim, 111, 112, 122, 123, 151, 152, 157, 168, 183
Kestenbaum, Israel, 25, 27, 28, 176, 183
Kielce, 91
Kindertransport, 57, 59, 62, 79, 91, 93, 170, 177, 184, 192
Kingsbury, 171
Klausner, Sarah, 43
Kleeman, Max, 103
Koenigsburg, University, 28
Konigsburg, Pesye, 43
Kook, Rabbi Abraham, 13
Kovno, 28

Kristellnacht, 55, 57, 58, 62, 123

Labour party, 29, 135, 146
Lachosky Room, 10
Ladies guilds, 45
*Lady Chatterley's Lover*, 103
Lag b'Omer, 68
Lancashire CC, 140
Landau Morley, 166
Lansbury, George, 29
Laski, Neville, 38, 52, 186
Law, Richard, 84
Lawrence, D.H., 103. 103
Lazarus, Dayan, 32,
League of Nations, 37, 50
Lebrecht, Solomon, 60
Leeds University, 95
Letchworth Abattoir, 115
Letchworth Shechita Board, 136
Levene, Dr Abraham, 68, 79
Levin, Salmond, 114
Levy, Rev. Isaac, 87, 88
Lew, Dayan Myer, 168, 169
Liberal Judaism, 24, 47–9, 103, 135, 147
Lincoln, Ashe, 64, 114
Lipton & Jeffries, 41
Lithuania, 5, 7, 28
Litman Hall, 152
Liverpool, 66, 92
Liverpool Street Station, 192
Lobenstein, Joe, 66, 100, 113
Loewe, Herbert, 23
Logue, Valentine, 132
London, 8
London Board of Jewish Religious Education (LBJRE), 105, 107, 114, 125, 126
London Board of Shechita, 115
London County Council, 105, 107, 109, 110, 113, 114, 125, 126
London County Council Education Staff Sub-committee, 110, 112–14
London Philharmonic Orchestra, 116
London School of Economics, 21
Long Island, NY, 66, 94
Longford, Earl of, 143
Lonsdale, Kathleen, 135
Lord Chancellor, 31, 114
Lord Mayor of London, 63
Lord's Day Observance Society, 31,
Loyters Green, 79
Lubavitch, 5, 124
Lunzer family, 183
Lunzer, Fanny, 81
Lunzer, Hugo, 55, 56, 143
Lunzer, Jack, 143, 173
Lunzer, Julius, 10
Lunzer, Ruth, 68, 69, 96, 193
Lyon/Herschell, 70
Macchiavelli, 59
Magdalen College, Oxford, 23

Maimonides, Rabbi Moses, 39
Mamaroneck, NY, 142
Manchester, 61, 93
Manchester Grammar School, 140
Mansfield College, 104
Mapai, 125
Marble Arch Synagogue, 77
Marks & Spencer, 63
Master of the Rolls, 113
Matching Tye, 79, 137, 144
Maudesley Hospital, 24
Mauritius, 78
Megarry, Mr. Justice, 170, 171
*Mein Kampf*, 58
Menorah School, 103
*Message to Jewry*, 9, 83, 119, 129
Messiah, 88, 89
Mett, Dr, 169
Middle Ages, 4
Middle East, 49
Middlesex Hospital, 132, 176
Mikvaot, 10, 42, 79, 87
Mill Hill Emergency Hospital, 96
Ministry of Education, 32, 33, 68, 98, 106, 107, 125, 136
Ministry of Food, 82
Mintz, Louis, 92, 173
Mitnagdim, 5
Mizrachi, 13
Mizrachi World Conference, 13
Montagu, Ewen, 115, 116
Montagu, Lily, 80, 99
Montagu, Samuel, 7
Montefiore family, 6
Moravia, 11
Morgenthau, Henry, 94
Morrison, Herbert, 85
Moses, 1, 33, 57
Muslims, 1, 50
Muni, Paul, 32
Munich Agreement, 55
Munk, Rabbi Eli, 22, 27, 28, 31, 42, 56, 87, 104, 122, 135, 153
Mussolini, 71

Nassau, 78
National Council for Rescue from Nazi Terror, 185
Nathan, Lord, 34
Naturei Karta, 13
Nazis, 2, 4, 10, 22, 40, 51, 56, 61, 62, 73, 74, 77, 82, 84–7, 112, 116, 170
Needy Clergy War Fund, 185
New York, 64, 94, 128, 142
Niettos, 70
Nitra, 22, 25, 28, 48, 73, 138
North Hendon Adath, 134
North London Beth Hamedresh, 10
North London Yeshivah, 86
North West London Jewish Day School, 104

Northfields, 60

O'Dwyer, William, 94
Ordman, Jack, 141
Ordman, Nachum, 141
Ostrowiec, 92
Oxford University, 23, 31, 95
Oxford University Jewish Society, 117

Pace University, New York, 142
Padwa, Rabbi Henoch, 117–19, 124, 133, 154, 192
Page Street, 145, 146, 148, 150–2, 175
Pakistan, 8
Palestine, 12, 13, 37–9, 42, 49, 57–9, 64, 70, 71, 77, 78, 84, 85, 87, 88, 118
Palestine Crown Colony Association, 42
Paris, 112, 113
Paris Claims Conference, 112, 126
Parson Street, 122, 145, 151, 152
Passover, 55, 56, 68, 80–2, 97
Paul, Pincus, 30
Pearl Harbour, 77
Pentateuch, 3
Perse School, Cambridge, 104
Permissive Society, 147
*Personality and the Frontal Lobes*, 96
Petrie, Asenath, 68, 95, 104
Petrie, Ernest, 95, 104, 120, 142
Philadelphia, 129
Philipp, Oscar, 32
Poland, 5–7, 10, 23, 34, 46, 50, 58, 68, 84, 91, 92, 94, 96, 111, 118, 181, 193
Polish Union of Synagogal Communities, 119
Port Erin, 75
Posen, Dayan, 113, 118
Prefrontal leucotomy, 96
Progressive movement, 99, 103
*Protocols of the Elders of Zion*, 50
Przeworska, Zuzanna, 23, 24

Quakers, 24
Queen Elizabeth School, Barnet, 155
Queensboro Bridge, New York, 94
Quota System, 37, 39

Rashi, 141
Reconstructon of Jewish Education in Great Britain Conference, 99
Reform Movement, 10, 32, 35, 47, 59, 80, 99, 103, 121, 147, 148
Regency, 15
Regent Street Polytechnic, 30
Registrar General, 70, 71
Religious Reconstruction Fund, 185
Reith, Lord, 31
Retter, Marcus, 58, 68
Richer, Isaac, 26
Roberg, Rabbi Meir, 139, 140, 144, 150, 151, 157, 160, 175, 183, 192

Romania, 6, 40
Romans, 2, 12, 126
Rome, 70, 71
Romer, Lord Justice, 114
Rosen, Aubrey, 167
Rosen, Rabbi Kopul, 114
Rosenfield, David, 177
Rosenheim, Jacob, 51, 52
Rosh Hashanah, 76, 97, 189
Rothschild, Edmund de, 34, 107, 126
Rothschild family, 6, 15, 100
Rothschild, Jimmy de, 84
Rothschild, Lionel de, 52
Rothschild, Lord, 47
Royal Artillery, 96
Royalties, 128, 136, 137, 144
Rubin, Nat, 105, 106
Russia, 5–7, 29, 58, 77, 116

Sabbateians, 3
St Michaels Hall, Shefford, 67
St Paul's School, 23
Salomans family, 6
Salonika, 13
Sandomierz, 92
Sanhedrin, 132
Sanhidriya, 13
Sassoon family, 6
Satmar, 5
Satmarer Rebbe, 119
Saxony, Lower, 86
Scarcity Value, 132
Schenirer, Sarah, 34, 111, 123
Schiff, Otto, 38, 48, 51, 54, 58, 59, 62, 101, 153, 186
Schmidt-Bodner, Adolf, 173
Schmidt-Bodner, Bennie, 173
Schonfeld, Aaron Ebenezer, (David), 13, 19, 24, 30, 95, 96, 120, 134, 142, 192
Schonfeld, Asenath (Senath) 19, 24, 27, 28, 30, 68, 95, 96, 104, 119, 120, 132, 142, 192
Schonfeld, Daniel, 11, 19, 24, 26, 64, 104, 116, 120, 142
Schonfeld, Deborah, 112
Schonfeld, Edith, 64
Schonfeld, Jeremy, 96, 128, 133, 134, 177
Schonfeld, Jonathan, 96, 128, 137
Schonfeld, Judith, 22, 71, 79, 80, 96–8, 128, 129, 136, 144, 170, 176, 177, 192
Schonfeld, Moses, 19, 20, 26–8, 30, 42, 64, 74, 95, 104, 105, 112, 120, 142, 160, 192
Schonfeld, Rachel Leah (Ella), 11, 13, 19, 20, 23–7, 32, 44, 62, 69, 75, 79, 104, 105, 119–21, 131, 142, 176, 179
Schonfeld, Ruth, 64, 105, 128
Schonfeld Square, 193
Schonfeld, Rabbi Dr Solomon,
    Adath Rabbi, 27
    Air Ministry ideas, 75

# Index

Archive, 179
Articles, 21
Assassination attempt, 91
Audience control, 33
Author, 82
Avigdor School closed, 128
Barnet Council, 145, 146, 148, 149
'Bill', 72
Bluff, 76
Born, 20
Bureaucracy, 53, 85, 101, 182
Career assessment, 159
Chief rabbinate, 69
Children, 66
COBRA, 94
Community Centres for Israel, 121
Confrontational, 184
Crystal dismissal, 109, 110, 112, 113
CRREC Director, 51–3, 55, 56
Death, 177
Demanding help, 48, 57
Democracy, 183
Divorced author, 71
Doctorate 28
Driver, 67, 133
Education, 20, 43, 44, 80–2, 182
Expertise, 29
Father's secretary, 15
Flexibility, 49, 78
Founder's Syndrome, 182
Fund raising, 31, 44, 46, 70, 75, 83, 89, 92, 116, 143, 152, 169, 185
Funeral, 178
Gardening, 98
Golden Jubilee, 166
Hasmonean structure, 95
Hertz relations, 43, 51, 52
Hertz royalties, 128, 136
Heter rabbi, 28
Internees, 75, 76
Israel, 110, 120, 190
Kestenbaum, Rabbi Ephraim, 111, 112, 151, 152
Ketubah, 71
Kindertransport, 62
Kibo relations, 24
Last illness, 176, 177
LBJRE, 105
Legacy, 180
Litigation, 113, 139, 141, 145, 157, 161, 163–5, 170–3, 182, 184
Marriages, 41, 69
Mobile Synagogue Ambulances, 86
Nitra, 28
Organizations created, 119
Page Street, 145
Parent-Teacher Association, 159
Paris Claims Conference, 112
Personal finances, 136, 144
Personality, 2, 3, 70, 114, 185, 193

Post-war Poland, 91. 92
Post-war reputation, 100
Post-war working life, 98
PR, 34, 113, 131, 185, 187
Presiding Rabbi, 124, 137
Problems approach, 30
Receiver, 161, 166, 169–72
Refugee children, 55, 57, 58, 62
Royalties, 128, 136, 137, 144
School organization, 35
Self-confidence, 33
Semicha, 22, 25, 26, 28, 71, 179, 181
Seventieth birthday, 176
Siberia, 58
Singing voice, 33
Shefford, 65, 67, 68
Slobodka, 28, 70
State aid for Girls' School, 145–7
Successor to father, 20
Tumour, 132–4, 170, 176, 191
University, 21, 112
UNRRA, 94
UOHC head, 27, 117
UOHC resignation, 117
UOHC Silver Jubilee, 119
Visas, 39, 53, 56–63, 66, 78, 85, 92, 93, 101
Walnut Tree Cottage, 79, 112
Wartime education, 80
Westminster Office, 74
Schonfeld, Rabbi Victor, 8, 10, 11–20, 23–6, 30, 141, 176
Schonfeld, Akibo (Andrew) 16, 17, 19, 23, 24, 26, 27, 96, 104, 105, 120, 134, 142, 176
Schonfeld, Jacob, 19, 24, 29, 72, 95, 96, 104, 105, 120, 192
Schonfeld, Victor, 96, 128, 137
Schonfeld, Zuzanna, 96, 176, 177
Schreiber, Rabbi Moshe, 5
Second World War, 8, 89, 186, 193
Seder Night, 55
Sem, 123, 188, 191
Semicha, 7
Sephardim, 41, 50, 99, 115, 118
Shaftesbury, 3rd Earl of, 10
Shah of Iran, 149
Shanghai, 78, 140
*Shatnes*, 81
Shavuot, 68
*Shechita*, 10, 19, 42, 136, 137
Shefford, Bedfordshire, 65, 67, 79, 81, 89, 96, 100, 111, 135, 146
Shell, 8, 47, 80
*Shema*, 93
Shreiber, Rabbi Moshe, 5
*Shulchan Aruch*, 7, 10, 157, 180
Siberia, 29,
Slobodka, 28, 29, 34, 82, 181
Slovakia, 47

Smith, Dr C.A., 16, 23, 27
Sobell, Michael, 34
Sofer, Chatam, 5
Solicitor General, 110
Solomon, 83
Solomon, Rabbi Elijah ben, 5
Solomon Schonfeld Hasmonean Primary School, 193
Somerville College, Oxford, 23, 79
Soncino Press, 129, 144
Soskice, Frank, 110
South Africa, 75
South America, 63, 78
South Hampstead High School, 79
Southampton University, 179
Space Shuttle, 75
Spanish Civil War, 65
Spanish Inquisition, 2
Spitfire, 187
Spragg, W.E., 27
Stalin, 17
Stamford Hill, 35, 60, 61, 64, 71, 74, 81, 115, 137, 148, 153, 193
Stanton, Walter, 95, 103, 132, 140, 150, 151, 155–9, 169, 170, 183, 190, 192
Stebba, Sam, 173
Stepney Jewish Schools, 43, 98
Sterling, Louis, 34
Sternberg family, 11, 28, 181, 183
Sternberg, Hazel, 69, 176
Sternberg, Sigmund, 67, 173
Stoke Newington Registry Office, 40
Strangers Cay, 78
Sugar, Alan, 138
Suicide, 29
Sunderland, 60
Swaythling, Lord, 7
Sweden, 39, 73, 78
Switzerland, 41, 75

*Tallit*, 40, 68, 87
Talmud, 3–5, 7, 9–11, 15, 29, 31, 34, 39, 44, 111, 116, 118, 125, 132, 180, 181, 190
Talmud Torah Trust, 99
Talmud Tractate Kerithoth 6a, 35
*Tashlich*, 189
Tchebiner Rov, 118
*Tefilat Haderech*, 65
*Tephillin*, 68, 81, 82, 124, 135, 149
Teheran, 58
Teitlebaum, Rabbi Yoel, 5
Tel Aviv, 118
Television, 119
Templeman, Lord Justice, 172
Thames, River, 189
Thatcher, Margaret, 136, 174
*The Mark of the Swastika*, 74
*The Times*, 68, 91, 131, 151
Torah, 4, 30, 67, 117, 131, 177, 180, 189
*Torah im derech eretz*, 4, 5, 10, 31, 32, 34,
112, 117, 137, 180, 181, 191
Trade Unions, 3
Trinity College, Cambridge, 31
Trotsky, 17
Trustees Act, 1925, 163
Trotsky, 17,
*Tsitsit*, 14, 53, 68
Tuck, Gustave, 32
Tumour, 132–4, 176, 181, 191
Tylers Green, 56
Tyrnau, 48, 138

Uganda, 12
Ungar, Rabbi Samuel David, 28
Union of Hebrew & Religion Classes, 99
Union of Orthodox Hebrew Congregations (UOHC), 14, 16, 27, 29, 42–4, 64, 80, 81, 100, 101, 113, 115–20, 122–5, 133, 135, 146, 147, 154, 160, 165, 174, 180, 181, 192
United Nations, 84, 94, 142
United Nations Relief & Rehabilitation Administration (UNRRA), 94
United Synagogue, 6–9, 19, 29, 31, 33, 34, 40, 42–4, 47, 48, 50, 52, 64, 70, 80, 86, 95, 97, 99, 101–3, 114, 115, 118, 119, 128, 137, 138, 140, 147, 150, 158, 165, 166, 168, 174, 181, 188, 189, 191
Universal Bible, 183
University of Calgary, 96
University College, London, 24
Untermann, Rabbi Maurice, 77

V1, 75,
Van den Bergh, Henry, 32
Veidt, Conrad, 64
Vienna, 10, 40, 60, 62, 70, 61, 118
Vienna University, 21
Vilensky, Rabbi, 87
Vilna Gaon, 5
Visas, 38, 50, 53, 56–63, 78, 85, 92, 93, 101, 115, 123, 170, 186, 190
Von Runstedt, General, 187

Walnut Tree Cottage, 79, 112
Walters, N.B., 103
Walton, Mr Justice, 163
War Office, 75
Warsaw, 92, 94
Wedgwood, Lord Josiah, 64
Weidenfeld, Rabbi Dov Berish, 118
Weinstock, Lord, 34
Weisman, Rev. Malcolm, 113
Weissmandl, Rabbi Michoel Bar, 28, 48, 51, 57, 73–5, 138, 176
Weizmann, Chaim, 21, 38
Welsh, 7, 31
White Paper, 49
Whitehall Theatre, 83
Whitford, Mr Justice, 172

Whittinghame College, 104
Willesden Cemetery, 51
Wilschanski, Rabbi Chaim, 192
Wilson, Harold, 146
Winegarten, Aaron, 30
Wolfson, Solomon, 43
World Jewish Congress (WJC), 84
Wouk, Hermann, 129

Yarmulkes, 95, 121
Yavneh Grammar School, 140
Yeshivah, 123, 139, 141, 154, 183, 191
Yeshiva Beth Jacob, 79
Yeshiva Ohr Yisroel, 61

Yesodey Hatorah School, 98
Yiddish, 7, 10, 63, 93, 116
Yom Kippur, 12, 24, 33, 70, 97, 176
Young, Rabbi Moshe, 171, 172

Zangwill, Israel, 106
Zionism, 8, 11–13, 21, 38, 39, 77, 85, 88, 89, 110, 120, 121, 158, 190

Lightning Source UK Ltd.
Milton Keynes UK
UKHW021423250819
348394UK00005B/50/P